THE BIG PUNCHERS

By the same author

My Bleeding Business
(with Terry Downes)

Let's Be Honest
(with Jimmy Greaves)

The Great Ones

THE BIG PUNCHERS

Reg Gutteridge

Seconded by Henry Cooper

Stanley Paul
London Melbourne Sydney Auckland Johannesburg

Stanley Paul & Co. Ltd

An imprint of the Hutchinson Publishing Group

17–21 Conway Street, London W1P 6JD

Hutchinson Group (Australia) Pty Ltd
30–32 Cremorne Street, Richmond South, Victoria 3121
PO Box 151, Broadway, New South Wales 2007

Hutchinson Group (NZ) Ltd
32–34 View Road, PO Box 40–086, Glenfield, Auckland 10

Hutchinson Group (SA) Pty Ltd
PO Box 337, Bergvlei 2012, South Africa

First published 1983
© Reg Gutteridge 1983

Phototypeset in Linotron Plantin by
Input Typesetting Ltd, London

Printed in Great Britain by The Anchor Press Ltd
and bound by Wm Brendon & Son Ltd,
both of Tiptree, Essex

ISBN 0 09 153640 5

To Dad, Granddad and Uncle.

Born and bred in the game, they died in harness,
caring for boxers. I hope I live up to their expectations

Contents

Photographic acknowledgements

For permission to reproduce photographs included in this book, the publisher and author would like to thank The Associated Press Ltd, United Press International Ltd, Sport & General Press Agency Ltd, Central Press Photos Ltd, *Daily Mirror*, *Daily Sketch*, Wide World Photos, Graphic Photo Union and P.A.-Reuter Photos Ltd.

Introduction

Henry Cooper, whose heavyweight hitting induced a great deal of discomfort, also felt the pain of being hit hard on the chin. Pain? Cooper disagrees. When the flashing punch of Floyd Patterson, a world champion, put Cooper down and out, he commented, 'A knockout doesn't hurt. I know. Patterson's punch came at lightning speed. I didn't see it. I didn't feel it. When I woke up a few seconds later I didn't even have a headache.'

I have heard it said that the impulse to punch destructively comes from the bowels and the physical movement should involve everything from the toes up. Yet the game's acknowledged big hitters have rarely been able to explain how they do it. Comparable to Belloc's nimble water insect: 'If ever he stopped to think how he did it, he would sink.'

Boxing is not predominantly about the strong, muscled puncher; I could name dozens of contests where the lighter hitter, with skill, put the bigger puncher in his place. But there is no denying that the man capable of taking another out with one well-planted, or even lucky, blow is imbued with confidence. And, usually, he is the crowd-puller.

Boxing is the most basic and uncomplicated of athletic competition and, at its best, achieves the status of an art form. I admit a prejudiced preference for the purist part of the game because my pedigree comes from a long line of boxers ('Except Uncle Fred who was a cocker spaniel,' says the pantomime patter). My grandfather, Arthur, who trained and seconded until a few years before his passing, aged seventy-seven, was the first professional in the ring at the opening of the National Sporting Club, at

Covent Garden, in 1891. (He won, of course, though dreadful rumour has it that Cooper's grandfather defeated mine on another occasion.) My father and uncle, Dick and Jack, identical twins, were amateur club and school coaches, professional tutors of champions and between them seconded every champion of their time.

Detractors contend that the sport's essence is brutality. It has come a long way since Athenian heroes of several thousand years ago required two contestants to sit on flat stones, face to face, and pummel each other until one fell off. The winner then beat the loser to death. Since then, gloves of varying sizes became obligatory, foul-proof protectors and gumshields were introduced, padded rings, four ropes, decreasing number of three-minute rounds for championship contests, with strict referees and doctors in attendance.

Yes, it can be, and often is, a brutal occupation, but, strictly controlled – safety aspects tightened by the hour – it is less dangerous than many others (for example, fifty-six postwar players died playing soccer, twenty-six with head injuries; twelve were goalkeepers). Abolitionists argue that boxers are trying to inflict damage, to knock out an adversary, never to succeed by skill and will, and contend that boxing has no place in a civilized society. There is always scope, especially in America, for tighter administration. The knockers are wrong because those who think boxing can be legislated out of existence will not accept that it has been tried many times, yet there are always men ready to fight for money in a field, on a barge, in a barroom. It is hard to believe a nation of such men would be less strong or better for it.

This is a collection of fascinating fighters, characters with courage – where do they find such men? – whom I have reported around the world, with the exception of the marvellous old-timers Ted Kid Lewis and Jimmy Wilde. But I knew them well during their retirement years. Each hit with authority. Each had a varying method. No matter how long or short the punches travelled, opponents got the message.

I do not totally subscribe to boxing's time-worn axiom that big punchers are born, not made. Obviously it is easier to coach a natural-born hitter to success but frequently the strong boy fighter with the big KO punch fades into obscurity when he fights the men. Timing and ability to deliver a blow correctly are the champion techniques. Lucky hitters, whatever their strength, seldom stay at the top.

Punch power is associated with body strength, but the best are often lithe-built without rippling muscles. Two modern examples are Bob Foster, light heavy, and Tommy Hearns, when a welterweight, who are not included in this book. I saw them as rising amateurs. Neither was known for exceptional hitting power. Yet both became poleaxe punchers as professionals and were built pencil-slim for their poundage.

Listing the big punchers over the years would require a volume. Omitting Muhammad Ali, Joe Frazier, George Foreman and Sonny Liston, whom I often watched in the flesh, seems a glaring misjudgement. But there are hitters, at lower weights, who claim my attention and admiration, having watched them at work from the closest ringside seat. I present them in profile, in no particular order of merit, with reflections from the ringside and the occasional anecdote. I do not necessarily contend that all included in this collection would have stiffened all others at their weight – but they would have taken some beating!

When the going was hard it was a pleasure to return unbowed to the stool between chapters and listen to the words of Henry Cooper, in his first role as chief second. Thanks, 'En.

Henry Cooper says . . .

If this keeps up I won't be needed for many corner repairs. I agree with your summing-up, especially about my grandfather beating yours! The perfect punchers are lithe-built, able to get a swift reaction from brain to muscle, able to sneak a punch when others are still thinking about it. I have never been impressed with heavily muscled boxers. It usually slows them down. I wondered whether Frank Bruno, for example, would be hindered in the long run by having such a heavily muscled body. We shall see.

Jimmy Wilde

Jimmy Wilde, who weighed 6 st 10 lb (soaking wet) in his prime, had the comparative whack of a mule's kick. A freak-built flyweight, Wilde is established as a legend beyond the rust of time in the Welsh valleys where they lauded marvellous boxers from peerless Jim Driscoll to Freddie Welsh, Dai Dower, Eddie Thomas, Howard Winstone and their best big 'uns, Jack Petersen and Tommy Farr.

Incredible Wilde – tagged the Ghost with a Hammer in his Hands, the Tylorstown Terror – is the only non-American to be rated No. 1 in the all-time great list of *Ring* magazine. He was entered in the American Hall of Fame in 1959, forty-six years after his final fight. American boxing men do not award an accolade to a Fancy Dan; they cherish a puncher.

My judgement of Wilde is, of course, based on film playback of some fights. But my grandfather, Arthur, frequently seconded Wilde in his prime, including the dreaded occasion of handing the little wonder's manager, Teddy Lewis, a towel to throw in the ring during the seventeenth round against Tancy Lee in 1915. The defeat rankled because Wilde had dragged himself from a sick bed rather than seek a postponement and his ear had painfully blown up to a cauliflower early in the fight. Granddad helped attend Wilde's wounds and was not the least surprised when the champion angrily kicked the surrender towel out of the ring: 'If the other fellow can put me down and out, let him have the credit for it,' he said.

A year later Wilde KO'd Lee in eleven rounds, putting the world title at stake along with the British and European. Lee was the only Briton to defeat him in a sketchy record of 140 fights, of which seventy-seven were won on KO's or stoppages, forty-eight on points and one foul. At least a hundred went unrecorded.

It took an extraordinary combination of speed and timing for a boxer, weighing less than a sack of Rhondda Valley coal, to clout all-comers from the 8 st to 9 st divisions, and once perform the near-impossible of knocking over twenty-three opponents in four hours in a fairground booth. Wilde conceded parcels of poundage and, though built with the frame of a gnat (Mighty Atom was among a dozen endearments), he could make bigger men crumble. He did it chiefly by overwhelming opponents. He rained punches rather than aimed them. Measuring purely on single-punch power, the vote would go to another great flyweight, Scot Benny Lynch, whom my grandfather and his twin sons, who seconded for and against Lynch, believed could have overcome Wilde.

It's nitpicking to suggest that cagy management by Mr Lewis, on a par with Al Weill for Rocky Marciano, beat many opponents at the scales before Wilde gave them a hiding. The manager was entitled to try any ploy to give his man an advantage. But Lewis did frequently make natural bantam and featherweight opponents boil to an unhealthy limit before permitting his wizard to perform. Wilde never had a boxing lesson in his life. But he would have fought Jack Johnson, Carnera or King Kong, if they had provided stilts for Jimmy to reach their jaws; he had no occupational fear.

His aptitude for boxing was natural. His punching at such a freak weight – a lot lighter, for example, than jockey Lester Piggot – was not heavy or crushing, but was sharp, sudden and usually directed at the exact spot where the blows would be most effective. He could pick a spot and plant his steely little knuckles bang on it. He had the natural talent for being able to box without much tension in his body, which had as much fat content as a humming bird, yet be able to explode his pipestem arms at a furious rate. He fought, often, like an enraged octopus.

Yes, there were numerous occasions when a single blow won fights for Wilde, but usually when facing fierce or bigger opposition it was the speed of Wilde's blows that confused and normally downed them. He also had a knack of being able to read an opponent's next move. Uncanny anticipation was Wilde's success with his punching. There was no secret.

During the First World War, when Wilde was overweight at 7 st 6 lb wearing his army greatcoat as a company sergeant major, he was matched with stiff hitter Joe Conn at Chelsea football ground. Because he was a serving soldier, Wilde was not permitted any pay. Promoter Jack Callaghan paid him in diamonds.

Conn at 9 st, noted as a fine craftsman, was worn down in twelve rounds. Check the current world flyweight champion and consider if he could defeat the featherweight champion. I doubt if the so-called controlling bodies of the sport would sanction such a match. In Wilde's day nobody bothered about weight differential.

When Wilde was fed up being sidetracked out of a fight against American Pete Herman – otherwise Pietro Gulotta, Brooklyn born – he cleaned up in the States and returned considering retirement to a new house in Cardiff. Then an American actor, Rube Welch, offered him £8000 – an incredible amount in 1921, five years after Wilde had won the world flyweight title – to fight Herman in London. No sooner had Herman agreed and contracts been signed, than a typical fight-game stroke was pulled in New York. Herman just happened to lose his world crown against a fellow American, which made it certain that Wilde, if he won, would not lock up the crown in this country.

None the less the fight went on, following threats, pleas, promises, and finally an appeal by the Prince of Wales and Lord Lonsdale. Herman maintained he agreed to weigh in at two o'clock on the day of the fight, and not, as Wilde understood, at the ringside. It was a cockeyed set-up. Herman came off the scales at 8 st 6 lb, ate a meal and was probably not an ounce inside 8 st 8 lb when the first bell sounded. Wilde, fretful and fuming, weighed in at 7 st 1 lb. Such a weight disparity would not be tolerated in a championship match today. Inevitably the extra weight and the evenness of ability was too much for Wilde, who fought with a black jockstrap above his thigh-length woollen bathing trunks. He did not bother to dress up for royalty at ringside.

My grandfather, I recall, was always generous in his praise of Wilde's bravery. He worked in the will-o'-the-wisp's corner against Herman. He remembered having constantly to plug Wilde's ear, the result of a gash caused when heads clashed. Yet it took seventeen rounds of aggression by a fighter who was still world champion, other than by name, of a weight above Wilde's finally to subdue him. Wilde was battered, but at least was spared the indignity of a count-out. The referee, Jack Smith, complete with evening dress, waistcoat and watch chain, gathered Wilde in his arms and waved Herman away. 'I'm sorry, Jimmy,' he said, 'I have to pick you up because you don't know how to lie down.' Wilde came back two years later, lost his world title and retired in 1923.

I frequently talked to Wilde about his punching ability. I remember his hands were chunky and gnarled. They were buckled by the years of force needed to combat every name fighter from 1910 until 1923. 'I dunno, boy,' he'd say, 'but I just hit 'em all with everything I'd got 'till they dropped, see? I never tried to win a fight on points.'

We shared a press pew at a big show when Jimmy put his name to a regular boxing column in the *News of the World*. The topliner was a championship fight at flyweight. Promoter Jack Solomons invited the little great one, then a cuddly 10 st and sporting a bowler hat, to be introduced in the ring. The crowd loved it. Then Wilde grabbed the microphone and, while pointing to the champion and challenger, announced: 'I'd beat the pair of them.' He was in his sixties. The crowd laughed, the boxers blushed and the promoter was angry.

It was the last time Jimmy Wilde was publicly introduced. He reckoned the flyweights of the sixties were 'bloody slow'. In the history of the British flyweight division only Lynch and perhaps another Scot, Jackie Paterson, could match Wilde's freakish punch power.

I was among the last of boxing scribes to see Wilde. It was a foggy damp night at Cardiff when I visited him in February 1969 at the Tegfen Ward, Whitchurch Hospital, where he had been a patient for four years. He was senile, a diabetic, who was bedridden and suffering loss of memory. He was not aware that his wife, Elizabeth, whom he had married as a teenager, had died two years earlier.

His blue eyes glowed and he smiled at everyone. The nurses adored him. His body still had the sheen of a newborn baby. And his knuckles still looked imperishable. I sat and wondered how many times those hands had crashed into a rival's face and body. How much they had earned. He could not converse.

Jimmy had looked after his money, but his health had deteriorated after being beaten up by teenage thugs on a lonely Welsh railway station. (If the culprits are ever found – take it for granted – retribution will occur long before the case gets to court.) He had also never fully recovered from a serious car accident in Glamorgan.

He died, aged seventy-six, on 10 March 1969.

It was an honour to have known him.

Henry Cooper says . . .

It's difficult for me truthfully to assess Wilde's greatness. I met him, of course, and have seen films of his fights. For such a tiny mite – he looked like a matchstick with the wood shaved – he was exceptional. It proved that sheer strength was not the secret of hitting power. He must have had the perfect timing and the correct leverage in his punching.

My manager used to give Wilde's manager a lot of credit, as managers should do, because he cleverly made matches for Wilde where the other guy had to dry out to make the weight. It was never Wilde. But how do we know that Wilde would not have whacked them at the natural weight? You can't blame a manager for doing his job. It's hard for a heavyweight to think like a flyweight. The speed of Wilde's punches would be bewildering to me. He had the ingredient of being fearless, which made him able to wade in and hit where it hurt. The little fellow was a one-off. He must have been marvellous for the Americans to rate him the best at 8 st.

The Bantams

The weight division of 8 st 6 lb, 118 lb or 53.524 kilos has a natural attraction for me, because I scuffled at the poundage during an easily dismissed amateur career, wrecked by the interruption of a war, and finished permanently by failing to understand what 'Achtung, minen' meant on the battlefield of Normandy.

The earliest, barely remembered, introduction to a world champion of the division came during the thirties, when I sought the autograph of Al Brown, Stick o' Liquorice, from Panama, who won five fights in England and was held to a draw in the featherweight division by the nimble Scouse master, Nel Tarleton. Brown stood an alarming 5 ft 11 in. He had 152 recorded bouts, lost only fifteen, and was still fighting, at forty, to win his last Panama fight in 1942.

Scot Peter Keenan first caught our eye as the British team reserve at flyweight for the 1948 Olympic Games. He was probably a fiercer competitor than the selected Henry Carpenter (no relation to the chap on the other channel), but a doubt that Keenan could remain strong, having to make 8 st at each weigh-in for a lengthy competition, swayed the ABA vote. Scots would argue, with some validity, that the weight of London prejudice favoured Carpenter, but the selectors were obliged to prefer the reigning ABA champion. Keenan was too busy scheming a fight-for-pay career to bother about domestic medals.

At Wembley Pool – the ring was pitched across the open pool – Keenan eyed Vic Toweel, a South African beaten in the preliminaries, who was to become a brilliant world champion at bantamweight.

Four years after those Olympics, Keenan had won thirty-one paid fights – his first ending, inevitably, in the first round – and he had drawn one for the European title. As the proud unbeaten British and European kingpin, Keenan challenged whirlwind Toweel for the world title in Johannesburg. He had earned the chance by beating the London monopoly system, without boxing for Jack Solomons, the ruling promoter, but permitting Sassenachs a look at his skill with two non-title wins at Empress Hall (now demolished) at Earl's Court, where Braitman and Ezra, from the fashion trade, broke into fight promoting.

Keenan's stubbornness, backed by a punch that matched many lightweights, served him well for an eleven-year career. They came no bolder. But Keenan fought Toweel at the peak of the Springbok's reign, and did well to take him the full fifteen rounds.

I had watched, with disbelief, Keenan knocking out the O'Sullivan brothers, Dickie and Danny – Londoners with a natural hardness. I lived near their home and tracked their careers. During wartime, Dickie and I had the private use of the Arsenal Football Club gymnasium, because my father was among the Civil Defence section who worked the air-raid precaution barrage balloon, then a resident on the Highbury turf. Arsenal played their matches on the rival Tottenham FC ground. Dickie and I played pat-a-cake punches. He was the hardest hitting tot at the time. Later Dickie jumped ship in Australia, launched his pro career in a twelve-rounder, and fought a draw for the European title.

Dickie matched any flyweight in the world for strength. Keenan had to be favoured to outbox him clearly in a bantam match, but to flatten him seemed nigh impossible. It happened. When Danny later won the bantamweight title in 1951, he could not resist avenging family honour by accepting Keenan's challenge in hostile Glasgow. Fair-haired Danny, whose career had been curtailed while serving with the RAF in India, could unleash left hooks at a speed quicker than most can flick left jabs. A beautiful mover, Danny suffered from having to reduce to bantam because he was too short for success in a heavier class. When they met in Glasgow, Keenan could have whacked O'Sullivan at any weight. The champion went out in six rounds, having the doubtful honour of lasting twice the distance of his brother.

Keenan could have been fancied to win a world title from a London neighbour of the O'Sullivan brothers, Terry Allen, but he would not consider punishing his willowy frame with a deceptively chilling punch, having to make the required 8 st. Pity that Keenan was at bantam peak when Toweel was outstanding and forced all his challengers to fight in South Africa.

Keenan finally left the confines of Glasgow, Paisley and, occasionally, Liverpool, to campaign with honour in Sydney, Melbourne, Manila and finally Belfast. He took the Commonwealth title with a spectacular KO against Zulu Jake Tuli, a polite little man who was reckoned highly in the famous Jim Wicks stable. Keenan also successfully defended against a South African and a Canadian in Scotland. He feared nobody, official or unofficial.

Keenan at work was a combination of artistry, arrogance and artful butchery. He could box with the best and out-hit the punchers. Even in his declining years, Keenan was always able to give the crowd a show. In Paris we watched him playfully kicking the backside of European champion Alphonse Halimi. At home he outsmarted Billy Peacock, an American classified in the trade as dangerous. He stopped local rival Dick Currie, now a prominent Glasgow sportswriter, in ten rounds.

Keenan's farewell, at thirty-one in his seventy-second fight – knockouts backstage do not count! – was a marvellous and tearful occasion in Belfast, losing in eleven rounds to slick southpaw Freddie Gilroy. Winning the British title was the moment for Gilroy's fans to sing 'When Irish Eyes Are Smiling', but the cheeky Keenan took centre stage and led the crowd in a chorus of 'I Belong to Glasgow'.

Gilroy's Ulster rival, John Caldwell, took us to an unlikely fight arena in São Paulo, Brazil, for a sight of the polished, calculating punching champion Eder Jofre. Caldwell, the Cold-Eyed Killer – a tag he understandably hated – had twice beaten Alphonse Halimi for the European recognized version of the world title. He was unbeaten in twenty-five fights.

Jofre, the handsome Golden Cockerel, was also unbeaten – forty-four fights, with three drawn. Just the kind of match to make King Solomons a bob or two! Jofre, holding the then NBA American version of the world title, reckoned the match would draw more money in Brazil because the country had never produced an undisputed champion. So Solomons became co-promoter for the showdown to clarify the rightful title owner, at the Estadual Do Ibirapuera on 18 January 1962.

I had watched Caldwell, with Gilroy, when they were teammates for Ireland boxing at the European championships in Berlin in 1955. Caldwell, at best, matched the skill and class of any British bantam. But Jofre was to prove special. His only two amateur losses were on points against a Chilean and a Uruguayan, one at the Melbourne Olympics in 1956. As a professional he hammered both of them.

Often the way a boxer behaves away from the ring or training area indicates his attitude in the ring itself. On the whole, the best champions have humility. Bullies are seldom brave. Even Ali frequently resorted to whispering backstage.

I first sought Jofre's mother, Angeline, forty-six, who ran a bazaar, aptly named Golden Bantam, among the soil-red undeveloped hills overlooking a skyscraper city. 'I am the champion because I brought Eder into the world,' she said. 'I encourage him to fight because he makes it easy.' She travelled from Caracas to Los Angeles to watch him.

She met Eder's father, Aristides, at a Brazilian boxing academy – 'For thirty-two years he trains boxers.' Because I had discovered her roadside shop, Mother Jofre introduced me to wide-eyed bystanders, and we walked almost in procession in hot, choking, changeable weather, to her recently constructed home – a gift from Eder.

Her parents were Italian. Aristides was Argentinian, of French extraction. She sported a Scottish plaid skirt which she might well have changed had she realized that Caldwell's manager, Sammy Docherty, was a Glasgow bookie.

We later ambled along a dusty road to the champion's home, which sparkled in comparison with the neighbours'. It was built in an unroaded area, Rua Santa Euxodia, a working-class district. Eder liked living among his own. His home did not have a telephone – 'I see all the people I want to see every day,' he explained. The granite front of the house was emblazoned with a golden engraving of an Olympic discus thrower. Eder and wife, Maria, twenty-three, a former beauty queen and secretary, were a striking pair. They offered captivating smiles like film stars at work. But Eder's determination not to break away from his people even extended to refusing to drive home the Cadillac which was part of his prize when he won the world title. A modest four-seater was parked nearby.

After pleasantries were exchanged, Jofre confirmed he was a strict vegetarian – a rarity among prize fighters – but considered it helped keep his weight down. He admitted that the constant reducing to bantamweight was difficult. 'But mid-summer, São Paulo is my friend. In winter it makes things harder,' he said.

Caldwell's camp was not overconcerned that their man's need for liquids in the South American heat would play havoc with his weight. British reporters speculated that an overweight Jofre meant that Caldwell would win the title by default, and it was a long and expensive way to travel to cover a non-title meeting.

At weigh-in time we shuffled outside the medical room where both boxers were shoved to avoid the crowding of fans and the risk of unbalancing the scales. For both, ounces were important. Adding to the publicity was the appointment of Willie Pep, ex-featherweight champion, as referee; he shocked some of the less well acquainted when he preferred to leave a decision about the extent of expected injuries to each boxer's seconds. 'If they bleed, they bleed, 'cos they're in a business to bleed. You musn't pamper them,' he said, having been conditioned after twenty-one pro years.

When word filtered from the weigh-in room that 'he' was a pound above the limit, we considered Caldwell was virtually the undisputed ruler, without a punch being thrown. We 'experts' had reliably informed our readers that Jofre was outgrowing his division. Then the shockwave followed – it was Caldwell overweight. Following a period of stunned silence, the *Daily Telegraph* correspondent, known affectionately as Saunders of the Liver, popped a consoling pill in his mouth.

Caldwell had to trot around the neighbouring streets, wearing blazer and flannels in the rain, attempting to discard the offending pound within the regulation hour. At a second attempt he was half a pound too heavy. At a third scaling he was considered exactly 8 st 6 lb and given the go-ahead.

A further surprise was the invitation to Peter Wilson, of the *Daily Mirror*, to be an official judge. This gave him the unacceptable advantage of being able to criticize the judges from America and Brazil if he disagreed with their verdict, but he also ran the risk of criticism from rival newspapermen if they disagreed with his scoring.

Jofre saved Pep and Wilson embarrassment. His greatness
stripped Caldwell of everything except his instinctive Irish urge
to go on fighting. Caldwell's hitherto impregnable defence
became a blown safe. Though he took only two counts, in the
fifth and tenth rounds, Pep threw his grey-shirted body between
them when Caldwell's handler, Docherty, climbed on the ring
apron frantically waving a surrender in the tenth.

Caldwell's drastic weight-shedding might have been a
contributory factor, but he simply could not cope with the weight
of the shock inflicted. Nineteen thousand, three hundred and
sixty fans hailed Jofre's victory of cool calculated force over
comparative fragility. When the fight ended, judges marked
88–82 and 90–73 for Jofre, with Wilson, proving totally impartial,
also marking 89–83 for the Brazilian.

Caldwell had boxed deftly and defiantly, but the harsh truth
was that he looked a dainty pretender to the crown. He ended
on his feet, with raw courage, fitness and pride, but these,
historically, are possessions of losers. He tottered in drunken
amazement when Pep clasped his arms around him. As he did
so, Jofre threw his arms wide apart as if to embrace the world
of which he had become undisputed champion.

Jofre literally punched his way out of an invading melee, who
were dancing in the ring as though a band were playing. The only
music was the earlier introductory fanfare, familiar to Solomon's
patrons at Harringay and Wembley, that had been played to
encourage Caldwell. The ropes were appropriately wrapped with
green gauze. The only time Jofre exposed himself to danger was
to gain a calculated advantage. He lathered Caldwell with salvos
of accurate blows, and when the game Irishman appeared
resigned to defeat, he yielded to a combination of vexation,
exasperation and plain futility. Long before the finish, manager
Docherty tugged a towel from cut man Danny Holland,
borrowed from the Henry Cooper camp, in a determined bid to
signal an armistice and save his fighter and friend from total
slaughter.

Solomons proudly led the losing party back to the dressing
room, acknowledging that Jofre had proved a master. Caldwell
had not previously even slipped in the shower, let alone been
hammered twice to the canvas. 'He punched like a lightweight,'
said Caldwell. The loser stepped over a prostrate Brazilian

outside his dressing room. He had been flattened by a Glaswegian who caught him pick-pocketing. All had not been lost!

Jofre, inevitably, lost his battle with the scales and the title with it. He retired for two years, then made a remarkable comeback to capture the world featherweight title, defeating Jose Legra and Vicente Saldivar, whose ring deeds were well known in Britain. Jofre lost only two decisions – one a split vote – in seventy-eight contests before hanging up the gloves in 1976.

Masahiko 'Fighting' Harada, a gardener's son from Setagaya, Japan, was the villain of the piece when he twice outpointed super Jofre in bantamweight title clashes. Both were in Japan when Jofre needed everything short of an amputation to make the title weight limit. Form books can lie, because Jofre was unquestionably a greater champion than Harada. But there was an impressive unbuttoned force in Harada's fighting – he had previously held the world flyweight title.

For ten years, Harada punished his muscles as a full-time fighter, and bowed out when he failed in a bid to win a world title at a third weight – feather. His body resembled that of a dwarf Sumo wrestler, with shoulders powered by regularly delivering sacks of rice from mill to shopkeepers, on a bike. His legs were muscle-bound.

We met on Harada's Tokyo territory, with the champion bowing sedately – the way bullfighters accept applause – following a week of slanging in the Tokyo press between Harada's manager, Sasazarki, and myself. The old warhorse manager, who had 115 fights, kept Harada behind closed doors whilst preparing to defend his title against England's Alan Rudkin in 1965.

We requested at least a brief view of Harada, who belonged to the world, during the build-up for the big fight to take place within the Imperial Palace grounds. Harada conceded to my complaint that it was discourteous to stay in hiding. We were entitled to get some gen for our yen.

Harada's home was above a gymnasium, ten miles from the city centre. At twenty-three, his bulging frame must have required inhuman discipline to reduce to his fighting weight. Wearing a lime-green sweat suit, the stubble-chinned champion put on a rehearsal, without sparring, to satisfy our curiosity. We treated this with a pinch of rice. On the way out I spotted a line of sparmates, hands bandaged in readiness for action, and obviously about to swap practice punches with Harada. The first show was trimmings for the tourists; the second was the serious stuff, for workers only.

Assessing Rudkin's chances was not easy in the malodorous air of suspicion, where it would do Liverpool's Mr Nice Guy little good relying on the niceties and sensibilities of the local referee and judges, one of them an American based in Japan. Harada was the hero, with a television station sponsoring the match. But Rudkin, only one cut-eye loss in twenty-four fights, was no little boy lost. His boyish good looks belied his ability, both to take and to dish out punishment. He could box cleverly when demanded, and fight desperately when needed. His fanclub had increased in Tokyo because he came from Beatle-land. Schoolgirls yelled 'Aran Ludkin', and rushed to mob him.

No British bantam had won the world title since Joe Bowker in 1904. No Briton had won a world title away from home since Ted Kid Lewis in 1915. The previous English world title challenger in Tokyo was Terry Allen, a flyweight who lived only a left hook from Rudkin's London lodgings. Allen's conqueror, Yoshio Shirai, was a commentator, and he publicly announced his fancy for Rudkin to win.

At fight time, Rudkin's trainer, Freddie Hill, who drove a newspaper van – Rudkin was then a member of NATSOPA – took his time inspecting a natty blue spittoon and testing the four-rope ring, before they played martial music and introduced kimono-clad ladies who presented bouquets, and even silver cups, to the fighters. Harada looked bullish in his red and white outfit, and Rudkin looked calmer than he had any right to be with the weight of the Union Jack on his shoulders.

Our reporting pitch at the Budokan Hall, amid 13,000 fanatical spectators, was in the second row of the paid ringside seats, with a telephone on our lap and a filmstar in front, who attracted an unbroken line of autograph hunters. The time change meant a blow-by-blow account being simultaneously dictated to London, so that evening paper editions, including countrywide syndication (at no further fee for the man at the sharp end of the deal) could begin rolling with the fight story at noon, British time. No doubt neighbouring paying customers considered me a nut making a phonecall for the entire fifteen rounds.

In the first round, Rudkin's task was firmly set when Harada clearly wrestled him over and the Japanese referee, Toyama, ruled a mandatory count. Harada was blatantly breaking convention by being permitted to protect his eyebrows with plaster strips before he even entered the ring. Manager Bobby Neill's protests won a psychological round, and when Harada realized that Rudkin was both capable and willing to contest every point, and punch, he punched out his evening's work. It was a thrilling, evenly contested event, with Harada frustrated by Rudkin's superior footwork. Once he tried to claw Rudkin's throat with his left, and also hit him with his right. Had Harada been an American heavyweight, I am sure he would have been cherished for his meanness.

Harada constantly attacked as though he were willing to commit harakiri rather than lose on points. By halfway the champion appeared resigned to Rudkin not being about to topple, and he threw himself at the challenger, striving to wrestle him into weakness.

But there was an admirable workrate from Harada, and despite a defiant gesture by Rudkin with a peach of a left hook in the fifteenth round, the champion was awarded the points, with only one sensible scoring of 72–70 by American Nicky Pope for Harada. The local officials made it a ridiculous runaway. Some British reporters, including Peter Wilson, believed Rudkin had won by a short head. Rudkin, to his credit, did not complain.

Harada was delighted to escape unscathed against his first European rival. He made three more winning defences of the title, including defending against Jofre and the crack Mexican, Joe Medel, before the battle of the bulge caught up with him and the Aborigine, Lionel Rose, dethroned him in Tokyo.

Rudkin's showing rated him a second chance, but again he was forced to fight in the other guy's backyard. Rose, a formidable little champion, outpointed Rudkin – again with some dispute.

It was Rudkin's misfortune to be top-ranked when the title was owned by three exceptional fighters. His third attempt was, yes, in hostile territory, against Ruben Olivares, a savage-hitting Mexican who was fight-based in Los Angeles. Olivares shocked the traders by stopping the seemingly unstoppable Rose in five rounds. He was a puncher of higher calibre than Jofre, but without the Brazilian's ring flair. Others would argue that Olivares, who finished his career with 101 fights, would have mown down Jofre and anyone else who claimed to be great.

When Olivares faced Rudkin at the Inglewood Forum, Los Angeles, in 1969, he had fifty-two wins, one draw with fifty-one knockouts. He was planning to break Henry Armstrong's consecutive run of twenty-eight knockouts. At twenty-one, Olivares was unbeatable.

As if Olivares's record and hitting power were not sufficient, the fight was hyped, with publicity director Bill Caplan trying to convince us that Ruben was of the Jewish faith, because his father was named Solomon.

During training I felt the wrapped fists of the Mexican. They were like bolts coated with emery paper. He almost drilled holes in sparring partners with every punch in extra-padded practice gloves. Poor Rudkin. The challenger had started and finished his training in tinsel town, in a sauna bath, which indicated that weight-reducing had become irksome. He needed every ounce of strength to win an argument with cocksure Olivares.

I felt depressed watching Rudkin, the charmer, working feverishly to whip his body into shape, and sharpen his mind for yet another uphill battle. He was a hard little man to hit fairly and squarely on target, but I was amazed as I watched Olivares drop useful sparmates like flies with a single blow. At least Rudkin had the consolation of being guaranteed £10,000, with more to come – then the highest paid Briton at his weight. There seemed no more than a slender hope of winning.

My troubles, flu-hit and struggling to overcome air conditioning, were minor compared with Rudkin having to face a genuine gunslinger. We were advised not to install telephones at the ringside, because the Mexican fans who invaded the Forum were bound to rip them out, especially those plugged in for Britain.

Rudkin was noticeably sombre, almost resigned to defeat, because his training had been troublesome. His mood was not helped when a policeman attending his dressing room proudly announced that a gun had been taken from a drunken Mexican spectator. 'What about the guns of the rest of them?' shrugged Rudkin.

Five minutes and thirty seconds after the start of the fight, Rudkin was led away, with all resistance punched out of him. Gold-toothed Olivares was able to back his boasts. His win was merciless and complete, against a fighter who never quit easily. 'He's the greatest fighter I've seen,' said Rudkin. 'Every punch numbs. I went down from punches I never saw coming. Those are the ones that hurt.' Rudkin had taken three counts, and the referee did not bother with the formality of the last one. He called 'Enough' as Rudkin bravely groped on his knees.

Rudkin's sciences were swept away by the stunning blows of an executioner that stamped Olivares in a different punching class to all others. He had finesse, too, and no pity. Saved the indignity of being counted out, Rudkin passed our ringside pitch and said, 'I still look better than you!' We flaked out after the words had been transmitted to London.

In the dressing room, somebody switched the lights out. 'That's the second time tonight that's happened to me,' quipped Rudkin.

Olivares, like Jofre, gained weight to win the featherweight title, and ten years after whacking Rudkin without working up a sweat, Olivares was still battling in title fights.

The belief among old-timers that 'they just don't make 'em like they used to' is exploded by Wilfredo Gomez, a Puerto Rican with a narrow ribbon of black moustache and the looks of a banker. He's a bantam or, to be definitive, a super-bantam – weight division 4 lb higher – who ranks with the greatest. He could be the Greatest.

Gomez began 1983 with all his wins being knockouts, one draw in forty fights, with only one loss when he attempted to step out of his weight class against the brilliant Salvador Sanchez, killed in a car accident at the height of his career in 1982. Gomez has held a title for six years, longer than any current champion; has scored a record seventeen title fight knockouts, with a consecutive run of thirty-two knockouts, the most for a champion.

My first sight of Gomez was in Munich in 1972, when he made no more than four words in a notebook at the Olympic Games. He was underage at sixteen, stupidly pushed beyond his pasture, and eliminated by an Egyptian who would not now be rated good enough as a sparring partner. The notes became longer when Gomez won the amateur World Cup, completing eighty-three wins in eighty-six bouts. He wanted to remain amateur and get a college education, when he was offered $15,000 for his first fight. He 'took the money and bought my Dad a cab.' Today, Gomez is the wealthy president of Bazooka Enterprises, and destined to relinquish his crown – at least at super-bantam – to become a film actor.

I rate Gomez's fight with Lupe Pintor, the actual bantamweight champion from Mexico, the best at the weight I have seen – and among the top at any weight. They called it a 'Clash of the Little Giants' in the giant Superdome, New Orleans, in December 1982. Flashflood warnings and wild horses could not keep us away. (It helped that ITV paid the fare.)

The fight was for Gomez's title, because Pintor had virtually punched himself out of opposition. The first round epitomized what kind of fight it would be, when the notoriously slow-starting Pintor was repeatedly tagged by Gomez's rights that were led and landed against teachings of the textbook. But Pintor did not buckle; he changed his pace almost immediately, pushing Gomez back.

Men with less heart would have caved in by about the eighth round. It almost defied description – a couple of cavemen clubbing each other without pause. Lupe's defence looked leaky, yet he could find a way to take the play away when Gomez had an impressive spell. As the old chroniclers put it – no quarter asked or given. At the halfway mark – fifteen-rounders for the WBC were about to be shortened to twelve – Pintor had absorbed the champion's best and he began his run, like a St Leger favourite coming round the final bend.

The wills of both champions surfaced in each round; the sheer intensity of the battle was frightening – Gomez was no goody-two-shoes in the ring. New York referee, Arthur Mercante, deducted a foul point for elbowing the Mexican.

Though my card had Gomez slightly ahead at the thirteenth, his face sprouted bumps, his eyes were increasingly becoming slits, and when Pintor won the round it seemed his staying power would get him home. I could not understand why Gomez's seconds kept dragging him back to the corner, even when he had clearly won the round! The way Gomez slumped into their arms, dragging his feet, must have inspired Pintor.

But Gomez possesses that indefinable thing called class. He sprang out in the fourteenth as though the fight had just begun and his gargoyle looks were only stage make-up. Blows that had been reduced to arm punches suddenly became spiteful again. A right dropped Pintor, who beat the count and did not appear too distressed. But Gomez knew by then he had to do more than rely on his immense skills. He waded in with a pair of hooks that sent Pintor down again, and though the Mexican made an attempt to sit up, as if to signify that he could again beat the count, he slumped backwards, and the referee, standing over him, stopped the fight two minutes forty-four seconds into the fourteenth.

Both came and left as champions. They owed us nothing. But they may never be as great again.

Henry Cooper says . . .

I can relate to Alan Rudkin, John Caldwell, and Peter Keenan, whom I saw. For Keenan to have whacked Jake Tuli showed me he was exceptional. Little Tuli was with our stable, as you mention, and he was a classy fighter who could hit. Jim Wicks did a fatherly job with Tuli and we were all disappointed when he slipped home to South Africa without saying goodbye. He could not criticize the way he was handled here.

Rudkin was certainly unlucky having to fight such classy opposition who could all hit. I'd pick Ruben Olivares as the most dangerous. Your behind-the-scenes reporting of Harada, Jofre and Olivares is new to me. In action they all seemed to have the necessary relaxed style that helped produce the old pay-off punch. Tightness stifles punch power. These little bantams, formidable at their weight, were genuine world beaters.

I'd hate to have worked in the corner of their opponents. I'd be stumped for words on how they could win!

Eric Boon

When Eric Boon hit, they stayed hit. Pound for pound, the 'boy' from Cambridgeshire matched the greatest. Many fighters at least two weight divisions above him could not produce such power. If the Second World War had not cut through his career, I am convinced the crashing Boon would have at least fought for, if not won, a world title.

For single punch ferocity he was a division higher than any other British lightweight. Scribes could regularly dredge up the old line about a Boon punch 'that cancelled out the arrears'. His come-from-behind wins were explosive. He possessed all the drama of the big puncher, together with good looks and a body built like a sawn-off Rocky Marciano. He stood only 5 ft 4 in, but he often strode like a giant. Perfect Mr Box Office.

He fought before and after the war; won the championship during the hostilities, becoming the youngest lightweight champion on record two weeks before his nineteenth birthday. Before he was twenty, Boon won the Lonsdale Belt outright. A record. The excitement he generated by just stepping into a ring would have been gobbled up by today's devouring television coverage. Pictures of Boy Boon at work would have been bounced off satellites to every corner of the earth.

Son of a blacksmith, he honed his muscles pounding the anvil. His biceps bulged; his neck and shoulders were moulded for the natural hitter. Boon explained that his father insisted he learned to strike the anvil in a way to help his hitting power. 'He taught me to swing the hammer and then pull it back at the point of impact. It gave me greater force and accuracy. When I began boxing I did the same thing. Times were too hard to be just a jolly good loser. I hit to hurt and win. Always did.'

It was a long time before country-boy Boon, from the pleasant town of Chatteris, which later produced a similarly built Dave 'Boy' Green, shook off his rustic image, though he returned happily to his shire in retirement. When Boon matured he became London's West End man about town, setting fashion trends, sporting the sharpest mohair and cashmere clothes. He had style, and the look of a matinee idol rather than that of a prize fighter who admitted meanness in the ring. They called him Golden Boy because he appeared in the play of the violinist-turned-boxer in South Africa.

I spent many hours in early postwar years watching Boon workout at Jack Solomons' gymnasium, opposite the Windmill Theatre ('We never clothed') in London. Sometimes we had High Court judges, spivs, show-biz stars, ticket touts and even a hangman for company. Even in practice gloves, all eyes were riveted just in case Boon knocked over a sparring partner. He often did.

It was Boon who helped make Solomons, then a hustling matchmaker in the East End, who worked for promoter Sydney Hulls at Harringay Arena. Solomons managed Boon to the championship and became boxing's big-time promoter with an amusing touch of bullshine that Barnum and Bailey would have envied. Boon's welterweight career was managed by Benny Huntman, who knew more strokes than Higgins and Davis combined.

Boon's brief amateur career ended with suspension at fourteen for taking ten bob for a bout in Chatteris. He was licensed as a professional at fifteen, though he added a year to comply with the then age regulation to compete for money. He fought for 3s 6d, made it big at Peterborough in 1935 earning 25s, and cycled to most of his fights.

It was Jack Hart, a London referee, who watched Boon at Peterborough and told him to report to London's Devonshire Club, a converted church hall within splashing distance of Aldgate Pump where Jack Solomons staged Sunday afternoon shows. 'You'd better get a good opponent, because this kid is bound to be champion,' he warned Solomons.

Boon's parents opposed his leaving home, but Boon was hungry for money and success. He set off to cycle seventy-two miles on the day of his first big fight, managed to scrounge a lorry lift, throwing his cycle on top of the cabbages, and eventually peddled to the East End fighting den. He propped his bike against a wall and was rebuked by the dressing-room whip for being late. His legs were obviously weary before the first bell, but he fought eight rounds for the first time and was awarded a draw against Young Higgins. So began the slog to the top.

In the thirties, the bad old days for many of us, there were no short cuts. (In 1982 American Davey Moore won a world title in only his ninth fight!) Boon had forty fights before being allowed to appear on a major bill, a mere four-rounder at Harringay Arena in 1937. That, too, was a draw. But there were many flattened victims along the way – nine out in the first round.

His return to Harringay a year later brought an impressive one-round knockout against Johnny Ward, a hard nut who had survived in higher company. A month later, Len Lemaux was also dispatched in the first round at the famous arena where Solomons later became Mr Boxing and attracted royalty to the ringside. Boon had an incredible sixty-seven battles in four years, losing three and scoring thirty-nine knockouts before he was considered ready for a championship match.

The proving fight was a non-title effort against the reigning champion Jimmy Walsh. There was an outcry – critics don't change – when Solomons dared pit his teenager against a cagey champion. Solomons, with his customary eye on the takings and also on giving his man an edge, signed the fight for Chatteris during an agricultural show. He didn't consider the unreliability of the English weather in May. It poured, and a few hours before the first bell was due the show was about to be called off. Solomons, copying the baloneying P. T. Barnum at his best, said, 'I've had a word with the man upstairs, and the rain will stop.' It did. Jack subsequently considered himself the official weather settler, and it usually worked for the fine open-air shows he promoted at White City and elsewhere.

The ground at Chatteris was waterlogged; bales of straw were spread around ringside seats; and Boon played his part by defeating Walsh. Unfortunately for Solomons, though it didn't bother Boon, Walsh made the mistake of subsequently losing his title to dapper Dave Crowley, a James Cagney of the ring, whose boxing moves fascinated me. I was a devout Crowley fan even though I recognized his inability to hit hard in the declining years because his hands were like putty. He fought with a mixture of proud caution and audacity.

When they matched Crowley with eighteen-year-old Boon in 1938, Crowley had fought the world's best and had been to the States. He was at his best and he simply dazzled. My father also enjoyed Crowley's Cheeky Chappie brand of boxing, but worked with Solomons, trainer Nat Seller and Mike Milligan in Boon's corner.

The best cornermen (now it's cornerpersons) are expected to work wonders in the sixty seconds between rounds. Cut men, con artists, nurses, father figures, they are expected to be a combination of all to keep a fighter winning. Dad had to become a traitor to Crowley, whom he'd befriended, when Boon's left eye had swollen, plum-coloured, in size. Crowley outboxed the comparatively raw kid, taunting him with cries of 'Taxi' when Boon's swings flailed and missed as though he were hailing a cab.

Their boxing styles were totally contrasted, but as people Crowley and Boon were two of a kind. Boon, though infuriated, understood and enjoyed Crowley's joke. As the fight wore on, Crowley maintained his lead. Boon's favoured, murderous right hand was badly bruised and his eye was closing to a slit. The fight was in danger of being stopped, but with an old-fashioned, though crude, method, Dad nicked Boon's swollen face with the tip of a razor blade, kept in his emergency pack, and actually sucked out blood to reduce the swelling. A human leech. 'Oh, how could you?' I remember my mother asking. Dad replied, 'I didn't like doing it, but it worked. I'm a pro.'

Crowley's confidence wilted when Boon's punching suddenly became more accurate – he could now see intended targets. He had not previously fought longer than ten rounds, but in the thirteenth, Boon, who could knock a man down with either hand, brought Crowley to his knees – counted out. 'Try getting up from that one,' Boon said as he winked at the clouted Crowley. (The World Boxing Council and European Union have since reduced championship fights to twelve rounds. The British Board of Control followed suit in January 1983.)

The ring became a carnival; Solomons had produced his first champion; writers besieged the teenage champion's dressing room; and Dad stayed in the corner, clearing the bucket, tidying the resin tray, and preparing to second the curtain-closing boxers on the bill.

A month later, Dad was in hospital suffering from a throat infection – suspected blood poisoning – which doctors attributed to his desperate first-aid act for Boon. Our family were upset because Dad was interned in the National Temperance Hospital, near Hampstead. A penance for a second who had enjoyed toasting Boon's victory.

A month after becoming champion, Boon, with his handsome features restored, kept fists flying with a visit to the outback of Mountain Ash, Wales, to knock out Boyo Rees in two rounds. Then came a match that caught on and has become boxing folklore – Boon *v.* Arthur Danahar, Fight of the Century, etcetera, etcetera. It was booked seventy days after Boon had become the boy wonder champion. Danahar, as Cockney as jellied eels, was a boxing hero after only fourteen fights. His left was the textbook English version, as reliable as the Greenwich time signal.

As a scuffling office boy in a newspaper sports room I listened to the informed talk of my seniors, and to the discussions between Dad and Uncle, who enthused about Boon *v.* Danahar, when they trained amateurs or pros at the gymnasium they ran in Islington. Rarely was boxing a topic at home – there were serious things to discuss, like the prospect of a Second World War. Dad had trained South African Ben Foord to fight Max Schmeling in Hamburg in 1938, and he came home fearing an impending big fight, having witnessed Naziism at its ugliest.

When the promoters considered staging the lightweight classic at a West End hotel for twenty-five guineas a seat, there was almost a national strike in protest. Thirty years later, when Solomons tried to convince us that he would promote in Hyde Park or on Wimbledon's centre court, it made headlines in the same way – newspapers don't change either!

Inevitably, Harringay was the site on 23 February 1939. Predictably, all 11,500 seats were sold in advance. The championship carved its own bit of history by becoming the first wired-for-closed-circuit screening to three West End cinemas – at one guinea a view. And the comparative few who owned television sets saw it live.

The fight surpassed even its massive publicity. Though Boon

was more experienced, many favoured Danahar, because Boon's
defence had been pierced easily by Crowley for the best part of
thirteen rounds, and Danahar was younger and stronger than
Crowley. My fears were for Danahar being comfortable, having
to weigh inside 9 st 9 lb. Weight-making is draining, and Boon's
opponents had to possess stamina as well as a strong chin.
Danahar had not fought beyond eight rounds, and public
demand had forced the match for Danahar's premature chance,
whereas Boon had needed sixty-seven bouts to qualify.

At 5 ft 8 in Danahar outreached Boon by 5 in. His defence
was sound but obviously not impenetrable. Bethnal Green's
product of the amateur school stood upright and left-jabbed
Boon into frustration. Boon's face was blotted from the first
round; his left eye trickled blood and the bruising began.
Danahar was on his way to becoming champion.

It was the pattern of several Boon fights – patiently waiting
for an opponent to tire; hoping his face could absorb blows
without forcing the referee to intervene. The sole arbiter was W.
Barrington-Dalby, later to become a Board steward and the
famous 'Come in, Barry' of radio commentary. Barry and I
became friends in his veteran years. He presented me with rare
books on pugilism, and he frequently referred to the highlight
of his career – officiating for the incomparable Boon v Danahar
championship. 'I had the closest view of two brilliant young men
giving everything they had, and more, and being able to keep it
sporting,' he said.

In Boon's corner, Solomons, not overconcerned about the
niceties of the sport, was hollering at Boon: 'Remember he's not
fought over eight rounds. He'll tire. Go to work.' And it was in
the eighth, with Boon trailing, that the fight switched dramati-
cally. Boon finally landed his jaw-busting right. Danahar
instinctively sought refuge in a clinch, but Boon denied him.
Another right sent Danahar down for a nine-count.

They came no bolder than Danahar, who miraculously recovered from nine knockdowns until the fourteenth round – at about
four minutes from armistice time – when Barrington-Dalby held
Boon off, collecting Danahar in his arms to prevent a brave
challenger from being counted out.

Boon had thrown punches like an outraged octopus, with
Danahar wilting but refusing to stay down. Boon's face was like
an affronted gargoyle; Danahar's was comparatively unmarked.

They hugged at the end and remained respectful opponents and pals. It was modest Boon who reminded us that when Danahar retained strength as a welterweight he stopped Boon, seven years later, in the same ring. But the intervening war years, and a serious injury for Boon, had taken the gilt off his fighting. Guardsman Danahar remained a successful welter, and was probably the best, at any weight, who was unable to win a title.

The lightweight match had netted Boon £3215, including his share of the television fees, then a record for a lightweight champion. Danahar took the pitiful loser's end – £500. The rematch with Crowley, ending with injury in seven rounds, brought Boon a belt outright – in eleven months and twenty-four days, aged nineteen.

Boon's wartime injury was played down. He had crashed at night on a motorcycle, wearing only an RAF forage cap, into a cow crossing a blacked-out country road. The cow was killed and Boon suffered skull damage. With today's admirable tightening-up of the medical requirements for boxing, Boon would not have been relicensed; he would not have passed the modern brain-scan examinations. Wife Wendy, a dancer whom Boon had twice married, told me: 'As he got older he sometimes lost his balance. He knew it had nothing to do with boxing; the accident was far more serious than he admitted.'

Yet Boon, the grown-up, was an exciting, nicely proportioned, if short, welterweight. He continued fighting from the Fens to South Africa, Canada and Australia until 1952. He returned to a four-hundred-year old cottage at Wicken, near Newmarket, working as a timber tools salesman and showing fight films, especially his clash with Danahar, for charity.

The great battle of the thirties was Boon's most memorable, but not most exciting. He topped it against Robert Villemain, a Frenchman who had earlier knocked out Ernie Roderick, a champion who had outpointed Boon and defeated Jake LaMotta, of *Raging Bull* fame, a former world champion. It was at Harringay, nine years after the memory of Danahar, when Boon, at twenty-eight and softened by bright lights and world tours, took on the unbeaten Villemain.

I rate that battle, which was not even top of the bill, among the best six I have seen. They fought like infuriated stags, both refusing to break ground. Boon was on the wane, but he had immense pride. He came out for each round signalling a potential knock-blow with a loud 'ooomph', and he sailed into Villemain as if the Frenchman were a false alarm. Villemain's footwork and strategy sneaked the opening rounds, but Boon's contempt was so fierce that he forced Villemain to fight, rather than box, his way out of trouble. The old Boy was ageing by the minute and started to make trips to the canvas. Yet each time he hauled himself up as though he hated the indignity of having to take a count.

In the sixth, Boon had almost punched himself out. His fight back was sensational. For forty-five seconds he maintained a nonstop aggression that made even teak-man Villemain wilt. The crowd were on their feet. The roar cracked the blue and yellow paint on the rafters. Villemain's right cheek was gashed. Boon was back in the picture. It was anybody's fight, and when the bell rang for the last round neither would have been blamed for hanging on. Instead, they kept up a blistering punch pace. It was not enough for Boon to contest points. There is no honour in caution. His awful pride was visible. With three minutes to go, he waded back seeking a pay-off punch. When Villemain cupped his gloves around his face in sensible defence, Boon kept pounding and actually broke two of the Frenchman's knuckles. But in the exasperating final thirty seconds, Boon dropped to his knees, caught by Villemain's well-timed counter-punch. He came back again, briefly took the play away, then buckled under a left hook.

On his knees again, Boon shook his head in disbelief, and though he was striving to get up his strength was sapped. His body finally betrayed him, officially counted out in the act of rising, only five seconds remaining of the fight. 'It wasn't his punches that did it. It was my own. I'd punched myself out. I couldn't stand up.' Boon gained more credit for losing this fabulous battle than he had by winning so many in his youth.

At fifty-four, a remarkably youthful-looking Boon sparred in a charity bout with Harry Lazar. Then Jack Solomons, running his Park Lane World Sporting Club, gathered admirers to raise a modest testimonial for Boon. I was privileged to propose a toast and speak of his deeds on the tribute night. Predictably a flickering film of Boon *v*. Danahar was shown – the bow-tie observers lapped it up.

Contented Grandad Boon went back to his country home, happy that he had not been forgotten. He was not wealthy, but was rich in friends. His only vice was being a near chain-smoker. When he collapsed with a heart attack in 1981, he still had a fighter's stubborn will – he tried to stop ambulance men from carrying him to hospital. Wendy Boon blamed smoking for blood clotting. 'I'll never smoke again if I come through this OK,' promised Boon. It was a battle he lost. At sixty-one, the great Boy had gone.

Henry Cooper says . . .

I knew Eric only for a few years before he died. He always looked so fit and sharp. I'd seen his fight with Arthur Danahar on film several times, when Eric asked me along to functions. He liked to stage boxing film nights. It's difficult to judge from a flickery old film, but it's obvious to anyone that Boon was an exceptional light-weight hitter.

His build looked perfect for the game. If you could make matches in heaven I'd like to see Boon against Charnley. He was certainly a funny character who lived it up and got the best out of his life. I regret not having seen him fight for real.

Dave Charnley

His southpaw style, uncommon at the time, may have been an abomination in the eyes of the straight-left purists, but Dave Charnley was a professionals' pro. The most consistent British lightweight champion produced for a decade, he fought reigning world champions of two weights and every ranked rival from 1954 to 1964. He battled for ten years against the toughest, without the restriction and, thereby, the protection of being tied to one promoter. He did it totally freelance, without producing any lurid adjectives, and I know many knowledgeable traders who would vote Charnley the most competent British boxer in twenty-five years, though he just failed to capture a world crown.

I witnessed fifty-five of Charnley's sixty-one fights, several of his amateur exploits, and had an unusual association with his career, though the relationship was professional, not personal. Rarely could I keep Charnley's name out of a newspaper chat column, but I cannot recall having commentated on a Charnley fight. The reporting trek covered Houston, Texas, to Rome, and more earthy sites from Southampton to Streatham, Harringay and Wembley.

I had almost daily reports of Charnley, the chunky kid with a Scottish accent from Dartford, Kent, because a Fitzroy Lodge amateur club official, Tommy Hallett, worked on a bench along-side me at the London *Evening News*. Charnley's instructor was Freddie Hill (later to train Rudkin, Finnegan, Sibson and others) who drove a newspaper van; and the club's matchmaker, Ray Bartlett, sold the paper outside St Paul's station.

Fascinated by their glowing words about terrier Charnley, crop-haired and dedicated, whom they genuinely believed to be the best thing since sliced bread, I bought tickets to sit on the stage of the now demolished Manor Place Baths in south London, to watch Charnley attempt to win his first novice competition.

A young lady, who happened to live in the apartment above our family's, accompanied me. Charnley, a featherweight, clobbered his opposition at the start of the show and, as was the custom, had to box his final in the last contest. Had my date insisted upon leaving, I would have missed Charnley's first title, which meant that he would qualify to represent Fitzroy Lodge at open shows.

My lady, who had never watched amateur boxing, was also interested in Tiger Charnley's final. We stayed. Charnley won. My companion later signed a wedding contract with me and has only watched one boxing show since. She never met Charnley, whose career as a pot hunter was crowned by becoming ABA champion, and then knocking out Dick McTaggart, later an Olympic champion.

His service-with-a-scowl brand of fighting was a cinch in capturing the professional lightweight title in 1957 from Joe Lucy. The glory was short-lived when, three months later, Charnley dropped a fifteen-round decision against Willie Toweel, from the famous South African fighting family, for the then Empire championship. The defeat rankled with Charnley for the next two years. He constantly pestered manager Arthur Boggis, exboxer turned wealthy London meat trader, to fix a rematch 'at any cost'.

Meanwhile, Charnley cashed in, moving up a weight to fight Peter Waterman, London brother of actor Dennis, who had retired as a brave and brilliant welterweight champion. Waterman came back for a natural match, the kind that made Jack Solomons lick his lips, at Harringay Arena. Charnley was at his cruel best. Waterman, once an Olympic competitor and having twice battled against Cuban Kid Gavilan, a world champion, was swamped by Charnley's punch avalanche and was stopped in five rounds. He never fought again.

Charnley's insistence on facing the top-notchers continued, and he defeated ranked Joey Lopes at White City.

He became David Fraser Charnley Ltd and also Corporal Charnley, D.F., 23391, Royal Engineers. He was chosen to star in the farewell to Harringay Arena show on 28 October 1958, against Carlos Ortiz, a sergeant leader of the Pioneer and Assault platoon, National Guard, East 28th St, New York.

They never made an easy match for Charnley. The boiler-maker's apprentice at Vickers Cray, Dartford, was now starring at the arena where Solomons had staged many great fights, and a few flops. Ortiz, Puerto Rican born, raised in New York, was managed by Bill Daly, who had been there and back in the fight business. We suspected Ortiz would be special after a glimpse of his boxing against George Guy in a London Boys Club v. New York match.

Ortiz had lost one of thirty fights, later avenged, and at twenty-two seemed a champion in the making. Charnley fought doggedly in a memorable scrap. But Ortiz stole the points. Nobody argued, including Charnley, who was more inclined to be rude to opponents who ran and lost rather than to those who defeated him. Charnley's showing was classy against a businesslike boxer, proving that British boxing was by no means beyond redemption. It was strictly a he-man issue for ten rounds, and Charnley did not bother to moan that his right hand was injured when he needed it most. Winner and loser were applauded by the greats gathered there for the occasion, including Americans Henry Armstrong, Max Baer and Gus Lesnevich, who fought at Harringay. Ortiz proved his class, as if we ever doubted it, by becoming world lightweight champion in 1962.

Before Charnley could brood they brought on Toweel at Wembley. Charnley learned quickly when he'd been, as he put it, 'messed about' by the hit-and-move boxers. Toweel, word had it, was struggling to stay strong at 9 st 9 lb. It needed at least welterweight strength to stave off a Charnley fired for revenge. Toweel knew sufficient moves to make it difficult, though he could no longer match the power or aggression of his chunky challenger. For nine rounds they offered a repeat of the first fight, with Charnley giving more evidence of his robust methods by drawing Toweel's leads and countering. It was a difficult fight to score: a fight of endeavour and expertise between fierce competitors. Charnley seemed a fraction in front when they came out for the tenth. He had to take charge.

Toweel's right eyebrow was ripped open and Charnley sensed the Springbok was trapped. With a perfect punch combination, a southpaw right lead followed by lefts in rapid succession, Charnley stopped the smart Toweel in his tracks. Nobody had hurt Toweel. He seemed totally bemused, and whilst he was making a brave try to seek refuge either in a clinch or a corner, Charnley pounced. He unloaded a leading right hand over Toweel's pawing defensive left; a following left sent Toweel floundering into the ropes and down on his knees. The roar of the crowd drowned Belfast referee Andrew Smyth's count, and though Toweel made a courageous attempt to get up, his arms were draped on his shorts, his eyes glassy and his body spent. He was counted out on his feet with Smyth spreading his arms wide to signal that the battle was over.

A thrilling match of will overcoming skill. Charnley at his unstoppable best. Toweel would surely have been a world title contender in the eighties. To defeat him in style was a measure of Charnley's class, and proof of his power.

British lightweights had suffered forty-four years of frustration in their assaults on the world championship. Freddie Welsh, the last holder, was punished by Benny Leonard in 1917. Kid Berg, a big hit in America, won a junior world title but lost two 9 st 9 lb challenges against Tony Canzoneri. Ronnie James wilted before the bolo-punch avalanche of Ike Williams.

Charnley, clearly the best in Europe, was given a crack at Joe Brown, nicknamed Old Bones, a one-time carpenter who ran a honky-tonk in Baton Rouge, Louisiana. At thirty-five Brown had had 112 fights and offered Charnley a tenth defence of the title he had won with a broken hand. He was ten years older than Charnley, had the hips of a Harlem dancer, with spindly arms that bulged at the biceps. He was pure pro – a correct hitter.

In the days when a British challenger going to America was an event, Charnley faced Brown at the Sam Houston Arena in Texas on 2 December 1959. His purse, before the benefits of television ancillary rewards, was a mere £4000. Brown, who had a welcome habit of saying things the news gatherers wanted to hear, took the precaution of staying isolated at Camp Holden for six weeks. 'I'm doing this guy Charnley a favour,' he assured us. 'I'm doing my manager Lou Viscusi and his friends a good turn giving the English fellah a break. I hate them lefties [southpaws]. I'd get more money fighting other guys.'

Brown's take-home pay was a guaranteed £8400. He was not a braggart and had worn his fighting years well. He was frank and friendly because I happened to be the only reporter who had bothered to travel to watch his final workout for the big fight.

He had risen from labouring in the cotton fields, finding the ring, as many have done, the shortest way from poverty to plenty. He talked about his wife, psychology and religion, and was itching to escape from the pine camp. 'A man gets lonely and fit enough out here to kill,' he said.

Charnley, always particular about his training, was testy with his entourage, which included his amateur manager Ray Bartlett, who travelled to Texas as Charnley's guest as a thank-you for his invaluable help – his amateur career had been plotted masterfully. Charnley's testiness began with dissatisfaction at the training facilities in the downtown Roxy gym. Texas wise-guy talk from sparmates did not amuse him. His then wife, Ruth, was permitted to visit him at feeding time only!

Backstage Charnley was rarely known to raise his voice. He disliked profanity and was reserved and reticent. He was by no means a typical typecast fighter. Yet gloved up, whether it be practice or reality, he turned into a spiteful puncher who gave the impression of enjoying trying to rearrange an opponent's face into as unrecognizable a shape as possible. Family and friends could not understand how the home-loving Jekyll became the ring Hyde.

Manager Boggis, who pouted his chest like a pigeon when he talked of Charnley's deeds, had attempted to spy on Brown in training. He stuck out like a sore thumb, and the champion's wily trainer, Bill Gore, a tall seventy-one-year old with watery eyes and the perpetual melancholic look of an Alistair Sim, was not amused. 'We can spot fakes a mile away,' he drawled. 'If he wanted to come he should'a asked. We'd have invited him and, maybe, got some mileage out of it. Brown has nothing to hide.'

None the less, Boggis felt he had boosted his own confidence, if not Charnley's, by seeing Brown in the flesh for the first time. The champion, aware of the intruder, offered little more than a soft-shoe shuffle workout. 'He's smart,' said Boggis. 'But I didn't learn anything I didn't already know.'

British morale was boosted, along with the box office, when Harry Carpenter, reporting for the *Daily Mail*, wrote in the *Houston Press* that Charnley was a 'Midget Marciano who had only once failed to spank a Yank'. George Whiting, whose words were devoured by both readers and writing competitors, like me, said in the *Houston Chronicle*: 'Charnley does not have to apologize to anyone for coming here. . . . He may win, he may lose,

but of one thing the good folks of Houston may be certain –
Dave Charnley will fight 'till the cows come home, and never,
never quit.'

At fight time, Brown's manager, Lou Viscusi, who spoke with
a whisper and made dollars drip from every facet of the fight
game, stayed in the arena box office when the first bell rang. He
employed others to flap towels, sponge faces or staunch cuts
while he kept a close eye on the takings; and he had infinite faith
in Brown.

A black-shirted Texan referee, Jimmy Webb, ordered the
Marine guard out of the ring, checked the near-black gloves of
champion and challenger, and motioned for battle to commence.

The brown mallet fists of Brown picked punches, while
Charnley, who sweated profusely during the drawnout introduc-
tions, took stock. Charnley, surprisingly, stayed at long range,
although his style demanded getting close in where his hooks
were capable of doing most damage. Brown's whiplash lefts may
have looked flicks from a few rows back, but from the press
bench at the ring apron they were purposeful punches that
reddened Charnley's right eye.

Charnley had trouble finding range, and Brown, a science
master, slipped away and taunted punches. It was not a thrilling
match; both were biding time, playing it safe. Charnley began
to have some success by the fourth round, correcting his
tormentor with looping blows. I made Charnley win the round;
referee Webb scored even. By the fifth Charnley finally moved
into gear. The searching start was not his style. He began
bobbing and weaving, attempting to get inside Brown's long
arms, and a right hook, his only notable punch of the fight,
tagged the champion. It had the undesired effect of rousing
Brown from his comparative slumber to swap punches.

Trading blows suited Charnley because it forced Brown into
errors and recklessness. Charnley stormed in, winning the round
beyond doubt. Then an incident, difficult to define, changed the
scene. Brown delivered a right uppercut and lowered his head
instinctively to protect himself from a predictable Charnley
counter. Heads clashed seconds before the end of the round, and
Charnley staggered away, shook his head in disbelief and
slumped on his stool, head lowered between his knees. His right
eyebrow was badly gashed – the first blood flow of his career.
He knew he had been headed off the title.

Referee Webb asked, 'Can you fix it?' to Charnley's cornermen. 'No way,' they said. So Charnley was forced to surrender, injured before the fight had really begun. A later television replay confirmed that a head clash which seemed accidental had caused the damage.

Charnley was subjected to the customary acerbic criticism of Jimmy Cannon and Dan Parker, as though he had welcomed being cut. 'Charnley is wearing a golf ball for a monocle today,' wrote Cannon. 'Brown acted with the boredom of a tavern keeper rousting a stormy drunk.'

George Whiting, who had assured Texans that our man would never quit, nudged me at the ringside and shrugged. 'It's a smack in the eye for both of us. At least Charnley got better paid for it.'

Brown insisted that his right had inflicted the damage and, after thirty-nine months of continuous defences, talked of 'not wasting all the training'. Only twelve days later, Brown yawned while earning his corn by outpointing Joey Parks in a non-title match at New Orleans!

Charnley returned to lick his wounds and concentrate on winning and defending the European crown. He proved a different class. An Italian and a Frenchman were whacked at Wembley and Streatham, and his claims for a rematch with Brown were considerably strengthened by a fine knockout against American Paul Armstead, who was world rated in 1960.

Jack Solomons baited Brown with $50,000 to face Charnley at the giant Earl's Court arena in 1961. Bookmakers, who rule with head, not heart, made Brown 5–4 on to retain his title – a shift from the unlicensed touts in Texas who laid 12–5 against Charnley in the first fight.

Charnley trained and pounded sparmates with an almost inhuman detachment. There was a sheen on his skin that denoted super fitness, and there must have been hate in his heart. The occasion had the electric, palm-sweaty atmosphere that Solomons enjoyed at many of his promotions.

Brown began the fight, attempting to play matador by craftily drifting out of distance on drumstick legs and carefully tucking his elbows close to his body to nullify Charnley's blows to the ribcage. This time Charnley was relentless. The frail-looking reed of a champion swayed before the gale of Charnley's attacks.

Brown's red-hot poker left Charnley's face again masked in

blood, but the damage was not serious. The cause this time was a blow that could be seen by the backrow customers, and undoubtedly heard by ringsiders. It was certainly painfully felt by Charnley. Midway through the fifth round Brown unleashed a right with swift accuracy and an obviously punishing result. There was a distinct crack as the punch connected flush on Charnley's putty nose. The bridge was slashed as if Brown was carrying a razorblade in his glove, and Charnley brushed his right glove across the injury to assure himself that the nose was still intact.

When all seemed lost, Charnley threw himself at Brown and forced the craftsman out of his stride. Brown was made to fight where he had earlier elected to box. It was an exciting touch-and-go championship that must have given referee Tommy Little palpitations when he entered fractions on a scorecard at the end of each round. Charnley magnificently lifted himself by crash-bashing his way to winning the thirteenth and fourteenth rounds. Was brilliant Old Bones ready for burial? The final 180 seconds had the crowd erupting as Charnley produced his finest yet.

The fight ended with the two super competitors enmeshed on the ropes, as though their arms had been spliced. They had both given all. When referee Little pulled them apart and hoisted Brown's arm, the crowd booed loud and long. The ring was littered with debris. We ducked coins and cartons. The biased crowd, raised to fever-pitch excitement by Charnley's final fling, had forgotten Brown's early rounds' lead which, I thought, had just entitled him to keep his title. But there were many, including Harry Carpenter, commentating for BBC TV, who considered that Charnley was robbed. Charnley, having come so close to glory, simply shrugged his shoulders and considered his next assignment.

This came the following year, defending the European title in Rome against Ray Nobile, a Sicilian who made the mistake of stepping up from the featherweight division to oppose the game's strongest lightweight. Twenty thousand shocked Romans saw Charnley annihilate poor Nobile, who was permitted to take punches by a Swiss official who was the most incompetent I had seen. 'How can you call yourself a referee? I shall report you. This is murder,' hollered manager Boggis when Nobile was being hammered and the slaughter was allowed to continue, even after a spectator had thrown a white coat into the ring. It was Nobile's manager, whose lack of compassion equalled that of the referee, who finally raised his man's hand in token of surrender.

Charnley collected his £6000. He'd hated having painfully to dismiss a rival who should not have been permitted in the same ring.

Because Charnley was totally superior to the home light-weights, yet another mismatch was to follow. The Board of Control nominated an eliminating series winner, Darkie Hughes of Cardiff, to challenge Charnley for three titles, British, European and Commonwealth. My story headline, forty-eight hours before the fight, read: 'Ban This Fight'. I liked the easy-going Welshman and felt no satisfaction whatsoever when Charnley clobbered him in a record forty seconds, including the count, at Nottingham.

'I had to finish him quickly,' said Charnley, 'but I was sorry afterwards; he looked in a bad state.' Hughes's manager, Benny Jacobs, lightened the despondent loser's dressing room by quipping: 'You must admit that Darkie was ahead on points before he got hit!'

Four years after Charnley had first faced his 'hoodoo' opponent Joe Brown, he was still determined to defeat him. But when the third match was made at Manchester, Brown had finally been deprived of his world title by the rising Carlos Ortiz. Nonetheless, Charnley still thirsted for revenge.

In 118 fights, Brown had only taken one count, against George Araujo eleven years earlier. At thirty-seven, Brown was creaking, and Charnley informed us there would be none of the reckless charging that had ruined his first world title chance. He now had the knowledge, gained in fifty-six fights, and was prepared to await his chance to catch Brown. When it came, in the sixth round, Charnley made no mistake. The ex-champion had ducked and dived to avoid being tagged, as old fighters do, until Charnley nailed him.

Brown's smoothed hair became a disordered mop as Charnley maintained his nonstop aggression. He cracked a right that made Brown blink as though he was temporarily blinded, and when he followed up with a crushing punch to the ribs, Brown turned sideways, clutched the ropes, stared vacantly at the crowd, then sank to his knees to be counted out. Charnley's revenge was merciless and complete. Pride, Charnley's great asset, was restored.

It became routine for Charnley to win his third British title fight, and claim a Lonsdale Belt outright, by chasing and cuffing Geordie Maurice Cullen for fifteen rounds in the Manchester ring. No home lightweight could compete with Charnley, even by sprinting, during his reign through the sixties.

It took exceptional welterweights to check Charnley. Brian Curvis, also a wrong-way-rounder, sneaked a ten-round points win; and when classy Emile Griffith, welter and middleweight world champion, was able to stop Charnley in nine rounds, Dartford's Destroyer knew it was time to quit – after sixty-one fights. Charnley went out in January 1965 where he belonged – at the top.

Since then, Charnley, divorced and remarried, has kept fight trim as a wealthy speculator and property builder. He has Park Lane offices and a Rolls-Royce to match his status, and puts the same verve into his business success as he did into boxing.

Henry Cooper says . . .

I boxed on the same amateur teams as Dave. I recall being with him in Germany. I think he was the only winner. He boxed with J. and E. Hall at Dartford, and I was with Eltham which is quite near so we saw a lot of each other. We trained in the same gym as professionals.

We turned professional within a month of each other. Twin brother George and I both won at Harringay Arena in September 1954 – George came off the floor to defeat Dick Richardson – and Charnley had his first fight at Harringay a month later and I won on the bill. He stopped Malcolm Ames in three rounds. He was still a featherweight then, having won the 9 st ABA title.

I've always thought Charnley the best of lightweights and it was bad luck that he was unable to win a world title. He was certainly good enough. He would probably have walked it today. Had a great body for his weight, worked very hard. He was a wicked body-puncher, a very cold little fighter, spiteful with it. His eyes were like steel. He was so determined. That's why he's made a success of his life. Yes, a good example in and out of the ring.

Roberto Duran

Roberto Duran reminded me of a bull rhino battling his way out of the bush; a grinding, rather than chilling, puncher, who seemed to resent the inhibiting presence of a referee.

When fight men gather, they acknowledge that Duran, a genuine throwback hungry fighter, with a startling violence, could have held his own with any lightweight in history. 'The only time Duran is serious is when he's sleeping or when he's fighting,' said veteran trainer Freddie Brown, who seconded Duran after being the cut man for Rocky Marciano. 'The guy ranked with the best lightweights in history,' said trainer Angelo Dundee, who always worked against Duran.

They called him Mano de Piedra – Fists of Stone – the product of a Panama poverty ghetto, who fought to live, then lived to fight. I had not seen a more ferocious fighter who lived up to his image of malevolence; an eccentric character with coal-black eyes, a bouncing mop of matching coloured hair, who always fought with hate in his heart. He was a captive of his own restless energy.

Duran had been 'discovered' when caught stealing coconuts from the estate of Carlos Eleta, airline owner, industrialist, sole cigarette distributor in Panama. The millionaire liked his looks – and his nerve. Duran had won sixteen of nineteen amateur bouts, but wanted to make it pay. Eleta bought his contract from a jockey, Alfredo Vasquez, for $300, later giving him $1000 bonus when Duran won big fights.

Eleta learned of Duran's hitting power from the Faefan beach gangs who were rounded up for Duran to flatten, bare-fisted, while his pals timed his wins. They called Duran's section of the

beach simply Duran Beach. I asked him why. 'Because anyone
come I don't like, I keel 'em,' he said. Nothing happened to
change my first impression of Duran.

With admitted bias, I will defend boxers from uninformed
attacks, because the vast majority are, in the words of an obser-
vant, totally uncommitted wife, 'like friendly cuddly bears'.
Regrettably, I find barely a redeeming feature in Duran, an
arrogant, ill-mannered fighter, who frequently made obscene
gestures to opponents and always bragged of 'killing' them. He
fought with a contemptuous grin. He changed management and
trainers when the loyal team disliked Duran's prostituting
himself by fighting when his flab reached middleweight proportions in the eighties. He became a parody of the former feared 9
st 9 lb fighter.

When Duran reigned as world lightweight champion in the
seventies he was brilliant and unstoppable. He punched himself
out of opposition, losing only one non-title decision in seventy-
two fights, with fifty-six failing to finish; and he vacated the title
to become welterweight champion. Ray Arcel, who handled a
long line of champions from Benny Leonard to Duran, and who
closely studied the boxing business, said: 'Duran has ring sense.
It's an art; a gift from God that flows out of a fighter like a great
painting flows out of an artist, or a great book flows out of an
author. Ring sense is a natural ability to cope with any situation
in a fight. It cannot be taught.'

I first encountered Duran in 1972, the week of his twenty-first
birthday, at Lake Kiamesha, New York, where they caged him
for weeks in preparation to challenge Britain's Ken Buchanan,
a ring Nijinsky from Edinburgh, for the world title at Madison
Square Garden. Duran had appeared earlier, in a supporting
role, at the famed New York boxing mecca when Buchanan
fought magnificently against Ismael Laguna. Duran took his
opponent out in sixty-six seconds.

Arcel and Brown – I tagged them the Sunshine Boys – were
attached to Duran's camp, using an interpreter because the brash
kid was uncomfortable speaking English, but he seemed to
comprehend.

Duran's long-time aide, Candido Natalia Diaz, forty-nine, was
also in the training camp. He was nicknamed Chaflan, which,
they told me, was loosely translated as 'punchy'. Chaflan had
trouble obtaining a visa because of a few disagreements with the

authorities; no felonies, just social errors. He had KO'd a police chief's brother in a pub brawl, followed by the son of a politician. Bound over to keep the peace, he was sent to Duran to keep him company. A man can usually be judged by the company he keeps.

'Sometimes he loves you, sometimes he wants to kill you,' said trainer Brown, who became cut man, counsellor, and often Duran's conscience. Brown always had the task of forcing Duran to run in the rain, or forbidding him to eat fatty foods when the champion waged a constant battle with the scales. Duran's prodigious appetite was always a bigger danger than opponents. During snack time on an airline, Brown once rapped Duran for overindulging. The contents of the tray were then thrown against a window, much to the horror of nearby passengers. 'But he always apologized later,' said Brown.

Duran's is the classic story of the kid who combined his ring-licensed fighting with the undisciplined winning methods picked up in the streets. His urchin days were in a windblown slum of narrow streets on the east side of the mouth of the Panama Canal. His young life was mostly stealing and scrapping. His father had deserted the family before he was born.

It was during the height of Duran's career that journalist colleague Mike Marley discovered Duran's father, Margarito, a gravel-voiced Arizona cook of Mexican descent with a splash of Indian. He had fathered Roberto when serving as a twenty-two-year-old GI in Panama, and said he had not intended to abandon him. They subsequently met and Roberto understood. Duran Senior had been shipped out of Panama to California and Germany, and at thirty-nine had served with an infantry battalion in Vietnam and had married a woman from Guatamala.

Duran's mother had eight children. Roberto, nicknamed Cholo, a friendly term between Spanish-Indian fraternities, became the bread winner. He would swim two miles for daily raids on bounteous mango trees, and swim back with a loaded sack. Once he came close to drowning, having bagged a splendid harvest, and a friend explained, 'Three of us had to grab him and drag him ashore. He wouldn't let go of the sack.'

The fire in Duran's belly remained when he fought, even when a millionaire, with an implacable will. That hardship upbringing shaped his career in the prize ring. The timeworn yarn of boxing's rags-to-riches.

Eleta shrewdly called on Arcel and Brown to knock the rough edges off Duran's raw talent. They preached the virtues of learning dexterity with both hands; how to set up an opponent; to keep temper under control. At first Duran resisted taking advice, but gradually the lovely old firm convinced him. So Duran became adept at hitting without too often being hit; he could slide expertly away from smarter boxers, and was generally a much better boxer than given credit for. He was able to cut down the ring against a mover, could left-jab with the best, and was not a mere clubber. He harnessed fury with finesse.

When Duran returned to Panama he had achieved the celebrity status usually accorded diplomats and generals. He was even exempted from paying income tax. Thousands awaited Duran's arrival at Panama airport chanting: 'The world championship belongs to the people of Panama.' Duran waved from an open car along fan-lined streets to tour the Chorillo slums. He gave beach parties for the poor. Away from his ruthless ring business there was obviously a lot of good in him.

I confess to having struggled over a period of years, viewing Duran from close quarters, at trying to cut to the raw ganglion of his character.

Ken Buchanan, by comparison, had been born with a silver spoon in his mouth, though his upbringing in Scotland was traditionally hard, and he fought with a pride to match the chip he frequently carried on his shoulder. Clean-cut, teetotal, and a non-smoker, Buchanan was the people's favourite when matched with Duran on 25 June 1972. Buchanan had won the world title in oppressive afternoon heat in Puerto Rico, defended against the ex-champion Laguna at Madison Square Garden, after putting a substitute Mexican, Ruben Navarro, in his place in Los Angeles. Buchanan was the best away exponent of the brutish game since Ted Kid Lewis and Kid Berg were domiciled in America.

Buchanan had the approval of New Yorkers, who were staggered that the Scot had not been a big hit in London. Except for a strong Panamanian contingent, few among the 18,821 crowd, paying a lightweight title record of $223,901, could favour Duran, despite his being unbeaten and putting twenty-four of his twenty-eight opponents away.

Duran's face, later to sprout stubble at fight time, was described as 'smooth as the handle of a rare Malacca cane'. He was trim and handsome. Bagpipes played Buchanan into the ring, sporting his yellow and red tartan clan trunks. Panamanians retaliated by banging drums; and there was between-rounds pandemonium throughout the entire fight.

The cool craft that had made Buchanan a Garden favourite was suddenly threatened by a ceaseless, satanic attack. Duran called it 'going to war'. And he meant it.

Buchanan had been prepared to abandon his classic style, mixed with a bit of spite, for a genuine cobblestone battle after Duran had insulted him at the weigh-in. Duran sneered and used the Spanish expression *marcon*, suggesting the proud champion was a Gay Libber. Buchanan turned pale with rage and there was a chance of a scuffle around the scales. 'The title will not be taken from me by words,' said Buchanan. He resented Duran's actions, dismissing them as being disrespectful to a champion who had earned success the hard way.

Ali could be fun when he taunted opponents, but Duran seemed nasty. We soon discovered that his snap and snarl were not a posture. He *was* nasty. Buchanan had sensibly hired Gil Clancy, a manager–trainer who was fully versed in both the niceties and the foul tactics of the fight game. He drilled Buchanan at Grossinger's, a favourite fight camp in the Catskill Mountains, a.k.a. the Borscht Belt. I had watched Buchanan behind closed doors during a week of torrential rain, preparing himself for the assault. Neither he nor I fully realized the extent of Duran's aggression: he used every part of his body in an attempt to inflict damage.

Because Buchanan had lost only one decision in Madrid in forty-four fights, a decision, incidentally, with which I disagreed, and had not been stopped, there seemed little chance of his being overwhelmed by a challenger making his first attempt. New York odds players bet 8–5 on Buchanan to win.

Duran stuck to Buchanan like a barnacle, and the Scot tried desperately to punch the impudence out of him; but Duran fought as a man possessed. He seemed impervious to punishment and his forbidden target blows were ignored by New York referee, Johnny LoBianco. A punch that landed on Buchanan's back in the first round, causing a slip, was ridiculously ruled a standing count. It was the only knockdown. Buchanan was too often forced to stay on the ropes, and his broomstick left, normally sounder than the pound, was not sufficiently powerful to keep Duran off. The drums banged, Panamanians bayed for

Buchanan's blood, and Duran fought as though he were mugging Buchanan. His gloves seemed to cover every part of the champion's body.

Duran had not previously fought over ten rounds, and there was hope in Buchanan's corner at the start of the eleventh. 'He's getting to Duran,' they were saying. They pleaded with Buchanan to make better use of the ring and resist being trapped in corners. His cheeks were swollen and blood trickled from his face.

By the thirteenth, Buchanan's defence became a blown safe, but his grit kept him battling and the judges seemed a bit harsh making Duran ahead by a long way. At the finish of the round Buchanan made the mistake of continuing a punch rally as he was propped on the ropes. This was interpreted as 'anything goes' by the free-form Duran, who unleashed a punch that travelled almost from Buchanan's knee, ruffling his trunks and landing smack in the groin. At that point, Buchanan was being barged over the ropes. He collapsed, grimacing, long after the bell ended the round, and the referee allowed Buchanan's seconds to haul him back to the safety of his stool. Duran was still snarling and stomping wildly.

Buchanan began to slip off his stool, clutching his body, and though he first signalled to the referee that he was prepared to fight on, I recall hearing him say, 'I'm hurt,' and the official stopped the fight.

Although film replays confirmed that Buchanan had been fouled, his claim provoked little sympathy from American critics, who hailed their new macho fighting machine, and blamed Buchanan for contributing to his own downfall. Since Duran was ahead anyway, there were the usual dismissive jokes about collapsible British boxers, but the Garden boxing boss, Harry Markson, strived to stage a return fight. Buchanan claimed that he was ready and willing, but they could not come to terms.

Meanwhile, Duran returned home to the expected hero's welcome and, for good measure, took on two opponents to give his fans a treat in non-title fights. Duran, as usual, was all business: he knocked both out in the first round.

To prove his victory over Buchanan was not a fluke, Duran successfully defended his title fourteen times and, bowing only to the demands of nature, gave up the lightweight crown after sixty-four wins, spoiled only by a single loss in a non-title match against Estaban DeJesus. Duran had fought off illness when he accepted the fight, and admitted he was not mentally or physically prepared. 'Sometimes the body will fight, sometimes not,' he shrugged. But in two subsequent fights, both with his title at stake, Duran knocked all the fight and half the life out of DeJesus, stopping him both times. It's a record that fully supports Angelo Dundee's appraisal of Duran, worthy of being an all-time great in his division.

Duran quickly developed into a full welterweight, and they fed him the usual quick-win opponent in Panama before forcing him to qualify for a title bout at the higher poundage. When Duran competently whacked Carlos Palomino, who had won the world 10 st 7 lb title and taken out Dave Green and John H. Stracey in London before losing to Wilfred Benitez, the way was clear for him to meet the game's golden boy, Sugar Ray Leonard.

The city of Montreal put up an alarming amount of cash for the privilege of staging the super-match at the Olympic Stadium – known locally as the Big O. New York promoters, Arum and King, who dislike each other more, even, than Leonard and Duran, made a brief peace and involved themselves in the ancillary rewards of the fight. Arum protected Leonard's interests; King, Duran's. Both were ecstatic and called it a dream fight. They were right.

Duran, who had walked out with the lion's share when tearing apart a decade of lightweights, settled for a paltry $1.5 million minimum; Leonard, as champion, had a bottom line of $5 million, which included pieces of everything from programmes to car parking. At count-up, both collected more, but the ambitious Canadian promoters lost money.

Things had not changed with Duran when I arrived in Montreal. Surrounded by Panamanian friends, some acting as bodyguards, Duran moved around with an accompanying tape deck the size of a suitcase, with the volume so loud that nobody attempted to speak within a hundred yards of it. Québeçois seemed to favour Duran more than Leonard, because he was outrageous, wore a T-shirt emblazoned with 'Bon Jour, Montreal', a white cap, a three-day beard growth and rainbow-coloured braces.

Duran trained at the Le Jardin complex, a splendid shopping

and hotel centre in the heart of Montreal, where passers-by could watch him during their lunch break. He impersonated a drunk skipping, bringing hoots of laughter; he beat the speedball with his head, and undoubtedly won over the locals who believed Leonard to be overpolite and less friendly. In fact, Leonard was entrenched nearby with a much more laidback group from Maryland, and disliked Duran's behaviour. Duran's showmanship, which included strange shrill cries as he boxed and skipped, not only sold tickets but also psyched him up.

The only downbeat in the Duran camp was when Carlos Padilla, a Filipino who lived in Las Vegas, was named as referee. Both Arcel and Brown believed Padilla would be a hindrance because he had previously not allowed Vito Antuofermo to fight 'inside' against Alan Minter. The constant instruction to break, they believed, had won Minter a world title. Duran was essentially an in-fighter.

Padilla got the message. He would leave him alone, unless one or other blatantly transgressed the rules. A referee, it seems, can change habits to keep people happy – especially the appointing World Boxing Council brass who were out in force at Montreal. By fight time, Britain's representatives on the WBC, Alexander Elliot and Ray Clarke, had arrived to be surprisingly relegated to $500 seats among the public, and were protected with black plastic garbage bags pulled over their expensive clothes. The weather did not match the splendour of the occasion, but despite the dampness, 46,317 customers turned up, with a full house a few miles away at the Maple Leaf Stadium where the customers, preferring cheaper prices and staying dry, watched a closed-circuit screen view.

The event proved a magnet for boxing traders. Hotel lobbies were packed with experts talking it up, mostly Americans who flocked over the border. Literary heavies, Budd Schulberg and Norman Mailer, were among those on press benches that had been rain-drenched during the preliminary fights.

The Canadian Installation Board, a government agency, had organized well and worked hard to recoup a $4¼ million layout as promoters. It was considered a boost for French Quebec Canadian separatists votes; but the fight made little political impact on the voters. With a $600,000 insurance covering loss, the agency needed a crowd of 55,000 to break even. The boxers' purses, of course, were big enough to wipe out a famine in Somalia and equip a few armies.

There had been promotional palpitations when squiggly lines appeared on Duran's first electrocardiogram test. It subsequently turned out that the machinery was faulty – the mean human machine from Panama never had trouble with his ticker. The high-rolling promoters breathed easily when they saw Duran jogging his way to the ring to the beat of drums through the loudspeakers. The ring was covered by a canopy, but there were water spots on the edges of the blue canvas.

Duran sported white shorts with red patches and his name, which made him look like a Marlboro cigarette packet. He fidgeted after stamping his feet in the resin tray, while the crafty old firm of Brown and Arcel were to have a final word with referee Padilla. Duran appeared charged with a predatory intensity, and though we were still uncertain about his carrying sufficient firepower in a heavier division, he gave all the signs of being a winner. He outweighed Leonard by ¾ lb.

The instructions were over without delay and, even without throwing a punch, both boxers had warmed up sufficiently to be steaming in the misty, humid, summer night air. Right from the off Duran was determined to show Leonard, with only twenty-seven fights, some of the rough secrets of his trade. Leonard, who had dictated the pace and pattern in most of his fights, proved to have extraordinary durability and gameness to resist Duran's furious charges. It became a fight to be indelibly etched in the memory, with everything except a knockdown. A marvellous encounter.

With total disregard for danger, their bodies steaming heavily, they fought with a fire that stamped the championship a great one long before it had finished. Angelo Dundee was yelling that his man was being wrestled, and was not particularly enjoying the battle, while Duran's cornermen were satisfied that Padilla was unable to say 'Break,' no matter how much the contestants were entwined. Punches were rained from all points of the compass, and the blows raised a constant sweat spray in the air.

At the end of each round Duran snarled at Leonard, trying to mouth through his gumshield, and swaggered back to his corner, excited by the wild joy of his own vitality. 'If Leonard is to beat me, he will have to fight me; he will have to apply pressure,' Duran had earlier confided. He was right. By constantly attacking, shoving Leonard into the ropes, Duran shaped the fight and gave it momentum. He pounded Leonard's body, and as early as the third round, the champion's wife, Juanita, was covering her face in tears at the ringside. By the eighth round she was out cold, being revived by Leonard's sister, Sharon.

No doubt Duran's forward march, more like a run, influenced the neutral judges imported from England, Italy and France – the referee did not score – and most of the American writers favour any man who attacks, ignoring the textbooks about 'milling on the retreat'. But Leonard hardly retreated. He frequently met Duran toe to toe, punch for punch.

'I showed I could take a punch. I didn't want to, but I had to. I had no alternative,' said Leonard. Duran set a pace intended to nullify Leonard, setting himself for counterpunches or dictating with his whiplash left. The rounds were so often fought with such fury, the judges scored them level, but the Italian, Poletti, was a monument to indecision, marking ten rounds even. If judges faithfully followed the guidebooks, 'marking for the boxer who does most part of the leading off, or displays better style, etc.', there would be no place for a drawn round.

Leonard made an incredible stand in the home-straight rounds, bringing the points to fractions; and when the boxers came out for the fifteenth, the stadium became the Standing O, with a roar from the crowd which more than approved the sheer theatre, albeit street theatre, of the fight. It was not surprising in its intensity or in the wonderful condition of both boxers. Despite the roughness, neither was badly marked. The only surprise was Leonard's willingness, indeed sometimes silliness, in electing to fight Duran's type of fight. It cost the champion the title. Harry Gibbs pointed 145–144 for Duran, though having handed over his score after each round, he had forgotten how the points would total at the World Boxing Council's adjudicating bench. Officials blundered when adding Poletti's card, and for over an hour it was believed he had scored a draw. A recount gave Duran a win with 148–147. Raymond Baldyrou had 146–144, the higher marking for Duran, who was twenty-nine that week, and became the first lightweight since Barney Ross, forty-six years before, to become welterweight champion.

Duran also became Leonard's only conqueror.

The return fight, five months later, became boxing's biggest shock. Duran's eyes that had smouldered with violence were dark and hooded in the replay. Duran, a quitter? 'If somebody had suggested that, I'd have busted them in the mouth. Not Duran – never,' said octogenarian Arcel, normally noted for his dignity. Maybe Duran had shirked his training.

Leonard used his dislike of Duran as a weapon. He completely changed tactics, hamming it up, taunting Duran, and seldom staying in one place long enough for Duran to catch him. Leonard had learned from the Montreal loss. Duran reckoned Leonard was not playing the game by hitting and hopping, instead of matching Duran's celebrated macho spirit.

The crowd at the magnificent New Orleans Superdome was stunned, and so was Leonard, when Duran turned his back, signalling a surrender in the eighth round. I gasped, 'I don't believe it!' into a microphone. It is generally forgotten that two judges, James Brimmell from Swansea and Mike Jacobs from London, had awarded Duran three and two rounds, because Leonard had barely landed a blow while playacting to frustrate Duran. The third official, a Belgian, also agreed.

We had assumed that Duran would go out biting and butting, rather than surrendering. He blamed stomach cramps. It was true he had gorged a steak a few hours before, and we must not expect that a boxer can produce his best in every fight, but succumbing to stomachache was so shocking that Duran's exit had to be analysed on several levels, including the mystical. It was ridiculous to consider a fix – the boring theme of Hollywood scripts and fiction books – because the manner of defeat, handing over a valuable title, ruined Duran's career.

There was no possibility of a third fight. Sugar Ray had skilfully orchestrated his own kind of fight, toying with Duran's rushes, and had learned, from a locked-door crash course in the gymnasium, how to deal with Duran's butting and elbowing. He absorbed the lore and logic of his mentors. Duran could accept physical punishment, but could not endure the psychological torture. Though Duran went to hospital – I was waiting in a hotel lobby when he rushed past me having been discharged – I doubt that his overindulgence with steak and fruit juices had really caused the humiliation. No doubt, as Duran fattened and lost speed, somebody would have beaten him; but Leonard will be remembered for destroying the legend.

Duran continued fighting, and I saw him in the final bout on the Arguello–Pryor title show in Miami in November 1982. At 18 lb heavier than his untouchable lightweight days, Duran refused to permit television to record his clash with Jimmy Batten, a Londoner who held a British title and was boxing out of Chicago. Americans called it 'the walk-out fight'. Duran was sure that he could keep the crowd in their seats, even after watching a sensational 10 st championship between Arguello and Pryor.

Regrettably, too many yawned and departed as Duran laboured to outpoint a sprightly Batten. Duran left the ring, gesturing and spouting to a Panama radio reporter alongside me that Batten was not willing to stand and fight. In fact Batten had fought well, but Duran could not be graceful either in defeat or victory.

The days of declaring a public holiday in Panama when Duran won had long gone. But the ring had turned the urchin into a millionaire, with a wife, four children, a plush home, five cars, and the owner of an apartment complex. He also bought a three-bedroom house for his mother.

He continued fighting, shuttling to and from gymnasiums in a $25,000 van equipped with stereo, television and telephone. Sooner or later his stubbornness would succeed. At thirty-one, Duran still had sufficient fire in his belly finally to overcome the humiliation by Leonard. Scaling a respectable 10 st 12 lb, Mr Bad Guy knocked all the fight out of Pipino Cuevas, once an exciting World Boxing Association champion, and Duran was again back in the world title business. He was 'wanted' in Sun City, the homeland patch in Southern Africa, to fight Davey Moore, American, for the light-middle title.

Duran, the also-ran, packed the rafters of the Madison Square Garden boxing mecca to challenge unbeaten Davey Moore, from the nearby Bronx, for the WBA Junior Middle, 11 st championship. He trained in Times Square for what seemed the final fling.

Bookies, who rule by head, not heart, laid 3–1 against Duran. On his thirty-second birthday, 16 June, 1983, eleven years after belting Ken Buchanan, the incredible Panamanian knocked all the fight and much of the life out of talented Moore to win in eight rounds. Bands played, trumpets blared, and they danced in the aisles again. Duran led the chanting of 'doo-ran, doo-ran' as he left the ring to become only the seventh in history to win world titles at three weights. Dare we consider a fourth when Duran challenges Marvin Hagler?

The appealing eccentric had proved us wrong and went home

a hero once again to lead a 680-lb lion, Walla, around his land like a pet dog on a leash. Odds players around Broadway will lay plenty of 6–4 that if the lion gets out of hand Duran will KO the animal inside two rounds.

Henry Cooper says . . .

This fellah is the classic of the hungry fighter who wants to make it in a rough world. He's the kind who kept winning in the survival of the fittest. It didn't seem possible after losing to Leonard that he'd be winning for a world title in 1983.

He scowled and fought like an animal. I never met him, so I can't vouch for him as a person. He is a strict fighter, great record, who didn't go too much on boxing. But guys like Duran always ensure a good fight.

Sugar Ray Leonard

Including Sugar Ray Leonard in a collection of the game's best hitters is a risky choice if judged solely on an instrument measure of a single blow. Many others at his poundage hit harder. But Leonard, whose regrettably abruptly-ended career fascinated me more than any other boxer's, had *exactly* the measure of skill and punch technique that creates greatness. His really was a sweet science. It attracted me far more than the brawling, powerhouse stuff that excites the crowds and brings in the money.

I charted Leonard's career early on, to Olympic and dual world titles. Alongside Ray Robinson, the original Sugar, I rated Leonard the most watchable. Muhammad Ali, of course, transcended sport. His fights were events, extravaganzas, rather than technical boxing matches. Ali was obviously a wider known figure, but in America was not as popular as he was the subject of contention.

Leonard was a student of sport and genuinely strived to produce an art form. He really loved the game. Old-timers assure me that Leonard's ring thinking was comparable to Benny Leonard's, reputed master of them all. Ray could make opponents do things they didn't want to do. Against an aggressive fighter, he'd back him up. He'd force a known counter-puncher to lead. He could think and feint quicker than anyone I had seen. And when an opponent was stunned by the speed and varying angles of Leonard's punches, he could finish him quickly.

Leonard's saucer eyes opened wider when he climbed into a ring. He seemed able to part-destroy his opponents mentally. He surprisingly had no noticeable occupational fear. This came from the knowledge of never having been stopped and taking only two counts – he considered them slips! In 145 amateur bouts he had only five losses (seventy-five stopped) and in thirty-three professional fights, one loss and twenty-three halted. After both knockdowns, Leonard got up and stopped the offender.

Two of Leonard's amateur losses – behind the Iron Curtain in 1974 – were, to say the least, highly controversial. In Moscow Anatoli Kamnev, awarded a decision, walked across the ring, hoisted Leonard's arm and gave him a trophy. In Poland Leonard knocked Kazimer Szczerba down three times, but judges disqualified Leonard because they reckoned he knocked the Pole out a split second after the bell.

I doubt whether any boxer bettered Leonard's performance of tackling four formidable opponents – all of whom had won world titles, all with varying weights and diverse styles – within twenty-two months, by defeating Wilfred Benitez, Roberto Duran, Ayub Kalule and Tommy Hearns. At the time they had a combined record of 177 wins, one loss and one draw.

Hearns and Kalule had never been put down – Leonard put them down. He stopped the unstoppable Benitez. It was unthinkable that anyone could make Stone Fists Duran quit – Leonard made him quit. Leonard became the world welterweight champion, both WBC and WBA, plus the WBA junior or light-middleweight kingpin.

It was Leonard's sole loss, well, adjudged loss, to Duran in their first clash in Montreal 1980 that stamped him, in my mind, a great one. The way Leonard fought impressed me more than all the wins I had seen. With luck, judgement is not blinded by a belief that Leonard seemed to have won by a nose, but he accepted defeat graciously against a rival who must be ranked among the best ever lightweight champions, though he had not an ounce of dignity.

Prejudice? No. I had written and spoken Duran's praises for years, having been at the ringside in 1972 when he waged a spiteful winning war to become champion against Scotland's Ken Buchanan at Madison Square Garden. Judges in Montreal seemed influenced by aggression, rather than by cleanly landed blows; but who am I to argue with the scoring of England's Harry Gibbs who, having turned in his card round by round, pointed for Duran?

Leonard's tactic, opposed by his cornermen, of 'fighting the other guy's fight', may have been foolish, but I respected him.

This was Leonard trying to mix it with the roughest guy at his
trade. The macho bit. Hit-and-run would have been the safest
and surest way of winning. Leonard was determined to make it
a man's fight. And I still think he just about succeeded. The
fifteen rounds of mayhem, fought at remarkable speed for
welterweights, ranks among the best four fights I have witnessed.

The return in New Orleans five months later gave us the
flashy, showboating Sugar Ray at his finest. The exact, carefully
conceived game plan was to frustrate, and finally to humiliate,
a fighter whose deeds had earned him continuous glowing phrases
on America's sports pages. When Duran walked away, raising
his hand, with a Spanish 'No; mas' in the eighth round, it created
more debate in saloons and sports columns than any fight of the
decade.

The dancing chipmunk with the red tassled boots and the
looks of an actor had actually forced the surrender of the bully
boy, by taunting and humiliating. Duran, who claimed stomach
cramp, knew the beating and humiliation would worsen as the
fight went on. Leonard barely lost a punch, let alone a round.
There was no fix. No fighter would belittle himself in this way.
Maybe Duran was unwell, but he took a long time recovering
from the disgrace. None the less, there was still a faithful corps
of writers, remembering Duran's greater days, who comforted
him in print for winning meaningless matches three years later.
He had earned that much loyalty.

It irritates Leonard when outsiders suggest that Duran robbed
him of true victory by quitting. What greater victory could there
be than to turn a dauntless Duran into a quitter?

Though Leonard had beaten Duran more with the threat of
punishment than being forced to deliver it, he had taken out
Britain's Dave 'Boy' Green with the kind of punch that becomes
etched in the memory. For Green, a game and likeable, if
limited, campaigner, it must be a nightmare watching constant
television slow-motion replays of the left hook Leonard landed
to knock him cold. ('One of these days I think I'll get up,' he
says.)

Green, grittier than many, was not found wanting at the start
of their fight in Leonard's virtual backyard of Landover, Maryland. But after the local hero had put on a show, dazzled Green
and us with his punch combinations, he delivered the pay-off
straight out of the picture book. One hit. Green was out before

he hit the canvas. The referee abandoned the formality of a count and Green's manager, Andy Smith, darted into the ring to remove his man's gumshield to prevent him from choking.

'I didn't feel a thing,' Green recalls, 'I was in the dressing room before I remembered what might have happened. What a punch!' (In 1981 Leonard and his wife visited Green and family at their Cambridgeshire home. All was forgiven.)

Andy 'Hawk' Price, an American who had given Green a photofinish fight in London, was also pitted against Leonard, and fancied as a fair test. He went out in one round.

Leonard's highlight fight was, inevitably, clashing with Tommy Hearns, who won the WBA version of the welter crown (and later became WBC 11-st title holder) and had a mule kick of a punch. The hit man from Detroit stood 6 ft 1 in, at least, and had an extraordinary reach of 78 in – longer than some heavyweight champions. His fists were bolts on pipestem arms.

Hearns was unbeaten in thirty-two fights, thirty stiffed in style. Like Leonard, I had seen Hearns in his amateur days – outpointing George Gilbody at Wembley – and though his record was impressive, I was surprised when the smart-odds players in Las Vegas made Hearns 7–5 on favourite. Now Leonard had to penetrate the defence of a good opponent, never knocked out: a worthy champion who had boxing ability to match his power.

We watched, almost afraid to blink, on the hot night in the neon desert of Nevada, as Leonard attempted to break down Hearns's defence. By the thirteenth round the judges, to my amazement, had Hearns ahead, though my card (was it again blind prejudice?) had Leonard a shade in front because his winning rounds were, unquestionably, worth more points than those of Hearns, who snatched them. However, the hailed puncher Hearns – another big favourite with American writers – was up against a smarter puncher.

Leonard had Angelo Dundee in his corner, which is comparable to a classic horse having Lester Piggott on his back. Dundee did not know the official scoring, but he was wise enough not to count on favours. He pleaded with Leonard to finish the job. Leonard, his left eye badly swollen, looked straight ahead, as if transfixed. 'I heard every word Angelo said, but I didn't respond because I already knew what I had to do.'

In the fourteenth round there could be no measure of cuteness, just crucial attacking. Hearns, who may well have been drawn

at the weight, was fading fast. Leonard whistled a right that
glanced Hearns' chin. He wobbled. Leonard raised his arms in
victory salute. He had hit enough men to know when it was
over. He gestured to referee Davey Pearl to step in. But he
allowed Leonard to follow Hearns along the ropes, pummelling
him with blows, while Hearns sought refuge between them.
Leonard did not look for the one-shot ending, biding time to
pick his spot. He merely unloaded a salvo, a product of the years
of hard work in gymnasiums and fights, forcing the referee to
signal the armistice.

There were a few, particularly those who had tipped Hearns
or bet on him to win, who thought referee Pearl may have been
a bit premature. When they watched slow-motion replays they
apologized. Here was Leonard at the height of his powers – and
the highest paid of all. But he was not satisfied. 'History,' he
said, 'drives me now. I want to do bigger things. I just don't
want to be in the record books because of the highest purse. I
want to be there for my talent, my class.'

He never mentioned punch.

In February 1982 Leonard resumed his campaign. The long-
term plan was to move into the middleweight division and satisfy
his ego, besides a bonanza payout, to challenge Marvin Hagler,
undisputed awesome holder of the 11 st 6 lb crowns. His management, probably the most successful and uncomplicated in
boxing, had no ties with promoters. Frequently deals were
arranged direct with arenas. Reno, Nevada, in competition with
Las Vegas for gambling customers, eagerly sought Leonard's
publicity. He was clearly the most marketable boxer of his time.

'I'm a personality apart from being a boxer,' said Leonard.
He ordered two thousand monogrammed hand towels to give
away to his training camp visitors. He boxed exhibitions at
schools; ran in community road races; kissed lots of old ladies
and talked at father–son breakfasts. Despite the adulation, he
remained very much a country boy – born in North Carolina –
with a warm demeanour and a friendly wink that made anyone
feel he was on their side. He always calls people 'Pal'.

Bruce Finch, a have-gumshield-will-travel type of warrior, was
ranked No. 4 and was hauled in to accept Leonard's punches in
Reno where, in 1910, Jack Johnson, a great champion despised
for his arrogance and, disgracefully, for being a black, had fought

James J. Jeffries. Leonard *v.* Finch was the first world title fight in Reno for seventy-two years.

Times, thankfully, had changed and Leonard was accepted as a prince at the Centennial Coliseum. Finch, also black, was a public relations worker in a Las Vegas hotel, and had respectable ring credentials. He was, if you'll pardon the idiom, no mug. Thirty wins, three losses, and North American Federation champion. But the tip-off that Finch was really a no-hoper on the night was because Hearns had beaten him in two rounds.

I may have been the sole European reporter in Reno. Had we known it was to be Leonard's last fight, the world and his brother would have been there.

Finch was not overawed and chased Leonard to win the first round, perhaps by courtesy of Leonard, but he gave the champion more trouble than he bargained for. Finch's mistake was being good enough to rattle Leonard. Later the champion was to admit that he had doubts about continuing his career during that fight, because he was lacking incentive. However, the job had to be done. 'I don't carry anyone,' Leonard had often said.

Leonard hit Finch with a vicious hook to the body – a blow intended to stop his gallop – and fired two head punches that made Finch buckle. A hard right to the head dropped Finch. 'Oh, no,' Sugar thought. He was remembering a dream that had bothered him only the night before – about standing over a boxer whom he had knocked down and who wasn't moving.

Instead of instantly retreating to a neutral corner, he stood staring at Finch. The referee chased Leonard away, then counted over Finch, who lurched to his feet at nine. The fight continued, but the end came after one minute fifty seconds into the third round, after Leonard had assaulted with straight rights and a left uppercut. Staggering Finch was wrapped in protective custody by the referee. It was Leonard's quickest win in eight championship fights.

In the dressing room were Leonard's wife, Juanita, and her mother, Gertha. They were the first to applaud when the game Finch walked in to shake hands with his conqueror. 'Win some, lose some,' he said with the philosophy of a true Reno gambler. We sensed that Leonard's family were itching for him to retire. But by his own demands, not by prodding from friends or the professionals around him, Leonard sought work to keep him punch sharp and 'able to pay for the groceries'. Eight minutes action in Reno had earned him $2 million from television rights alone.

Next was Roger Stafford, willing and able, with yet another arena wanting Leonard's services for nationwide exposure, in Buffalo, the United States side of the Niagara Falls. Take-home pay for this exercise was $3 million. Twenty-two days before the fight Leonard ran five laps of an indoor track in Buffalo; he whipped his head back and forth every few seconds – 'As though trying to shake-off an annoying thought,' wrote Pat Putnam in American *Sports Illustrated*. 'I have a floating spot in my left eye,' Leonard reported calmly.

At first it was thought the condition was fatigue from training. But within hours, eye surgeon Dr Ronald Michels, who had successfully operated for heavyweight Earnie Shavers, diagnosed that Leonard had a partial detachment on the lower part of the left eye retina.

At twenty-five Leonard's career was over, though he kept us wondering will he/won't he retire for seven months after an operation. The farewell, as undefeated champion, was staged like a coronation in Baltimore.

We had a rapport dating back to an amateur match, New York *v.* London, at Madison Square Garden, when a then willowy, flashy lightweight Leonard outpointed Graham Moughton, a London milkman. He defeated another London boxer, Clinton McKenzie, at the Montreal Olympic Games in 1976. (McKenzie was still British champion in 1983.) Leonard won the gold medal with six bouts in thirteen days, taking the votes of all five judges for each outing – a feat in itself, without going on to prove exceptional as a professional.

By chance I was first to greet Leonard when he came to the press interview room in the Maple Leaf Stadium. He bore the medal around his neck and seemed shy. I could only manage a polite 'Well done' before he was besieged by news gatherers. 'I recall all I wanted to do was get home,' he says. 'I was overcome and my hands hurt.' He instantly became a media creature, as though the gold medal were an Oscar.

Leonard genuinely had no intention of turning professional – brittle hands were only a contributory factor – because he wanted to study at Maryland University. His son, Ray, was born out of wedlock, and his girlfriend, Juanita, whose photo he pinned to his socks in the ring, had applied for Welfare to help feed their son.

When the euphoria of the Olympics was over, and no endorsements were offered, Leonard married. 'I was trapped in a web of nothing,' he said. Then, as if schemed by a publicist, Leonard found himself the desperate breadwinner, because both his mother and father were taken seriously ill and were unable to work. He sought advice from Janks Morton, an insurance broker with whom he played softball, who introduced him to Mike Trainer, a lawyer with unpretentious offices in Silver Springs, Maryland. Dundee was later brought in, after Leonard had interviewed others, to be the professional minder, the approving matchmaker, of his paid career.

Leonard became sole stock owner of his own company. Trainer negotiated purse moneys and was paid by the hour. Morton, a close friend, was an able coach. Trainer's clients and friends raised $50,000, to launch Leonard, asking for a four-year repayment at 8 per cent interest. The loan did not entitle them to any stock. Within two months Leonard had returned the money – interest paid. 'It was a terrible investment, but it got the kid launched,' said Trainer.

Leonard retired a multi-millionaire, still the same, super person I had known when he was broke.

We can never know how great he might have been. A phenomenon cruelly beaten by injury in his prime.

Henry Cooper says . . .

His eye injury was an absolute tragedy. There is no telling how great he could have been. He was already great enough, but he was comparatively untouched and had years of fighting left. He'd matured so much since his amateur days. Mind you, he made the right decision when he had retina trouble.

He was such a big attraction and was earning even more than Ali in his prime. It didn't seem possible that a welterweight could follow Ali and become every bit as big.

He was a natural talent, but I must give credit to Angelo Dundee. His best fighters from Ralph Dupas to Willie Pastrano and Ali were great movers and boxers. He'd yell, 'Stick and run!' which meant left hand and move, and they'd do it. I was the first here to box with Pastrano, who became world light-heavy champion. He had great movement and told everyone that Cassius Clay of 1964 would upset Sonny Liston. Leonard, like Pastrano, was a student of the game. I enjoyed Leonard boxing Roberto Duran. Although he lost, or they reckon he did, in Montreal, he burst Duran's bubble. I know who I fancied in the return fight. And I was dead right. Leonard broke Duran's heart. I think Leonard would have stayed unbeaten. Only going up a weight to fight Marvin Hagler would have been the real test. Yes, a modern who would more than have matched the old-timers. Full of speed, accuracy and the habit of coming up with the right blow at the right time.

Ted Kid Lewis
and Terry Downes

They came from the heart of London, chatty Cockneys to the core, confident characters with big hearts, in and out of the ring, who were fight-fashioned in America. Both served with the US Forces. The peaks of their careers were forty-six years apart; both won world titles; both were challengers in Boston. Their styles were considered close enough to apply the tag of 'crashing, bashing, dashing' to both. Truth is, Lewis the Jew from Aldgate and Downes the Protestant from Paddington (he also fought for the Catholic Fisher amateur club) had a considerable amount of skill, but their brashness was food and drink for the hyperbole of us sportswriters – perfect copy.

I had watched Lewis on film on numerous occasions at his home. I relived his fighting life through an association in his retirement years, regularly ghosting articles for the great Kid and proud to have him as my guest for some twenty years at the annual Boxing Writers' Club dinner. It was a moving moment in 1966; when Lewis was seventy-three, the club awarded him a silver ring engraved 'The best old boxer of this year – and any other year'. For the first time in his life, Lewis was speechless. He cried with pride. There wasn't a dry eye in the house. Again the comparison is remarkable, because Downes won the Best Young Boxer Award in 1958, and the Bromley award for meritorious services, similar to Lewis's, twenty-three years later.

I reported all Downes's forty-four paid fights, four for world titles, four for British, plus some amateur, when he returned to the USA after five years' service with the Marines. I produced Downes's forthright views for his autobiography *My Bleeding*

Business (Stanley Paul) which was published within days of his last fight in 1964.

Gymnasium lawyers and ringside punters might question my inclusion of Downes for the big-hitter collection. I interpret hitting not necessarily by the measured force of a single blow, but also by the cumulative effect. Twenty-eight of Downes's opponents failed to finish. Some were counted out, others were totally nonplussed by the speed and effect of his punches. Downes, more than any other fighter of his class I know, is a student of the game. He knows it backwards, yet has little to do nowadays with the active part of the sport. He was disillusioned, I suspect, when boxers he briefly managed or coached did not possess his determination and discipline. He fought with a heart beyond any ordinary man's endurance. But he rarely misses a big or small fight and has become as much a part of the scene as the Lonsdale Belt or the promoter's cigar.

The measure of Downes's skill, frequently hidden to the onlooker and somewhat overlooked by the pundits, was displayed against Joey Giardello, a Brooklyn-born craftsman from Philadelphia, at Wembley in 1960 – three months before Downes was granted a world title challenge. Giardello had fought in the toughest rings since 1948 without winning a title, but brought the experience of 107 fights to test Downes, with only thirty fights, in what we considered a proving match to meet Bostonian Paul Pender, twice conqueror of Sugar Ray Robinson, for the world middleweight title. Downes, the threshing puncher, turned into the technician – a remarkable transformation. He jabbed when Giardello, a product of the true-pro school, expected him to hook. At the end of ten rounds of cut and thrust, Downes won, and deserved, the points verdict.

No British middleweight since then has been given a more qualified workman to defeat than Giardello in a lead-up to a world title fight. He was acknowledged as world No. 3. Peter Wilson, giving Downes his Paddington Whizz-Kid tag, wrote: 'Downes got his BA . . . a degree, believe it or not, of boxing artist, by outpointing Giardello.' George Whiting reported: 'Downes found a most successful formula and stuck to it most sensibly. He harried and hectored Giardello at every conceivable opportunity, cupped his head in his gloves to minimize the effect of counters that got through and finished every round breathing easily.'

Yet there were still surprising disbelievers that Downes was the goods, because Giardello was thirty, had previously lost to Dick Tiger and had recently fought a fifteen-round draw for the then National Boxing Association version of the world crown against Gene Fullmer. A good match for Downes, they reckoned, catching Giardello on the wane. Critics never learn. Three years later the allegedly washed-up Giardello became the world champion by defeating Dick Tiger!

Tiger, real name Ihetu, from Nigeria, fought Downes in the Cockney's third pro fight. Tiger, a painter in Liverpool, had lost the first four of eleven fights in England. Downes was the promoters' pin-up. They paid him a handsome £125 to face Tiger at Shoreditch Town Hall, an incredibly atmospheric arena in the heart of London's East End. Tiger accepted a pittance of £60. A few years later they could not match them for £50,000. Both became world champions.

I still recall almost every punch of that incredible battle. Downes had fought fifty-one times in the US Marines, against the best, and had never been off his feet. Only when they discovered that he was British born was Downes dropped from representing America at the Olympic Games, though he had beaten Pearce Lane who became the US competitor at the Melbourne Games.

Conceding 6 lb to Tiger was an overgenerous act by Downes, but the betting boys, caught up with the Downes blaze of publicity, laid 5–1 against Tiger. Downes entered the ring with his warm-up jig, in scarlet and gold Marine colours, bringing cheers and jeers from the crowd who, at Shoreditch, somehow managed to bring the best out of fighters – the balcony wags practically breathed down the necks of the contestants. Downes waded into Tiger, who had won a fight two weeks earlier at the National Sporting Club, but was tagged with a left hook. 'I thought, " 'Ello, Tiger looks a lot bigger than me." But it was because I was on the floor looking up at him,' Downes later quipped. It was the first of a continual flow of cracks that Downes delivered during a seven-year career.

The only count Downes had taken was against Mickey Rosette, an amateur in Atlantic City. He instinctively jumped up at three, expecting a mandatory eight-count – the American practice. ('The resin dust wasn't 'arf dirtying my nice scarlet shorts.') He went down again, but had quickly learned to stay put until the count reached seven. He fought back for the crowd to be lifting the roof with noise when the first round ended. Some had rushed to the ring apron, banging for Downes to get up. He did. He finished his career without having taken a full count.

For six rounds Downes and Tiger waged a frightening war for a combined £185. Finally, cuts caused Downes's cornermen to retire him. The curse of scar tissue, the tendency to cut, severely hampered Downes's career. His nose took more shapes than putty, often bled profusely, and the most famous proboscis of its time was affectionately called Downes's hooter. He introduced a personal doctor, who attended fights, as a hooterologist!

In the dressing room at Shoreditch, a Press Association reporter inquired of Downes, 'Who will you fight next?' Came the reply, 'The silly so-and-so who made that match.' But Downes continued to have a successful quip-and-counter relationship with Mickey Duff for the rest of his career. Duff imported a long line of varying-styled middles so that Downes could develop and take heed of defence. All the matches, many for Jack Solomons, took place in London. Downes was always hot box office. Having outpointed Pat McAteer in a non-title fight at White City, a defeat so complete that McAteer announced his retirement, Downes was ready to become British champion.

He did it with a genuine crashing, bashing display, worth only £1500, against Welshman Phil Edwards, stopped in thirteen rounds at Harringay Arena. As they fastened the Lonsdale Belt around him, Downes was chiding me at the ringside for daring to suggest he might not have possessed the stamina to win.

The same year the dream of a world title was shattered when Spider Webb, an executioner avoided like a virus in America, came to London to cut up Downes in eight rounds. Downes was written off – the bleeder who fought with his face – in the same way that many critics, including the trade paper, suggested that Charlie Magri should retire when he forgot to duck in two fights. Magri came off the canvas to make them choke on their words in 1983 – the emotional fight event of the year.

It took Downes three years, in a three-fight serial with fireman Pender, whose nose was shaped like a big dipper, to prove his point. A defeat, a drop of blood, does not cripple a capable fighter. Pender, at thirty, had been fighting twelve years. He'd retired and made comebacks, complaining that his hands were brittle. But putty fists on a putty nose can still cause damage. I remember we parked a typewriter on a beer keg at Boston Arena because they had run out of press benches. Pender's propaganda about damaged fists was dismissed by Downes, because he knew Pender had hurt durable champions – Robinson, Fullmer and Carmen Basilio.

I had written a series of articles for the *Boston Record-American* on Downes's London build-up for the fight, and I hoped they were objective. Pender called me aside and said, 'Your man won't beat me, but after what I've read at least I'll give him respect.'

Pender's stance was old-fashioned British; he was an exceptional punch picker. He used his left like a fireman's axe, coming at all angles, cutting blows that Downes would find difficult to block.

Downes revelled in the fight atmosphere of America, and though he attracted a good share of support from Baltimore, where he spent his teenage years, the Irish-favoured Bostonians were solidly behind Pender, whose forebears came from Killarney. But Downes seemed a diminishing breed of Briton, with a mean dedication, prepared to torture his body to produce teak toughness. His style was not shaped by apprehension. He walked in without fear. He did not scurry from contact behind a flickering left, but he could not expect to box his way in against lean-back Pender. He had to hustle and bustle.

The game's greatest exponent of taking an opponent out of stride, yes, Ted Kid Lewis, had visisted Downes with me at a White City drill hall. It made a handy confidence line in Boston that the old Kid, who had conquered in the Bean City, had put words of wisdom into Downes's ear.

Downes's impetuosity, an attempt to stamp his authority on the fight, came unstuck in the first round. He was caught by Pender's right, the punch believed to have been in a scabbard of indecision, and was sent sprawling. Downes took the mandatory eight-count, shook his head in disbelief, and piled back again. Pender tripped over Downes with the force of his own punch; Downes strived to get past Pender's tantalizing left that found his face time and time again. Pender clutched whenever pressured. 'I was a bit pig-headed wanting to do it my way,' said Downes. The referee permitted Pender a great deal of licence, especially when clasping both arms around his challenger to nullify close-quarter hitting. Inevitably, the raking left and the chopping-action right lacerated the bridge of Downes's nose.

Dan Florio, who worked with Jersey Joe Walcott and Floyd Patterson, was Downes's hired cut man. But Florio, with Londoner Tom Ryder, could not hope to staunch the blood flow, because Downes could hardly hide his nose from Pender's punches. Twice the referee visited Downes's corner; the Commission doctor checked; and it wasn't until Downes's face was masked with his own blood that the referee stopped what had developed into a gruelling slog in the fifty-seventh second of the seventh round. American papers called Downes 'Mr Courage'. *Boxing News* headlined 'Gallant Failure'.

Downes's mentors, Jarvis Astaire and Sam Burns, with Harry Levene playing, would you believe, an honorary role in Boston as Terry's stand-in manager when Burns was ill, schemed a quick replay. Pender was tempted, at the right price – over £30,000 – to defend at Wembley five months later. Downes's brutal wound healed for him to pound the fight out of two Yanks, Willie Green and Tony Montano – both retired hurt with Downes unmarked – at Wembley. The wisecracking Whizz Kid was punch sharp for part two of the world championship.

Pender was the first of the modern trend to be lawyer-represented instead of having the cartoonist conception of a haggling manager. John Cronin, still seen in happy retirement at front-row ringsides around the world, squeezed every penny out of the London promotion, had every 't' crossed and 'i' dotted on a contract. Cronin had cleverly cashed in on Pender's win over Downes with a quick defence against fading Carmen Basilio, whom Pender outpointed, but he had pre-fight troubles making the title poundage. He weighed in four times, had vigorous exercise wearing a raincoat to shed 1¼ lb rather than forfeit his title at the scales. Downes was glad Pender didn't.

Pender, cushioned in a Knightsbridge hotel, fretted being away from home. In warm weather he trained in woollen pantaloons, suggesting he was concerned about shedding stubborn ounces. Cronin made sure his man had the right counsel – Al Lacey, sixty-three, a walking encyclopedia on boxing. He was given the task of conditioning the champion. He made many English trainers look mere bag carriers!

But Lacey was concerned that Pender was not right for the fight. His man moaned, fidgeted, disliked hotel food, fought off a cold and hoped that everything would be all right on the night. It wasn't. Pender discovered that Downes was a discouraging man to fight. Again Downes was cut around the eyes, but Pender also bled. In a seesaw fight Downes's punch belligerence, and his constant nagging blows, like a Chinese water torture, wore Pender down. The champion posed and looked the part of a class boxer, but Downes inexorably punched out his night's work.

Pender's best round was the ninth, giving what the Americans called his 'best shot'. We did not then realize he had shot his bolt. When Pender flopped on his stool – a stool that had dissatisfied him from the start – trainer Lacey called tiny Welsh referee, Ike Powell, to the corner and announced Pender's retirement. Quitting was unthinkable. 'I hit Downes with my best shots, but he kept coming on and I was getting weaker,' said Pender. Lacey blamed the stoppage on Pender's brows being cut. It was a convenient excuse. Downes had outgunned and outgamed Pender, despite the narrow scoring when the fight finished. 'If I had known the ninth was also going to be my last round, I promise I'd have won it. Pender only looked good in that round because he'd made his mind up he wasn't coming out for more. He tried hard to stop me. Truth is, he quit cold,' said Downes.

Ten years earlier, to the night, Britain had hailed Randy Turpin as world middleweight champion. Because Pender had abandoned the fight, Downes was deprived of a comparable glory. Ten-guinea-seat customers were stunned. None the less, Downes's name was etched for ever in the record books, and no fighter worked harder to win.

There were the inevitable tales that Pender had merely loaned his title to collect better rewards for a third decider. True, Downes was forced to leave a sizable sum in escrow in the States in order to lure Pender to London. Champions call tunes, and Cronin made certain that in the event of Downes dethroning his client, a rubber match would take place. But big-time boxing is not the silly, seedy stuff screened in Hollywood B-pictures. Cronin was angry that Pender had failed – there were bigger fish to fry; and who wants to represent a loser? A champion who gives a crown away can never be sure of regaining it, or even getting the chance.

Downes was not considering sidestepping Pender. Without

even a bargaining plea he accepted the showdown battle again in Boston. But it took nine months to settle it. Both champion and ex-champion stayed inactive. Downes decided to travel in style aboard the *Queen Mary*, with his wife Barbara, new trainer Danny Vary, and a sparmate George Aldridge. ('They'd never eaten so well,' said Downes.)

Pender, who had taken a two-year course in public oratory, was camped within splashing distance of Plymouth Rock, nurturing his dislike of Downes and the Americans who had branded him a quitter. He trained with a plastic covering over his dented nose. He confided, 'I'm hurt by criticism. I'd been away from home five weeks when I fought Downes in London. My wife was expecting a third baby; I was off my food; and I simply ran out of gas. It's been hard to live with.'

For a boxer who had spent twelve years of sweat, swap and swipe in a profession he didn't relish, Pender did not spare himself in training. We were not subjected to the scriptwriter line about 'I'll murder the bum' from Pender. He preferred: 'Downes's style is appropriate for my style of winning.'

Downes had not been forced to finish a fifteen-round scrap, and Pender planned to win on points. Barring cuts, he knew Downes could absorb his best blows. Boston referee, James McCarron, a bank vice-president, leaned heavily for Pender, who was guilty of the Boston grab. When Downes ploughed in, Pender clutched, in a match that failed to excite until the final round. Both bled, and the referee's shirt was stained because he constantly had to prise Pender off. 'He spoke to Pender like a Sunday-school teacher,' said Downes. 'Come on, Paul; break, please.'

When officials gave the unanimous verdict to Pender, the referee at least called it close with 144–143, though a 1-point advantage for Pender still produced the same result as 10.

Downes's dad, Dick, a forthright man, said he would be happy if Terry retired. It was not only the newspapermen who were concerned for Terry's welfare. But when they made Terry Downes they threw the mould away. He was wealthy; his investments were shrewd; yet he still loved the roar of the crowd. ('Me batteries ain't run down yet.') He won seven fights in a row, including one against Sugar Ray Robinson who Downes knew was well past his peak, and turnstiles clicked again for

Downes to fight for another championship. This time a move up to light heavyweight.

Willie Pastrano, managed by Angelo Dundee, a master boxer who had thrilled crowds in London and Glasgow, risked his 12 st 7 lb title at Belle Vue, Manchester, in 1964, with the first intercity closed-circuit television beamed to the Phoenix Theatre in London.

Pastrano, who incidentally did not have a splash of Italian blood but went to night school to learn the language, might qualify as the most mobile light heavy of all. Downes was prepared to sacrifice his face to weave his way past Pastrano's flashing left that harvested respect. After an uncertain start, with Pastrano the textbook opponent, Downes, a gloriously game and obstinate man, completely took over the fight. It was easily his finest hour. The crowd chanted his name soccer-terrace style, and for ten rounds Downes forced Pastrano into errors. The champion was fast being drained of stamina. Downes was safely on his way to becoming a world champion at two weights – the first Briton in modern history.

The eleventh round brought a totally unpredictable transformation. Downes's cornermen advised a relaxed round, time to coast and come out steaming for the finish. The winning post was in sight. In Pastrano's corner there was desperation. Heavily sweating, Dundee screamed at Pastrano, who rarely required harsh words to perform his duties, and as the champion hauled himself off the stool, Dundee whacked the seat of his black trunks in the way a jockey brings out his whip in the last furlong. It worked. Pastrano looked angrily back over his shoulder. Without realizing that Downes was set for a quieter time, safely holding an unassailable lead, Pastrano lashed out to prove that a single well-planted punch can frequently change the pattern of a fight.

Had Downes's advisers sensed that Pastrano, seemingly on his way out, was coming out for a final fling, they would certainly have pushed Downes to carry on at top speed and not to spare the consequences. Downes went down, shocked as much as hurt, and staggered up with legs like a kid in a playpen. Pastrano abandoned his customarily styled punch-picking to wildly flurrying punches. Again Downes went down, sensing that he was safer taking a count until the Pastrano whirlwind had subsided. But in the few seconds before Downes went down, sixty-six-year-old Belfast referee, Andrew Smyth, was slapping Pastrano's back in a còmpassionate act to stop him punching. So the fight was over. Smyth had stopped it after seventy-seven seconds. Dismayed, disgusted, Downes argued with Smyth that he was entitled to the benefit of a count and not to be halted while waiting for it. But there are rarely home favours in Britain, and Smyth, regarded as the leading referee, remained unmoved. Pastrano had clawed back his crown and Downes cried unashamedly in his dressing room. I recall the boxers showering together with Downes chiding Pastrano: 'You were dead lucky, mate. The ref made a mistake. I knew what I was doing and he knew I would get up. You knew I had you beat.' Pastrano shrugged. 'I got you at the right time, man.'

There were constant attempts to make a rematch, but Downes walked out of the game he loved – and stayed out. He owns property and ran a betting shop before his manager, Sam Burns, teamed up with a chain of them and later became managing director of the William Hill Organization. Downes became a sizable shareholder. His sons were educated at public school – one bowled and captained a schools' cricket team, the first to win in India – and the 'ole man' doesn't change.

The larger-than-life character who went on the wagon after a few years of trying to recapture his lost youth – boxing ruled his teenage life – smokes the best cigars, drives a Rolls-Royce and travels the country, raising funds to purchase Sunshine coaches for distribution to handicapped children's homes by the Variety Club of Great Britain.

For some years, Lewis lived a similar lifestyle, spending money as though it were going out of fashion. 'In the twenties, I reckoned a thousand pound a week was my running cost,' Lewis had told me. He loved gambling, diamonds, furs and fast cars. His heart was too big, because he became an easy touch for a hard-luck story, and roamed the streets of Whitechapel showering silver coins like confetti on poor kids. Some rose to become wealthy and always courteously doffed their hats to the old champ.

Lewis did not die poor, because his only son, Morton, paid for his stay at the Clapham Home for Aged Jews where, just hours before his passing, Ted Kid was still outsmarting others at cards. He took a secret to his grave in 1970 – he was a year older than recorded in boxing record books. He died three days short of his seventy-eighth birthday. He had won his first British title at seventeen, twenty-two days before his eighteenth birthday, not at sixteen, as reported, when the East End wonder boy stopped Alec Lambert for the 9 st crown in 1912.

I have never doubted that Lewis would be rated Britain's best-ever pound-for-pound fighter. His achievements are mind-boggling. He looked almost anaemic; fought with hands dropped, his mouth open; but was years ahead of his time, producing the incredible salvos of blows that are now termed 'combinations'. He was welterweight champion of the world, British feather, welter and middleweight champion. In all, the incomparable Kid won eight undisputed titles and was a claimant to three others. A twenty-year career with 500 battles, many still unrecorded.

When he weighed 11 st 6 lb, his heaviest, Lewis knocked out Tom Cummer, a leading heavyweight of 13 st 10 lb, in the first round. He fought the mighty Georges Carpentier, world light-heavyweight kingpin, matinee idol of France, first $1 million gate fighter, with an outcome still frequently debated in the thick-ear industry.

Lewis was 10 st 12 lb against Carpentier's 13 st 7 lb. A match with this weight discrepancy would not be sanctioned today. Royalty was at the ringside at the London Olympia in 1922, with gate takings an indoor record of £43,000. The fight generated so much excitement that Very pistol lights, coloured green for victory, red for defeat, were to be fired outside the Olympia to signal the result for anxious Londoners.

Lewis complained that Carpentier was holding in the first half-minute of the fight. London referee, Joe Palmer, forcibly separated them. Lewis mumbled his disapproval, but hurled himself into battle. The Frenchman showed his anger when Lewis caught him with a blow on the break – permitted at that time. Again Carpentier clutched. 'Stop!' cried the ref. 'This clutching must stop.' Lewis lowered his arms and turned to protest. I have viewed the film a dozen times. Palmer was admonishing Lewis and also touching his wrist, when Carpentier unleashed a right, straight as a dart, to Lewis's defenceless jaw – the knockout point. Lewis crumpled like a sack and stayed on his knees from one to out – to the tune of thunderous protest – and Lord Lonsdale led the contemporary opinion that Lewis had been cheated.

He bounced back to capture six championships, yes, six, and a Lonsdale Belt within two years. In America he fought the legendary Benny Leonard, had the record serial with Jack Britton, sparred with Jack Dempsey and Jack Johnson and was not asked back; and long before Muhammad Ali arrived with his gimmick, Lewis often nominated the round he would finish an opponent. He won a three-fight series against Johnny Basham, a favourite of my grandfather who seconded both of them. He ended, aged thirty-five, defeating the classic Welshman at earthy Hoxton Baths. Thirty-five years after he retired, Lewis was honoured in the American Hall of Fame.

I have been lucky to have shared a part of the personal life of both Downes and Lewis – the ring is a Klondike for great characters.

Henry Cooper says . . .

I understand why you include the punching of Downes. He was similar in many respects to Ali because it was the cumulative effect of his blows that won fights. He'd hit opponents with half a dozen successive punches and they'd wonder where they were. You don't have to be a one-punch artist to be reckoned a good puncher. Terry came to the Thomas A'Beckett gym, where I worked out, when he returned from America. He sparred with Peter Waterman, Dennis's brother, who was a very good welterweight and champion. We'd boxed for Britain at the 1952 Olympics in Helsinki. The gym was alive with chat because this unknown Downes, who had boxed only as a junior here, had given Waterman plenty of trouble. In fact, Terry looked brilliant.

There is obviously a similarity between the lives of Terry and old Ted Kid, whom I met on your table at the Boxing Writers' dinners. Jim Wicks was always relating how Ted Kid had left England as a straight-left merchant and adapted to the American style to beat them at their own game. He and Terry stunned and overwhelmed opponents. I often thought a fighter like Downes, who could crowd and move inside, despite being cut at times, would have been the right type to give Marvin Hagler a good fight. Lewis, from your account, could have fought Hagler and his sparmate on the same night. But Ted may not have been able to concede weight to Hagler. Yet the old boy's record is remarkable.

Marcel Cerdan

If a promoter or manager could cast a mould for the fighter they would most like to handle, Marcel Cerdan would become the article. Striking in looks and hooks, courteous, crowd appealing, a world champion, a nation mourned when he was killed. He was, arguably, the most complete European-fostered fighter of all – dedicated and deadly.

Born in Algeria, Cerdan was the idol of France, though he had less than a third of his recorded 114 fights there. He looked as if he had wandered off a film set: the typecaster's dream of the perfect macho man. Gold-toothed and with jet black crinkly hair, he laughed a lot and women swooned. He was the only fighter I knew who attracted crowds to follow him at a distance, without actually exchanging words. They bantered with Muhammad Ali and fought to touch him; but people seemed in awe of Cerdan. He was untouchable. One hundred and nine opponents touched him and paid the price. Sixty-six were stopped. There were many that were unrecorded.

Four losses were totally accountable: a disputed points loss, subsequently avenged; two startling disqualifications; and a torn shoulder muscle that forced him to throw away a world middle-weight championship. Cruel fate denied him revenge.

I first witnessed Cerdan in a fight generally forgotten and, in truth, I could not have readily recalled his name until he hit the big time eight years later. Yet either my father or uncle was Cerdan's second when he fought north countryman Harry Craster, at the now demolished Empress Hall, Earl's Court, in 1939. He was ruled out for an alleged low blow in the fifth round.

I cannot forget his face; the welterweight champion of France oozed ring class from every muscle.

A war, and almost a decade later, Cerdan's reappearance in London needed a policeman astride a white horse, ushering locked-out fans off the steps of Seymour Hall, Marylebone, where a former refugee, Benny Schmidt, who was broke when he came to Britain, had the foresight to promote Cerdan against Bert Gilroy. The Scottish opponent, with respect to the work-manlike Gilroy, meant little. Cerdan could draw a crowd just to gaze at him. He had won the European title only nine days earlier.

Once the polite Cerdan was satisfied the customers liked what they saw, he dispatched Gilroy in the fourth round. He was clinical and close to perfection. He had a crouching, typically French style, with a minimum of wasted punches, tucking his elbows and gloves close to his body and peering through them to line up his target.

I was fascinated, having seen Cerdan bring over a Paris bantamweight – four weights below him – for speed sparring at Joe Bloom's gym in the West End theatreland. Cerdan never laid a glove on the partner. He moved adroitly to cut down ring space, frequently trapping the darting bantam and pretending to fire the finishing shot. The sessions were planned to sharpen his reflexes, not to improve his power. By comparison, Gilroy was easy to catch. He was simply outgunned by a ring general.

On 29 March – my birthday – 1949, Cerdan was back in the Empress Hall ring as undisputed world champion, with crowds clamouring for seats, to watch him at work against Dick Turpin, elder brother of Randolph, least acclaimed of the famous family, who had stolen many a verdict in ninety-eight fights. A pro at sixteen, Dick (real name Lionel Cecil) won the British middle-weight title two years before robust Randy added his name to the belt.

Promoters Braitman and Ezra, upstaging Jack Solomons, could not afford to pay Cerdan fancy prices for a title defence. The match was overweight and the brand new champion was embarrassed, scaling 20 ozs too much for the agreed 2 lb above the middleweight limit. It cost him a £500 forfeit. First point for Turpin. Cerdan was also embarrassed at the start of the fight when Turpin, calling on lessons learned in grubby rings at marked-down prices, made the master flail punches into the air.

Cagy, upright Turpin knew his boxing business and continually stabbed corrective left jabs into the advancing Cerdan, who had obviously underestimated him. He really did box rings around Cerdan. By round six, the world champion's left eye was bruised. While Cerdan landed blows on Turpin's protective arms there seemed little hope of victory. The intended easy fight for Cerdan was becoming more than difficult, but he possessed the patience of a puncher.

In the seventh, Turpin had a fleeting moment when he did not smartly retrieve his left hand after lashing Cerdan again. It left his chin exposed. Cerdan cracked a right, literally travelling inches, but Turpin got the message flush on his chin. He pitched face forward to the canvas and did not move a muscle when the count-out became a formality. One punch, one professionally applied counter, made a mockery of Turpin's skills.

'I don't remember the punch that got me,' said the honest Turpin. 'Even when I play it on film I still can't spot the punch that knocked me out. He's a great fighter.'

The customary herd of news seekers who encircled the fallen Turpin in his dressing room pushed for an answer to their question, 'Can he hit harder than Randolph?' With typical family loyalty, Dick satisfied them with 'No.' Storyline complete. But the follow-up was ignored. 'But he couldn't beat Cerdan. Even Sugar Ray Robinson gives him a miss.'

Six months earlier Cerdan, the bold smiling boulevardier in Paris, had ranked alongside Charlemagne and General Foch, great French warriors. He went into enemy territory, took on the best, and beat him out of sight. Tony Zale, the Steel Man, of Polish descent, was a style boxer and sharp hitter who had cut down the wild and fearless Rocky Graziano to become world champion.

Cerdan fought Zale in New Jersey, at thirty-two, when a bit of his best had been left behind in fourteen years of hard campaigning in North Africa, Paris, Milan, Brussels and Barcelona. He never fought in Sidi-Bel-Abbes, the pseudo-romantic Foreign Legion fort where he was born. American traders were primed about Cerdan's relentless fighting; his cumulative punching was bound to destroy when he could not land the single poleaxe blow. Cerdan won the wartime Inter-Allies championship, defeating Americans in Algiers. Joe Louis sang his praises. So did ex-champion Jack Sharkey, who reckoned Cerdan 'was the best European I've seen'.

A bunch of trouble-shooters, men without the disciplined will and a licence to fight to rules, also testified that an Algerian, serving with the coastal artillery, had cleaned out a bar of soldiers, single-handed, after he had politely asked the offenders to stop insulting his wife. Cerdan laid them out in a pile and reported his action to the authorities, asking for care in case they came to harm!

Zale could not be intimidated by toughness, which is frequently unrelated to winning. He had successfully fought off rougher foe than the polished Cerdan. But the challenger's marvellous commitment, his ability to slip punches, to maintain a nagging hurtful place, simply rusted Zale by the eleventh round. The champion could claim winning only the fourth. An extraordinary performance even by Cerdan's high standards.

He timed a change of gear perfectly, with some rapid punches that not only hurt the brave Zale, but also totally bemused him. Cerdan walked through his defence, aiming his short explosive blows, in the way shellfire weakens armies for the infantry assault, where they did the most damage. Zale was backed on the ropes and wilting. It was a dramatic ending with Cerdan firing at full power, forcing the referee to haul him away as the bell ended the round. Many thought the official had stepped in because Zale had collapsed in a heap. Seconds hauled the admirably game Zale back to the corner and retired him on the stool. They don't surrender over there unless a man is close to dying!

Part of the ring collapsed when excited fans invaded. Cerdan knelt and prayed, in Spanish, his mother's native tongue.

What appeared an unending road of reward for Cerdan was abruptly ended when he faced Jake LaMotta, yet another uncompromising fighter with the toughest middleweight chin of all. Detroit, where a punch in the eye is a calling card, was the site on 16 June 1949. It was Cerdan's first big haul as a champion. Had it come too late?

Cerdan had suffered several injuries during his career, though not to his face, because of the force he used behind every punch. Sometimes he switched to southpaw stance and boxed 'en manchot' – one-handed – trying to hide a busted left hand. In the first round against LaMotta, a torn shoulder muscle wrecked his chances. Yet Cerdan, who had never ducked an opponent, summoned his remaining strength in the hopeless task of trying to stave off the Bronx Bull. He persevered, in pain, for ten rounds, when the majority of fighters pitted against LaMotta would have quit much earlier. Cerdan, a proud man, considered surrender a dishonourable settlement.

Inevitably, in tears and protesting, Cerdan was compassionately retired on his stool by a management who were certain he could recover and regain his title. He had outboxed LaMotta virtually one-handed. Few had even realized his shoulder was gone. But as the fight bore on it was like a peashooter trying to stop a tank. No one-handed man could hope to check LaMotta, who had a victory over Sugar Ray Robinson during Sugar's peak years.

They strapped Cerdan's left arm in a sling, flew him back to New York where the return-fight negotiations began, and the fallen frustrated champion returned home. On the flight Cerdan became his *bon vivant* self. Nobody could be sad when he was around.

They talked and laughed about the time when Nazi invaders ordered that a proposed European welterweight title defence by Cerdan, arranged for Marseilles, be switched to Paris during the occupation of France in 1942, where a German-controlled committee had replaced the French Boxing Federation. Cerdan hated French collaborators even more than the Nazis who had downtrodden them. He was determined not to entertain them, but had no option on where the fight was staged. He fought Spanish Jose Ferrer, who was no stiff, but did not belong in the same ring as Cerdan, who left his stool at the start, quickly sized up Ferrer's stance and knocked him out without raising a bead of sweat.

Cerdan ignored the invitations – or was it orders? – to attend the occupation officers' dinner, when Cerdan and his gunnery *poilus* were suffering ersatz rations. Cerdan photographed smiling with German brass and Vichy puppets would have made propaganda lunatic Dr Goebbels ecstatic. Cerdan and manager Roupp were exited by a back-door alteration to their travel papers from 'free conduct to Paris' to 'return to Casablanca'. It took more guts for Cerdan to sneak his way back to Casablanca, where he was raised, than to face LaMotta again. His career was virtually over, with the Germans angry at being snubbed. But the Allied

invasion of North Africa freed him and he frequently fought to
entertain the troops.

Five months after Cerdan's torn shoulder, and loss of face, he
was signed for revenge. Again the match was in America, where
boxing is a thing of booty, and LaMotta was demanding a bigger
reward as defending champion.

Cerdan left Paris on the night of 27 October 1949, with handler
Jo Longman, who wore tinted glasses because he suffered desert
blindness after serving in the Free French Forces in North
Africa. There were only thirty-seven passengers aboard the Air
France Constellation plane.

After being diverted from fog-bound Shannon, the plane
headed for a fuel stop at the mid-Atlantic Azores. Captain Jean
de la Neue, a veteran of 6700 transatlantic hours, announced
an expected on-schedule flight to New York, where Cerdan's
American agents, Lew Burston and Sammy Richman, were to
greet them at La Guardia Airport, complete with press and
photographers. The welcome was to be almost regal, because
they still regarded Cerdan as the kingpin who had only loaned
his crown.

Conditions were fine when the big Connie banked sharply to
land at Santa Maria. The passengers did not realize that the
captain had suddenly lost radio contact with the control tower
and had veered off course. They never knew. While seat belts
were being fastened, the plane crashed into the top of 2600
Mount Redondo. There were no survivors.

The tragedy shocked the world. In Casablanca the Tricolour
flew at half mast. Newspapers in France printed details of the
tragedy on black-edged paper. Waiting in New York was Edith
Piaf, an admirer and close friend of Cerdan's: gossip-columnists
enjoyed making a Piaf–Cerdan love match, but the great man
was a playboy with no stigma attached. He was married, with
the customary tribulations that most travelling husbands have,
to Marinette, a grocer's daughter from Casablanca. They lived
at a farm near Marrakesh – Winston Churchill's haunt – with
three sons: Marcel, René and Paul. Piaf cancelled her singing
engagements and was reported to have broken down. When she
returned to the stage, she cried at the end of the performance
singing songs she knew Cerdan liked.

At Stillman's gym in New York, the fight crowd, always
tender-hearted when one of their own dies, stood quietly. 'They

loved him before. Now that he's dead, they'll love him even more. Now they'll realize how great he was,' said a promoter who had no financial interest in Cerdan's fighting. 'I know he's dead, but I don't want to believe it,' said another.

Thirty years later, on 27 October 1979, the French press published hundreds of words and pictures paying their tribute on the anniversary of his death. French television screened prized black and white clips of Cerdan's fights. I can think of no other sportsman who had been lauded for so long.

Last round: During the early fifties I helped the Variety Club of Great Britain promote a charity match between England and Russia at Wembley Pool. I suggested inviting Cerdan's bright son, Marcel, a promising amateur, to appear in a supporting bout. I arranged a match, with ABA approval, against Lennie Wilson, of West Ham, who seemed capable of extending Cerdan II without hurting him. Wilson won. It was Cerdan's first defeat.

I'm sure Dad would have consoled young Marcel – and, no doubt, criticized my matchmaking.

Henry Cooper says . . .

It's the first time I've read all the details of Cerdan's career and sad death. He must have been some fighter because my manager, Jim Wicks, so often talked to me about him. Jim was the matchmaker for promoters Braitman and Ezra and went to Paris to sign Cerdan to fight Dick Turpin. The reason he got Turpin's manager to agree was by making Cerdan contract for an overweight forfeit of £500. Had Turpin allowed Cerdan to come in a bit heavier it would have been a mismatch. It was the biggest weight forfeit ever.

After listening to Jim's view of Cerdan I wished I could have seen him. Certainly an attractive fighter. Fascinating reading. I can fully understand now why he was such a hero in France. The old game certainly produces some incredible men. It shows the character building of boxing.

Sugar Ray Robinson

Sugar Ray Robinson would clearly win a fight traders' poll as the most complete, close-to-perfection champion of all. I guarantee it. Possessed of grace, style, rhythm and good looks, he was able to execute every punch in the book and, when provoked, a few not in any book.

The man was a marvel, as close to being indestructible as any prizefighter can be. Nineteen championship fights – never knocked out in twenty-five years. He fought the best; beat them at two weights; and came close to winning a third title at a higher weight.

Yet Robinson insists he was not a particularly hard puncher! He could have fooled me. One hundred and nine opponents failed to finish in 175 victories. He fought the toughest in each division, winning the world welter- and middleweight titles. He was five times middleweight king.

I had long discussions with the great one about his supposed lack of punch power. 'It's a question of timing and surprise,' he explained. 'I was really a weak puncher but I was accurate.' I was asked to face Robinson in boxing pose while he pointed a finger, ready to prod gently into my body. 'That doesn't hurt,' he said. 'Now look away and I'll hit you with the same strength somewhere else.' The prod was on another side of the body. I winced with mild pain and surprise. 'See,' he said. 'It's the punch you don't see coming that hurts.'

Robinson was able to double up the use of difficult-to-cultivate blows like uppercut and left hook, which virtually made certain that if the recipient saw the first one coming, he was bound to be shocked by the repeat second or third. Obviously Robinson was being modest about his punch, or alleged lack of it. There were many times when Robinson took an opponent out, clinically, without first having to wear him down.

When he first moved to New York as a skinny kid named Walker Smith – Smitty is still his nickname with old friends – his trainers tied his right hand to his side and taught him to rely on the left. The drilling paid off. Robinson's stabbing left paved the way to the majority of his wins, apart from vital point scoring, and he was able to switch a potential straight punch to a hook with perfection. The art of punch surprise.

Because New York State forbids pro boxing under sixteen, the eager, hungry kid from Detroit – he lived in a black bottom district, black being the family colour and bottom is where they were at – borrowed another boxer's identity card. Ray Robinson, the ringer, was on his way.

He had scored an incredible forty first-round wins in sixty-nine amateur bouts – not bad for a lad who reckoned he was not a puncher – and for good measure he outpointed the magical champion-to-be Willie Pep.

When statistics are gathered it's incredible that Robinson, arguably the best pound-for-pound boxer of all, could only win one of four fights in Britain. He laughs about it, though it's obvious he is irked. Randolph Turpin defeated Robinson beyond question at Earl's Court in 1951 – despite the famous misleading radio commentary – but the title was regained in sixty-four days.

Robinson knows that too much boxing at the time and a laugh a day on a continental tour – six fights in forty-one days – contributed to his downfall. He never argued about the decision in London (actual scoring by Eugene Henderson, the sole arbiter, was not announced at that time). He never remonstrated with a referee or dredged up an alibi. I reckon he had some cause when Welsh official, Ike Powell, voted Irish Mick Leahy a winner over Robinson in Scotland. Powell enjoyed giving decisions that made headlines. The third loss was undisputed against Terry Downes at Wembley, when the Sugar Man was aged forty-two and needed an oxygen inhaler between rounds.

Downes, who also won the world middleweight title, never gloated about his victory. 'I only beat a man who called himself Robinson. He gave me a great fight and I can't imagine how much harder it would have been fighting Ray at his best.'

The solitary win was against modest Johnny Angel for the

launching of the Anglo-American Sporting Club at the London Hilton. Even in his waning years, whether champion or not, Robinson was always aware that he was the man the crowd had come to see. He could have cheated winning fights the easy way – hit and hop it. 'I can't because it bores me,' he said.

I reported Robinson from the bow-tie clubs in Britain to Antwerp and Chicago. I never ceased to be amazed, yes, thrilled by his technique. The way he could feint an opponent into a mistake and execute the counter-punch; a right hand to disturb a southpaw-style rival; slipping inside a left lead and whipping a left hook; the short, sharp right or the more spectacular uppercut. His was the perfect example of punch delivery – surprise or not – being sufficient to down an opponent without needing the power possessed by so-called natural big hitters.

As befits a proud, arrogant ring artist, he collected an entourage and drove fuchsia-coloured cars. When he came to fight Turpin in London, fifty-three suitcases were checked by customs, including his own punchbag, plus manager George Gainford (who actually managed whom is debatable), two trainers, a valet, a barber, a midget and a golf pro.

Just before the fight, Robinson sent for Dr Vincent Niardello of New York. He was not excess baggage: he was needed. After the fight when Turpin's strength and style had bothered the champion, Robinson had eight stitches inserted in a gashed eyebrow and was lectured about more disciplined conditioning.

Robinson won the return fight with some controversy, but it was the hallmark of a great boxer to be able to end a fight at the right time. He was bleeding badly, but was able to summon strength and punch speed to halt Turpin in the tenth round. As the rounds rolled away, Turpin's youth and strength could have overcome the edge Robinson had in class. Yet when Robinson saw blood and realized it was his own, he opened the throttle all the way.

The beauty of Robinson's punch was shown in a brutal five-fight series with Jake LaMotta (portrayed in the film *Raging Bull*). One fight with rough-hewn LaMotta was enough for most boxers. Robinson, conceding 17 lb, whacked him four times. Bobo Olsen, who traded on gameness, was taken out by a peach of a left hook. Carmen Basilio, tough as old boots, had his features misshapened by Sugar Ray's blows. Even the super three-weights champion, Henry Armstrong, admittedly on the slide, could not cope with Robinson's masterly hitting.

Robinson's second fight against Basilio, an onion farmer from Syracuse and a genuine digger with a steel-built jaw and heart to match, took place in Chicago, 25 March 1958. Perhaps the drama and importance of the fight are magnified for me because it was among the first I had covered in America. Basilio had the crude fighting insistence of a Rocky Marciano, and had dethroned Robinson in New York.

Robinson reported for revenge aged thirty-seven by his own account, thirty-eight by the record books, and forty by the reckoning of some managers. By any calculation he was old as fighters go. I cannot think of another middleweight who would have been considered a match at the same age against Basilio.

In the snap poll among thirty-four reporters at the ringside, twenty-one tipped Basilio. I had little attention to spare for speculation. Western Union had just dispensed with their key-code system of tapping our words direct to London. I warily eyed the large lady with long earrings whom the company had sent to transmit my words, virtually as I wrote, to an anxious sports editor in London.

Police took a stance outside dressing-room doors and led the scowling rivals into the ring. When the parade of familiar old-timers had ended, Robinson and Basilio came out fighting as though it were round sixteen of their last encounter. Robinson's hair had been carefully marcelled, but within seconds it was disarrayed in the most incredible opening round I had seen. Basilio butted and palmed. Robinson looked appealingly at silver-haired referee Frank Sikora, who made no response. So Sugar retaliated, adding a rabbitpunch behind the neck for good measure. One of Robinson's seconds, Honey Brewer, had climbed into Basilio's corner, presumably to watch for hidden stimulants or illegal coagulants. Tubby manager Joe Netro wrestled him away, suggesting he also ran for his life. Honey obeyed.

Rule books, it seemed, were parked at the gate. For a massive $260,000 each, Robinson and Basilio were prepared to punch until the last man to remain upright was declared the winner. But once the rule-flouting had finished, they fought a spectacular further fourteen rounds with mutual respect. Points seesawed; Basilio's left eye blew up to look like a purple plum. The fight seemed in a different league to the hard, but fair, contests I had watched at home.

Robinson, long past his peak they kept telling me, was magnificent. He had tremendous grit; a jaw that could take Basilio's shots without wilting; and a pride that shone. What a fighter! When the final bell sounded, they exchanged pleasantries, neither having been put down, and we awaited the decision with sweaty palms. Basilio knelt in his corner, crossed himself and prayed. 'Not only to win,' he said, 'but for having survived and not hurt my opponent. I didn't hate Ray that much.' Robinson combed his flattened hair and, even after fifteen murderous rounds, looked like a black Clark Gable. He beamed with an almost girlish pleasure at being admired. He stamped his feet in the resin while acolytes wiped the sacrificial blood from their high priest's face. I had scored Robinson a close winner, but referee Sikora voted 66–68 against him. The judges, however, saved Sugar, scoring a wider 72–65 and 71–64 for him. He reached for his middleweight crown for a record fifth time.

Five years earlier, Robinson had fought Charley Fusari for $1, giving $33,000 to the Damon Runyon Cancer Research Fund. Runyon was a sportswriter with a love of boxing and its characters, particularly Robinson, long before his Runyonese stories were best sellers.

Robinson told me he hated being in retirement. The ring was his stage. When they staged a tribute retirement night at Madison Square Garden in 1965, many of the men Robinson had hit and hurt were there. They donned dressing gowns, Basilio, Olsen and our own Turpin, to shake hands again with the master. We all sensed there could not be another like him.

Robinson, like Turpin, wasted money – his phone bills were higher than a big company's. He turned to acting and tap dancing in cabaret, and he still managed to create sweet vibrations when he walked into a room. In London in 1969, they honoured him for 'his unprecedented contribution to boxing'. I was flattered that he wrote me a humble thank-you note just for making a tribute speech for the occasion. Just being in the same room was a privilege.

During the seventies Robinson enjoyed being a Los Angeles County appointed leader for a youth programme. By 1982 his face had finally rounded and he had bouts of ill health. But when he walked into the open-air arena at the Larry Holmes–Gerry

Above: Posing in their prime — Jimmy Wilde, the greatest at his weight; Eric Boon, the Boy Wonder

Below: Japan's Fighting Harada slipping through Alan Rudkin's defence to retain the world bantamweight title

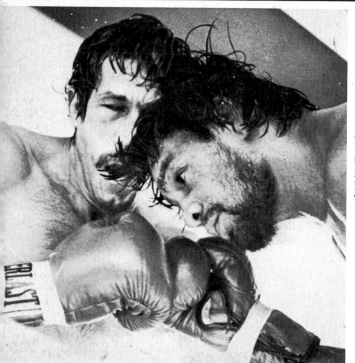

Above: Ken Buchanan overcome by the onslaught of Roberto Duran, winning his f world title. Eleven ye later Duran was worl champion again, at a higher weight

Left: Bearded Robert Duran in typical actio taking close stock of European champion Luigi Minchillo in La Vegas. Duran won

bove: The leading
ght-is-might of Dave
harnley (note the
shed nose)
allenging American
e Brown for the world
htweight crown

ight: Arrogant Ruben
livares, of Mexico,
oks to Alan Rudkin's
dy, blasting the
verpudlian out in two
unds to stay world
ntamweight king

Toe to toe between Roberto Duran and Sugar Ray Leonard in a classic battle for the world welterweight title. Duran outpointed Sugar Ray in this Montreal thriller, but was humiliated in the return match

gar Ray Leonard takes a bow after announcing his retirement and receives a gift from the
thor in London. Chief second, Henry Cooper, applauds

the left, and Tommy Hearns has a squashed nose when Sugar Ray Leonard lands a blow.
gar caned Hearns in fourteen rounds to stay world champ

Great Ted Kid Lewis displays the chiller right to the head of Johnny Basham and lands the blow with his feet almost off the canvas. Lewis won in the nineteenth round in London, 1920, to retain British and European welterweight titles

Crashing, bashing Terry Downes looks the stylist with a traditional straight left against Phil Edwards of Wales. Downes took the British middleweight title and went on to win a world championship

Cooney fight in Las Vegas, the crowd rose to him. Nobody could understand what he was doing in the stands. He should have been ushered where he belonged – to a super-star seat.

Henry Cooper says . . .

He was the perfect build and style for a middleweight. He and Joe Louis were my idea of the proper stance and make-up. They could carry hands low, especially Robinson, and be able to get a punch off quicker. He was a sneak puncher. He could flick and jab and then suddenly unleash a different type of punch at great speed. As you said, it was the surprise speed of Sugar's punch, as much as the power, that did his business. He could land a punch before the other guy tumbled what was happening.

Rating boxers pound for pound, I'd have to rate him in the top three. If you're talking about styles, I'd rather watch a Robinson than Ali. Yes, Ali was good to fight but Robinson was the proper boxfighter, using every punch and looking good doing it.

I remember being huddled around our wireless at home listening to his fight with Turpin in London. Now that I'm doing a bit of BBC commentating I often think how confused I was as a youngster listening to the different views of that famous fight. We all thought Robinson had won – then the result. We leaped around the room. Turpin did ever so well to beat him and it's unfair to suggest Robinson was not fully prepared, though we know he'd been larking about on the Continent. That didn't exactly help him. But Robinson had sold Turpin a bit short and he paid the price. None the less, a superb boxer.

Randy Turpin

Randolph Adolphus Turpin gave us triumph, tantrums, tragedy and tears. The first British undisputed winner of the world middleweight title for sixty years, he frequently severely hurt opponents but sadly punished himself outside the ring. He had a raw, untamed, kerbside toughness, harnessed with a natural power developed by his boyhood devotion to body building. With experience Turpin developed a high degree of craft, enabling him to outpunch and outpoint the world's finest at the weight, Sugar Ray Robinson.

Turpin's blows from tattooed arms seemed to explode on impact. There was no delayed action. He was a jaw- and heart-breaker. I saw many of his opponents, from his first to last professional fight, out to the world before they hit the floor. They called him the Leamington Licker, a sepia-skinned fifteen-year-old, punching holes in the toughest they could find at the Peoples' Palace in London's earthy East End. He was the first to become ABA junior and senior champion in the same season, at seventeen: and he won five professional titles.

Turpin's upbringing in fighting colour prejudice – he was the only black kid in his classroom – and itching to be a breadwinner, developed the inherent drive to be world champion. How else could he succeed? His father, a merchant seaman from British Guiana, died from the effects of being gassed in the First World War when Randolph was nine. His mother, Beatrice, who became partially blind, raised five children with only a 27s (£1.35) a week pension, living in one room. Brothers Dick and Jackie were successful professionals, Dick becoming middleweight champion, Jackie a top featherweight. They both served in the Forces; Dick from El Alamein to Berlin, and Jackie in the Far East.

Randolph, clearly the big hit of this most famous British fighting family, became a cook in the Navy. His knack of flattening opponents like pancakes riveted half the nation to their television screens. When England first took on the amateur boxing might of America at Wembley Pool in the postwar years, it was Cook Turpin, R., who scored the super knockout – in one round. No more chasing medals; no Olympics.

When service was completed, commercial managers began casting their nets for Turpin. Promoter Jack Solomons announced his undying faith in the ability of the Midlands marvel to become the saviour of British boxing in the fifties by guaranteeing to match him for the world title. At that time, coaxing Americans to come here and risk their world crown with our limited resources needed the patience of Job and, of course, the wisdom of Solomons.

Turpin turned down offers from the fashionable managers of the time and signed with George Middleton, a grocer in Leamington, who had known the family for some years. Turpin was not at ease with strangers, and part of his shyness stemmed from deafness in one ear that worsened over the years, caused by swimming too long under water.

Turpin trusted Middleton – their partnership lasted from start to finish – but it was Solomons, inviting the bright-eyed lad to gaze at the photos of the greats that adorned his office walls, who became the father figure – Mr Fix-It.

Few, if any, reporters were able to open up Turpin. He had discovered early in his career that he disliked being a peepshow. My old colleague, George Whiting, knew Turpin best because the respected wordsmith covered the amateur scene when Randolph was rising. His brothers were more outgoing, but Randolph was always pleasant to me and understood the need which occasionally caused his privacy to be interrupted. Big brother preferred to train well away from the bright lights, on the first floor of a gelatine factory on the road from Warwick to Leamington Spa. We had to climb over odd pieces of dead cow to watch Turpin work out. The roadwork clothes of the three brothers were dropped on the floor, and they got down to work with less fuss than you and I make when the missus reckons it is our turn to wash up.

All very ordinary; all very British. Manager Middleton would smoke a surreptitious cigarette in the short time he permitted himself away from the counter of his shop. Arthur Batty swung an occasional towel; Billy Hyam rubbed bodies; and when Randolph's knuckles were put out of joint by his fierce hitting, they carted him down to Watford for physio treatment from Eddie Mallett, who also promoted boxing when he wasn't playing around with broken bones.

Turpin was launched at Harringay Arena, September 1946, against Gordon Griffiths who lasted less than a round. Four of his first seven opponents were put out in the first. Yet the class of Turpin's early rivals was far superior to that of many present-day champions. Two of those whom Turpin took out, Bert Hyland and Jimmy Davis, were title class. The first setback was against Mark Hart, whom Turpin had beaten on points, in a return fight in 1947. They fought a six-round draw. Hart, from Croydon, is the only ABA heavyweight champion to drop to middleweight as a professional.

It didn't take long for Turpin to find his punch timing. The next two opponents were knocked out in the first. He rarely bothered with range-finding. He knocked a capable opponent down without realizing his punch was so explosive. Turpin, in the formative years, was tremendous.

I was witness to the plotting, at the basement gymnasium in the car-trading area of London's Warren Street, for Turpin's first eight-round shock. My Uncle Jack coached Albert Finch of Croydon, who could box with the best, to hit without being hit and teach Turpin a thing or two. Family loyalty hoped for the best, but feared the worst. But when Finch opposed Turpin in a non-title match at the Royal Albert Hall the plan worked. Finch won on points.

Randolph fretted and, surprisingly, lost to a Frenchman, Jean Stock, because his hands were so badly bruised that his power was reduced. It took two years of patience to fight Finch again, because brother Dick became reigning champion, and it was Finch who dethroned him. The perfect script for family revenge.

Finch's ring generalship and family knowhow could not save his title. Randolph was rampaging at Harringay Arena, and Finch was counted out in the sixth round. With his healed hands assuring normal service, Turpin socked Frenchman Stock in the rematch. But winning the British title, at middleweight, was not rewarding. Turpin was forced to vacate the throne for bigger fry.

Luc Van Dam, a Dutchman managed by a pretty wife, was shipped in to compete for the vacant European title. Mrs Susan Van Dam had no fears that the powerful young Mr Turpin would disfigure her husband because, like Finch, Luc knew the ring score. She was right. Turpin clinically knocked out Van Dam with his first serious punch of the fight – in forty-eight seconds – no damage done. Maybe Turpin was angry because the MC had wrongly introduced Van Dam as defending champion.

Soon afterwards Solomons imported an American, Billy Brown, who looked so ordinary in training at the Windmill Street gymnasium that was part of the promoter's office that he was quickly and conveniently dispatched. Nobody could bother Turpin at that time. With sound hands, his power at 11 st 6 lb was awesome.

Another American, Jackie Keough, a smarter mover, was brought in while Sugar Ray Robinson, the world champion, was engaged in a knockabout European tour. The great Sugar Man came to London, checking Turpin's form against Keough's, who was duly halted in seven rounds. It was more likely that Solomons's form was being checked by Sugar Ray's computer mind for money. There was the inevitable Fleet Street speculation that boxing's best Barnum could sign the match of the century, etc. Robinson could get whatever he demanded fighting in America.

Cross my heart, I knew Solomons had signed the big fight for the Earl's Court exhibition hall on 10 July 1951. Solomons told me first because he could not bear to withhold his feat a moment longer. He was driving me from a greyhound meeting at Harringay in June, where Mr Boxing regularly held court in the restaurant. He forced me to swear to keep his secret. Even his wife was not told! Solomons could not release the big story to the newspapers because, although the contracts were signed, they were still being copied and delivered to all parties concerned. I was on trial. Keeping the story bottled up was a newspaperman's heartache; but principle mattered.

Solomons had the customary business worries of a promoter, particularly having to guarantee Robinson £30,000; but he insisted he could sleep like a baby. He would wake and cry on the hour at the thought of Robinson ruining the biggest fight of the time by fighting in Italy only nine days before. Defeat was highly improbable, but injury was a possibility. Robinson did not fail Solomons. The ring king arrived on cue, with his retinue, to train at Windsor – at the Star and Garter, not the castle. Turpin trained at Gwrych Castle, North Wales.

Bookmakers did not hedge making Robinson clear favourite, and the official listed odds against Turpin winning on points were 33–1. There were few takers. It was Turpin's forty-fourth fight; Robinson's 134th.

Opinion at Earl's Court was that Turpin would not be humiliated; no one held a genuine belief that he could win. A good fight with a good loser was the most we could expect. A couple of sportswriters joined the incredible wave of emotion, forecasting the confident Licker to cane the renowned Sugar. It seemed more a sales gimmick than sincere judgement. Before the off, tension mounted, and a relation of the promoter collapsed and died in a ringside seat.

Solomons and the Turpin camp remained confident from the day of signing. For fifteen rounds Turpin defied Robinson, the odds and most of the forecasters. His deceptive 74-in reach kept Robinson away. His unusual wide stance, enabling both feet to be anchored, fooled Robinson, whose leads frequently fell short. Turpin's strength at close quarters was his way to victory. Robinson was 5½ lb inside the middleweight limit, and was turned, wrestled and pushed off like a baby by Turpin's brawny arms.

At no time was Turpin in trouble. The crowd could not believe by the halfway stage that Turpin had not only outpunched the master, but had outgeneralled him too. When 18,000 packed-in fans realized the underdog was bound to win, they roared. Robinson's corner, accustomed to success – he had lost only once – had trouble coping with the champion's gashed eyebrow. Once, I recall, Robinson grabbed a towel from a second and wiped blood out of his eye.

By the thirteenth round the crowd began singing 'For He's a Jolly Good Fellow', and Robinson was resigned to defeat. To watch a film of the fight with the sound turned off might disappoint, because there was much wrestling and little 'inside' hitting. But the atmosphere was indescribable when all sensed that Turpin was going to win. Strangers hugged each other; bookies willingly paid out; and at the final bell, Turpin followed

Robinson to his corner. Referee Eugene Henderson, in sole charge, walked towards them. There was a fear that Henderson would allow Robinson's reputation to sway judgement and lift his hand to retain the title. But he merely hauled Turpin away, anxious to give his decision.

Amid scenes of joy the nation had not demonstrated since the war victory, he held Turpin's hand high. The underprivileged kid who had come close to death in his childhood was the hero.

The Duke of Fife, later to become ABA president, told me that King George VI was holding a private party at Buckingham Palace, and the gathering fell silent while the King listened to the round-by-round commentary. The King, in great excitement, threw his arms into the air and announced to his guests, 'He's won it! He's won it!'

Boxing's iniquitous return clause, forcing Turpin to defend the title in America, was swiftly implemented. Such was the monopolistic effect of the International Boxing Club, for whom Solomons acted as European agent, that beaten Robinson took 30 per cent and champion Turpin only 25 per cent of the rematch rewards.

Turpin and brothers sailed in the *Queen Mary* to New York where he was received with disbelief because he had whacked the fight game's legend. Only sixty-four days after dethroning Robinson, Britain's big hitter was being asked to do it again before the Americans would really believe it. Turpin disciplined his mind – muscle was no problem – in an old airplane hangar at Grossinger's Catskill resort. Robinson, whose ego had been hurt more than his body at Earl's Court, was camped at Pompton Lakes (Joe Louis's training site) and he permitted a sparmate to wear a rubber bodybelt to protect himself from Sugar Ray's daily pounding. He also practised tug-o'-war with an iron bar, a technique fashioned for Robinson to combat Turpin's strength in the clinches.

The build-up was intense, described in a *Daily Express* leader article as: 'A human, understandable absurdity that a nation should consider its prestige raised or lowered by the ability of one man to stand up in a ring against another man from a different country.'

Any man capable of outboxing Robinson was no phoney in America. They fought for tickets at the Polo Grounds, New York, because there was no home television or even a radio description. There was a public outcry. The IBC were selling 31,510 seats at closed-circuit venues with 75 cents profit on each. Gate takings were an incredible $767,626. Only seven other fights, all at heavyweight, had bettered the return. Attendance was 61,370. Betting odds favoured Robinson at 11–5.

Turpin's comfortable corner crew were upset because a 'no-blood-relation' rule forbade Dick, known to keep his cool, to be among his seconds. But it pleased Randolph, swiftly tagged Randy in America, who was fidgeting and loosening up backstage when brother Jackie returned to the dressing room a winner of a six-round preliminary bout.

Robinson privately admitted he was wary of Turpin, because he had trouble trying to fathom his style and cope with what he considered an awkward strength. His training was severe, having been rebuked for his touch of *joie de vivre* in Paris, which friends considered was Robinson's downfall, together with a six-fight European stroll preceding his losing defence in London.

Again unruffled, Turpin took much of the play away from the master showman Robinson. For ten rounds it was punch for punch in a chess-match contest, each trying to huff the other and not succeeding. When they came out for the tenth, referee Ruby Goldstein scored the fight level. That says it all. But the judges, both American, had Robinson ahead by one and two rounds.

Turpin, at twenty-eight, remained stronger, though Robinson had increased weight from the first meeting to 11 st 3½ lb; Turpin was at 11 st 5 lb. Hearts sank in the partisan stadium when Robinson emerged from a clinch with a brutal gash above his left eye. It seemed all over bar the shouting. But Robinson became an enraged octopus, flailing blows – ripping, effective, cutting blows, with rifle accuracy.

Robinson surely sensed that his injury would prevent him fighting on much longer. He unloaded everything and, inevitably, a hook caught Turpin to send him down. At the count of three, Turpin got a leg under his sagging body, and when the toll reached nine managed gamely to stand up. Robinson rushed in wildly, pinning Turpin against the ropes, and punished him. In moments of stress Turpin had frequently dropped his hands, used the middle rope as a seat, and attempted to weave his way out of trouble, like a cobra swaying to a flute. It was a mistake. Had Turpin taken counts, mere rest counts, on his knees, time must have run out for Robinson. But he stayed rooted to one spot, his head sagging forward, and with only eight seconds remaining of the round, the referee stopped the fight. His job was to act wisely and not to be a timekeeper. Turpin was being hit without hitting back. At least he had the satisfaction of staying on his feet at the finish.

The wild, but remarkable, fling of Robinson meant Turpin had the shortest middleweight reign of all.

The late Red Smith, a Pulitzer Prize winner, with whom I was frequently honoured to share a working bench, scored Turpin the seventh, eighth and ninth rounds. He wrote: 'As Robinson turned towards his corner, Turpin straightened, refusing to fall, and lurched after him as though to resume the fight. His handlers leaped into the ring and tackled him, but he wasn't trying to hit Robinson; he only meant to congratulate him, and he towed his handlers into the corner for that purpose. . . . It was a genuine gesture of sportsmanship from a first-class fighting man. There haven't been many better fighters than Turpin seen around here in a long time.'

With a third decider fight not considered, there was a danger that Turpin would be relegated to becoming just 'another fighter'. But with the loyalty of Solomons behind him, the fallen hero was back in business. By moving up a weight and showing his punch skill, he stopped Don Cockell in eleven rounds for the British and Empire light-heavyweight title. Cockell, as a light heavy, was exceptionally talented.

Turpin boxed between weights, sweating back to middle to offer a fine showing of ability, without exploding, by outpointing George Angelo, a South African with a copybook style, for the Empire crown. He added the European title, at middle, by outpointing Frenchman Charles Humez, another quality opponent, at a Solomons summer spectacular. Because Angelo and Humez had stayed the course, Turpin's wins could be considered unconvincing, but his clear superiority at two weights in Europe earned him a second crack at the world middleweight title in his fifty-fourth fight. Carl 'Bobo' Olsen, although outpointed by Sugar Ray Robinson, had won fifty-five of fifty-eight fights and was nominated against Turpin for the vacant title when one of boxing's weird self-voted authorities decided Robinson was no longer in favour.

Unfortunately, Turpin's physical wellbeing was impaired by

a psychological mix-up. He had trouble living with the short fame of being world champion; had domestic bust-ups; a car accident; arguments with advisers; even a fallout with brother Dick. The bouncy Licker became a near recluse for his return to the States.

There was criticism of Turpin's training, or lack of it, discarding sparring a week before he was due in the ring at Madison Square Garden. Without wishing to detract from Olsen's ability – a tough, ex-sailor, always willing to fight – he could be rated a selling plater against Turpin when he was properly tuned for the game's richest prize. Turpin fought with other things on his mind, and lost a unanimous points decision.

There were victories to come – a smashing knockout of Alex Buxton for the home light-heavy title – but being clobbered in the first round by Tiberio Mitri in Rome showed that Turpin was virtually washed up. By the time his last fight had been contracted in 1958, a couple of years overdue against strong Yolande Pompey, Turpin's life had become a turmoil. Pompey duly knocked him out in two rounds, and we left the Birmingham arena with a newspaper story that could have been written beforehand. At thirty, when many are at peak, Turpin was a sad figure of a once superb fighter.

Income tax, surtax, false friends, courts, divorce, unwise investments, money tappers, girls, hangers-on, phoneys – Turpin suffered them all. He was virtually teetotal and a non-smoker, but without the strength of mind to match that of his body. He spent freely ('It's my money. I've earned it the hard way'), and gave too freely. A soft touch. Inevitably, becoming bankrupt. 'I'm the boxing sucker of all time,' he said. 'I earned about £150,000 and haven't got a penny.'

He drove a scrap-metal lorry through streets which were once lined with thousands of people cheering as hero Turpin waved to them from the mayor's car and RAF jets swooped past in a salute over Royal Leamington Spa.

With reckless enthusiasm, Turpin foolishly bought a hotel in Llandudno, and a share of the North Wales castle, a fake medieval fortress, where he had once trained. He again lost money. His heart and mind really belonged to a life of boxing where he had earned 'nobbins' – coins from the crowd – appearing at fairground booths as a boy wonder. So for a while he joined the grunt-and-groan wrestlers.

The Inland Revenue had collected over £40,000 from Turpin, but he was made bankrupt when he could not meet further demands for £15,922 which he was still owing, although he denied receiving the reported £68,145 for the second fight against Robinson. Manager Middleton, who had tried to help Turpin after his retirement, countered that Turpin had received every penny due.

Turpin's accounts, such as they were, were a pile of papers on a desk in a room above the transport café he ran with second wife Gwyneth in Russell Street, Leamington. He seemed resigned to having been fleeced by so-called friends. On the café wall hung a sign: 'That which seldom comes back to him who waits is the money he lends to his friends.' On 17 May 1966 another income-tax demand arrived – for £200. Randolph was joking with his two-year-old daughter, Carmen. Gwyneth took a photograph of them and went out shopping. An hour later she returned to find a note which began: 'I hope you will forgive me for this terrible thing . . .'

Turpin had committed suicide, shooting himself with a .22 revolver in the attic bedroom and wounding little Carmen. The first bullet lodged against Turpin's skull and was not fatal; a second went through his heart. In the end there was not even his own life to treasure.

At the funeral service, the Reverend John Haselden said, 'He was a simple, naive man, who needed friends to protect him from spongers. To our shame, he was let down.' It was a tragic price to pay, aged thirty-eight, for sixty-four days of ring glory.

I visited his grave at the Warwick cemetery where his handsome young nephew, Jackie, was a gravedigger at the time when the Boxing Writers' Club voted him best young boxer, 1971 – thirty years after Randolph had become the club's first winner. Paying respect was fulfilling. If only people and life itself had been more kind to a fine champion.

Henry Cooper says . . .

I still recall with honest excitement listening to the wireless when Turpin defeated Robinson. Randy had a fine English straight punch, as opposed to the jab. He hit like a prop with it. When he followed with a right that hit the target it was 'Goodnight all'. A natural hitter – and I still look at a photo of him, showing his Lonsdale Belts, and admire the ripples of his stomach muscles.

I don't think Britain produced a better one-punch middleweight than Turpin. And he could, as you say, box well to back his punch. What a tragedy that he was unable to cope with his private life. It takes so much discipline to become a champion, especially a world champion, yet we still have a few like Turpin who are unable to control their life in retirement. Very sad, indeed.

I was obviously a Turpin fan. He brought so much excitement and tension into the game.

Marvin Hagler

Marvin Hagler can box or brawl ambidextrously, a consummate pro who destroys the belief of misinformed boxing followers that the men of the eighties cannot match the old timers. Can anyone name a middleweight, with any genuine conviction, who would have whacked Hagler? Yes, the runners, the brave, the cuties may have frustrated or even outpointed Hagler, but none would have carried much of my money. To put Hagler in the mould of Greb, Walker, Robinson, Cerdan and Monzon is complimentary enough. He would surely have mown down most of the others with his relentless deadliness.

The accuracy of Hagler's hitting has not been surpassed by any champion. Others have exploded with single blows, but Hagler puts his combination of punches together with pinpoint accuracy. The first punch landed is merely the first rock of a landslide. Rivals are confused facing a champion with a basic southpaw style who switches when required. He destroys them with a versatility that not only hurts but also humiliates.

Decently equipped fighters like Alan Minter and Tony Sibson – they come no braver – both had moments in their clashes with Hagler when they turned away in the heat of the battle totally bemused – and embarassed. They could not cope with Hagler's classy butchery. Being hit and hurt was an acceptable occupational hazard; being outclassed wounded their pride.

No doubt the Wild West gunslingers knew they were bound to be hit, but they surely never considered dying without at least having got their gun out of the holster. They were blasted, presumably, without an audience. Hagler attracts millions to

watch him dismantle a man piece by piece. His television show-
ings should carry an H certificate.

I must have watched Hagler in the flesh more times than any
other critic this side of the Atlantic. Wembley, San Remo, Monte
Carlo, Boston, Worcester, Chicago, Atlantic City. The man is
simply awesome, an opinion offered knowing that by the time
this book appears Hagler could have been caught off-guard, quit
the ring, or had his reputation blown sky high. At the time of
writing, I'll lay plenty of 6–4 against it happening.

The shavenhead, bulging-muscle figure with riveting eyes that
squint when he punches enjoys his menacing image. He shaved
his head when an amateur and he has shaved it ever since. But
Hagler has never been a baddie outside the ring. His family
life was disciplined and his practically paranoid desire 'to be
somebody' contributed to him being a marvellously disciplined
trainer. The Pilgrim Fathers first landed at Herring Cove, near
Provincetown, Massachusetts, had a look round, pulled up
anchor and decided to disembark at Plymouth Rock. Hagler,
typically, chose Herring Cove beach for his daily 'yomping' and
to confine himself for weeks before a fight to 'get real mean'.
He takes immense pride in his fitness for the ring and in his
performance. A natural loner spirit in Hagler, inbred with a hard
upbringing in a broken family home in Newark, New Jersey,
makes his spells of self-imposed isolated training close to being
enjoyable. Yet another glowing example of the kid from the
streets who found boxing his only way, as they say, from poverty
to plenty.

Hagler became a fatherless loner as a child when Robert Sims
left the home of Ida Mae Hagler – they were then unmarried.
Marvin fought as Hagler; brother Robbie as Sims. Mae also
raised four daughters on Welfare – the Newark equivalent of
National Assistance. Producing Marvin as a millionaire champion, Robbie (at the time of writing) as a near champion, and
daughters as nurses is a fine testimony of mother Hagler's determination. She worked double shifts as housekeeper and caterer
to be sure her children led a decent life.

She gambled on packing the children and bits of their home
into a truck and moving from trouble-torn Newark, a black
ghetto scene of race riots, to Brockton, Massachusetts, a friendly
town originally known for its shoe factories and producing their
finest leather product – Rocky Marciano. The Haglers were

literally holed up, caught in the crossfire during the riots in Newark – twenty-six died – and have remained close. For three days the family moved about the house on all fours. 'It was like the end of the world,' they said.

Bill Nack, of *Sports Illustrated*, discovered how Hagler would shadow box in front of a mirror pretending to be Floyd Patterson. He also revealed that a figure known simply as Mister Joe, whom Hagler is still trying to find, came along to encourage him, taught him to counsel troublesome kids, and gave him his first pair of gloves. It took a kid with special talent and a lot of steel to survive. 'A rough bunch,' says Hagler.

His only friends at the time were pigeons which he trained for racing, and wounded birds. He also had a turtle that was treated to a swim in the family tub when Mum wasn't looking. He found pigeons more trustworthy than people. His understandable mistrust of people, especially white, was gradually eased in Brockton, a community of mixed creeds, with a small percentage of blacks and Puerto Ricans, that had not seen much social unrest since Shay's Rebellion in 1786.

In the days when Hagler fought with smart cropped hair he won the national AAU title – only two losses in fifty bouts – when Sugar Ray Leonard was beaten at the same tournament by Randy Shields. Hagler's prowess as a boxer, the flashy, Ali take-off type of the time, was proved in 1973 but it took ten more years before many traders accepted that Hagler was more than a lucky puncher. He'd worked hard at the game. Opponents were not beaten by accident.

Much of the credit belongs to Pat and Goody Petronelli, from the Italian section of town, who befriended Hagler and added the finishing touches to his fighting. It says much for Hagler's character that he remained with the Petronellis, with a friendship harnessed to a businesslike management, through frustrating times when he was blatantly cold-shouldered and promotion factions were luring him.

Brothers Pascuale and Guareno, who boxed amateur around Brockton – a son was clobbered by Belfast's Jim Montague – ran the best gym in town. At fifteen, Hagler hung around waiting to be asked to fight. When Hagler showed the desire required, reporting for duty no matter how tough the sessions, he was given the coarse schooling of fighting pro in Philadelphia, where champions come out of the cracks in the gyms. Survive Philly –

and you can fight. Hagler's background in equally rugged Newark, the slums, the hand-me-down clothes, winos on the corner, made him a survivor.

The only two losses when Hagler reached sixty fights, defeating Sibson in 1983, were in Philadelphia in the ring-blooding days. Victors Bobby Watts and Willie Monroe were cleanly taken out in return fights. Seven years without defeat rubber-stamped Hagler's fighting class. Hagler's followers enlisted the might of Tip O'Neill, top man on the political scene, to push his middleweight title claims. Hagler hollered that he was getting the runaround, that Vito Antuofermo and Minter were only pretenders to the crown. He was right – but a combination of caution and concern about staying fifteen-rounds strong against rock-hard Antuofermo caused a hitch.

Kevin Finnegan, who knew the ropes but never pretended to be a finishing puncher, twice gave Hagler a hard time in Boston, the nearest big-fight city to his adopted hometown. Finnegan swore he could have beaten Hagler, but for being cut up. But Hagler must have done some damage along the way. Finnegan's face required over sixty stitches. None the less, Finnegan was not counted out and obviously possessed sufficient knowhow to keep Hagler on his toes. Pity they were non-title fights.

Antuofermo, brought up playing a heading game with rocks then beating off the hooligans in Brooklyn, was eventually forced to give Hagler his first title challenge. It had taken him fifty fights to qualify. It turned out a rousing spectacle, a decent neutral crowd in Las Vegas rising to both fighters, and although referee Mills Lane, campaigning for sheriff's office in Reno, had indicated to Hagler that he was about to raise his hand after fifteen rounds, the result was a draw. Two judges scored for each man; the third a draw. A tie keeps the title for the champion.

Because Hagler had failed in one judge's view to take advantage in a fight he should have won – twice as good in every department as Antuofermo – there were a group of fight-game people, matchmaker Mickey Duff among them, who considered Hagler did not possess the backbone for the big time. I never understood the judgement and repeatedly stated my disagreement. Instead of ordering an instant rematch, justified by the drawn verdict, effective badgering by Mickey Duff, who has long had an influence on world boxing, persuaded the World Boxing Council to first give Minter his chance. Minter was rated

No. 1. Antuofermo was happy to oblige and Hagler went back into the shadows again, his bitterness festering. Minter fought splendidly in Las Vegas deservedly to take the world title, despite the closeness of the scoring (British official, Roland Dakin, excepted!).

Maybe Hagler had conveniently softened Antuofermo for Minter, but the bulldog Briton had the ability to have outboxed Vito on his best night. The emotional ending to the fight made Minter an instant hero, especially when he tearfully invited the millions, tuned in live on ITV, to celebrate with him by 'getting pissed tonight'.

Minter, to his credit, never suggested resorting to sidestepping Hagler because he was a ringside witness at the drawn-decision fight. But with Mickey Duff and Co. controlling the logic, Minter made the most of being allowed a voluntary defence and arguing Antuofermo was invited to Wembley. The replay was easy for Minter with the scarred ex-champion cut up in eight rounds.

In September 1980, Hagler had to come to England if he wanted to stop protesting and get on with the punching. While Minter evaded his growing army of fans by warming up in Jersey, Hagler and the Petronelli brothers joined the Lavender Hill mob, the gym in south London managed by Freddie Hill.

Regrettably, the fight had been hyped, surprisingly without pushing from the promoters, with racial remarks. Hagler vehemently denied making the slurs attributed to him by Kevin Finnegan. Minter replied, when asked about Hagler's alleged words, by not allowing 'any black man to take his title'. Later he retracted, asserting he meant 'any man'. The undignified pre-fight talk had been weaned by reporters and repeated in some previews to the fight. It was not another publicity gimmick, because the fight would have been a sure sell-out without either fighter saying a word.

Hagler trained furiously and the Petronellis even checked the accuracy of the gym clock just in case some interfering Limey messed up Hagler's timing. 'I feel this is it,' said Hagler. On his way to the ring Hagler said, 'I'm ready to die for this. Don't stop it.'

Flag-waving and anthems, Union Jacks everywhere, were a bit over the top – a procedure now requested by the Board of Control to be more restrained. A Minter fan dressed in a Union

Jack suit and bowler hat when he won the title later became an honorary inspector of the 'Board'.

Minter tagged Hagler early in the fight and made the mistake of immediately rushing in. Hagler retaliated with a frightening intensity, causing the first of four cuts that were to cause Minter's defeat. The crowd were quietened and by the third round Hagler was dominating. For the first time in his career, amateur and pro, Minter allowed a look of helpless resignation to spread over his face. At the end of the round, Minter drifted back to his corner knowing who but wondering what had hit him. His manager instantly reacted with compassion – he is also Minter's father-in-law – and called a halt. The referee agreed.

Without having his hand hoisted in the traditional victory manner, Hagler dropped to his knees in joy as beer bottles (plastic, but some half full) rained down upon the ring. Hagler's attentive seconds dashed to fling themselves protectively over the new champion. Hagler's lawyer, Steve Wainwright (later to shave his head), also rushed in and was at first thought to be an irate Minter fan. The scene was nasty, but short-lived. It was confined to a section of the crowd some of whom may have believed Hagler had caused Minter's injuries by butting. Minter sportingly admitted that Hagler had fought cleanly. Also clinically. I was struck near Hagler's corner by a flying Minter autobiography, hot off the presses and on sale at Wembley, and abused by two Minter supporters in expensive ringside seats because I had warned in a newspaper preview that I feared for Minter's safety.

Hagler's wife, Bertha, was distressed and suffered unforgivable abuse. The police acted swiftly, with Dennis Pollard, a chief inspector, leading the way because not only had he efficiently policed the arena for some years, but also fought well there for Britain against America. Hagler had praise for their rescue, but was deeply hurt at not being given public respect. (Pollard, incidentally, was not officially on duty and was the subject of a why-was-he-on-our-patch inquiry!).

I have seen much worse crowd trouble around the world, but rarely such a swift reaction with disgusting racial overtones. I am still embarrassed when the so-called 'minor incident', as described by the Boxing Board, is mentioned in Hagler's presence. It was totally out of character for a British boxing event. The next time I saw Hagler, he was holidaying, as a present from New York promoter Bob Arum, with his wife at Sun City, Southern Africa. He dismissed the Wembley scene as bad feeling from a few, but made it clear he would not consider fighting in Britain again for as long as he held the title. How could we argue?

Away from the strains of daily disciplining of mind and muscle, Hagler is an affable, easy-to-smile man with impeccable manners, who dresses like a stockbroker. No comparison with the champion who climbs into the ring without permitting the slightest distraction and who seems prepared to commit anything short of murder to win. ('When I'm not fighting I try to be a good human being, instead of the terrible monster you see in the ring'.)

Without prodding – and certainly without paying him a fee! – Hagler became our expert inter-round summarizer ('the colour guy' they say in America) for the WBA heavyweight battle between Mike Weaver and Gerrie Coetzee, screened live for 'World of Sport'. His first attempt was first class, as though he'd been a regular broadcaster; he quickly adapted to television techniques, like commercial breaks.

The route switched to Boston, in 1981, for title defences against Fulgencio Obelmejias, a tall, useful boxer from Caracas suddenly favoured by the often weird ratings system. Fully Obel put up a show, but Hagler dispatched him in eight rounds. A rematch with Antuofermo hardly seemed justified since the bold Vito had become the catcher for any capable pitcher in the division. None the less, we were treated to argument and objections when heads clashed and the ex-champion bled on cue before Hagler put an end to the argument in the fourth round.

On a personal note, I sat on the penitential stool for having been overeager, responding to an eager producer, to interpret a roar for Hagler's arrival from the dressing room to the Boston Arena aisle: 'The crowd must have spotted the champion's bald head.' The first pictures showed the champion's cranium hooded by his black gown. Duly reported, of course, in the dreadful Colemanballs collection of commentators' bloops in *Private Eye*.

Mustafa Hamsho, an Arab from New York, who had, surprisingly, eliminated Minter from the championship eliminators, was carted out for Hagler to display his ever-increasing power and guile in Rosemont, Illinois. Hamsho and family had been gracious hosts at their Brooklyn home when they celebrated bull-like Mustafa's win over Minter, though they knew I had doubted the justice of the decision. Maybe it was too close for serious argument. I certainly could not agree with Hamsho's Runyon-character handlers, Al Braverman and Paddy Flood, who considered their man had the body strength and undoubted heart to dishearten Hagler. They were hooked on the mistaken theory that Hagler would break under pressure. Hagler's desire was being doubted because he was smart in dangerous moments and able to back off instead of the expected instinct of battering his way out of trouble.

Hagler's display was planned to perfection, except for running into Hamsho's head and causing a worrying cut over his right eye. Goody P. staunched the bloodflow with the efficiency of a trained surgeon, having spent twenty years in the US Navy medical department.

Hamsho stormed bravely while Hagler showed the world he could adapt his style for varying situations. He boxed brilliantly, hit effectively, without allowing Hamsho to draw him into foolish slugging that could worsen his injury. By the eleventh round Hagler, who had not lost a round, had punched everything except the spirit out of Hamsho. Even Braverman and Flood admitted misjudging Hagler's ability and wrongly questioning his will to win when pressured. Braverman bolted into the ring just ahead of the Mexican referee who was about to call a halt when battered Hamsho had become another pitiful victim of Hagler's hard-cased professionalism. Hamsho had begun with contempt for the champion, just another example of naive misjudgement, sneering at him, challenging his manhood. He ended by almost paying homage, extending handshakes, looking as forlorn as a boy who has had his bike stolen, admitting he was whacked in style by a better man.

Ray Leonard's retirement left Hagler the sole owner of both WBC and WBA titles and he suffered the stupid statesmanship ruling of having to repeat his win over Obelhejias, who had the blatant bias of the South American swayed WBA, which considered him No. 1. All other rating systems made Tony Sibson the chief challenger.

The Ariston Cinema in San Remo, where the Venezuelan had fought in a preliminary bout, was the best away-from-it-all site, an admirable studio which had the backing of the Tourist Board and the local casino. Hagler was fitted in hours before Liza

Minelli arrived for a one-night stand. We had watched many tourist-attracting spectaculars on the tiny stage of the cinema, a straight left down the road from Monte Carlo.

Tony Sibson accepted ITV's invite for a three-day look at Hagler at work and to supply inter-round comments – his first attempt at the mike. Sibson, with an ideal temperament, had Hagler under his microscope, admiring his dedication but considering he had spotted some flaws. None the less, Sibson duly paid sensible respect when I introduced him to Hagler, who, in turn, made it clear that he bore no malice against Sibson because of the dreadful aftermath of his fight with Minter. Sibson had publicly sympathized with Hagler for not having been given the credit in London that was due to a fine champion. Sibson, too, had had an argument with Minter, who wore a blatant plug for a truck company on his trunks when Sibson knocked him out. It caused the BBC to blackout the fight. So Hagler and Sibson had something in common.

Fully Obel had been beaten only by Hagler. I liked his style, but laughed at his brashness which we knew would be silenced when Hagler got down to business. F.O. arrived with his stunning, dusky wife, showed off to the crowd and had several moments of glory before Hagler finished yawning at 3 a.m. – a start time demanded by American Home Box-Office TV – and delivered his near-dawn knockout. Obel swiftly lost interest when Hagler ignored his blows and countered. Sibson was most impressed – but was not the slightest impressed by Obel's showing. It was no more than a warm-up for Hagler, who was satisfied that the world had come to regard him as master of his class and, more important, Top Rank were prepared to put up $2,106,000 to stage Hagler v. Sibson. Home Box-Office were only prepared to chip in if Top Rank bid $2 million.

The deal suited easy-going Sibson nicely, thank you, with a gross income of $526,500 that became inflated when the pound sank. The fight was fixed, if you'll pardon the idiom, for Worcester, Massachusetts, in February 1983, a beautiful arena in a middle-class township some forty miles from Boston. All seats were sold within thirty-six hours of the fight being announced. Hagler became two years younger overnight when he legally registered as 'Marvelous' (with one 'l') Marvin, and tracing his birth certificate revealed him as twenty-eight, not thirty. Sibson's chances became slimmer.

Sibson and I never discussed his prospects because it seemed traitorous dismissing his chances. But I kept warning him, 'Remember when you get fed up with training, the other fellow will always be in the gym or out on the road.' Typical fight fever gradually convinced loyalists that Sibson had a genuine puncher's chance. Yes, a lucky blow could make a mockery of Hagler's skills. Rah-rah and all that. So Sibson, known on occasions to become bloated between fights, worked hard to hone himself for the big one. He trained diligently – perhaps a bit too hard. Sometimes strength can be left in the gym.

Trainer Ken Squires, who runs a neat gym behind the Victoria pub, Syston, Leicestershire, liked the nickname of the Animal because he put all his boxers through a course more designed for the SAS or mountain climbers than preparation for ringwork. Sibson has been inclined to be his own boss, which suited his rustic nature, and it was his decision not to spar for the twelve days spent in America for the final preparation. There was talk of Sibson having a sore nose. He dismissed the talk as false and explained that he was not inclined to try to impress by beating up sparring partners or take it easy and be beaten up by them. Truth is, training decisions should not be made by the competitor. Whether sparring close to the fight would have sharpened Sibson became academic when the real thing started, but the inaction could not have helped. With Hagler playing his Garbo-in-gloves act, ducking interviews, and Sibson not displaying, there was a disturbing neurosis among the mass media, holed up at a Worcester hotel, escaping winter conditions that even warranted lagging brass monkeys.

By fight time a blizzard was in force. Sibson's cheeks were ruddy, he remained good-humoured and a little too calm for the job in hand. He playfully prodded Hagler at the weigh-in ceremony, which did not amuse the champion. Pre-fight arguments about Hagler being allowed to wear a foul-proof protector that padded the upper parts of his body were dismissed curtly by Hagler because nobody objected when he wore the same cup at Wembley. The heart rooted for Sibson but the head ruled for Hagler simply because we could not spot a flaw that Sibson could exploit. Everything Sibson could do Hagler could do better. The odds of 5–1 on Hagler were justified. There was an obvious aching gulf between the performers.

From the off, Hagler displayed his most inspired skill and

power. He picked Sibson off with a right-hand lead, turning to a scything uppercut, with unbelievable accuracy. Before the first round ended the best judges around the ring reckoned it was Hagler's most complete exhibition in sixty fights. Just Sibson's luck!

Sibson did not lack grit and there were moments when he rushed at Hagler and a clamorous crowd of 14,000 were quick to encourage him. But when Sibson was cut, an unusual happening for him, Hagler, switching stance more than customary, applied a destructive technique. He dug hooks to Sibson's body and used consecutive straight rights as though he were hammering a stake into the floor.

Sibson's effort, despite the constant chastisement, managed a level round on the card of referee Carlos Padilla. Tony Perez, a referee turned judge for the occasion, flattered Sibson with a 10–9 winning round. It was not all one-sided but Sibson's customary slow start contributed to his downfall. Hagler came out firing early. There was a sickening inevitability about the fight. 'I figured I'd find him sooner or later, but I never did,' said Sibson. 'I asked myself, where did he go? I knew he was there because he kept hitting me.'

The sixth round had Hagler, in his words, 'Just dipping into my tool kit' and producing punches that both bemused and damaged Sibson. After one alarming attack, Sibson dropped in an ungainly squat. He completed the eight count on his feet, but adding to the indignity was Sibson's foul-proof protector which had broken and threatened to drag his trunks down. ('I felt my pants were full of water'.) Having a protector that had been resewn instead of replaced was another amateur-night-in-Dixie act. Sibson's camp might have been worried that the crowd thought their man was being rude when he bared a bit of cheek trying to recover the broken implement. But before they could replace it Sibson was sadly taken apart. There was no escape. The downward punches from Hagler destroyed him. Sibson stumbled forward pitifully for another count. He got up, of course, with his gumshield held in his gloves and glancing away as though attempting to explain to his supporters that it was not his night. The referee did him a favour by stepping in before Hagler caused more serious damage. He had inflicted sufficient injury for Sibson to need sixteen stitches.

Sibson's humility won many American hearts, even Hagler's,

and he could always come again. But only when Hagler had decided to move over. The *Observer* headlined 'Six of the best from a Master'. Hugh McIlvanney wrote: 'There are currently two middleweight divisions. Hagler and the rest. An orchid would have more chance of thriving in the kind of snow-laden winds that were howling across Massachusetts than his obvious rivals have of dispossessing him.'

I can't follow that. Hagler can.

Last May Hagler was briefly put out of business by fluid on his knee caused, he said, by running in heavy combat boots for long distances in the sand along the bleak tip of Cape Cod. ('The sparring partners go bananas having to live there and also take Marvin's punches,' the champion's lawyer, Steve Wainwright, told me, 'but he likes it, he talks to the gulls, and gets himself into unbeatable condition. He's some man.')

A challenger may have risked fighting on with a comparatively mild injury. Hagler insists on perfection. He felt no pain going backward (a rarity) or forward, but the knee hurt with a lateral movement. He asked for a brief postponement to dispose of challenger number seven – arrogant Wilford Scypion, a black Texan who made the mistake of overdoing his chat.

Hagler's first-round left hook turned Scypion's legs into jelly, though he resisted a count at the Civic Centre, Providence, within easy riding distance from Hagler's residence. The town, Italian-dominated, was brought up with Rocky Marciano. They were ready for Hagler; Scypion was not. By the fourth he fell from a flurry of blows, obviously totally disinterested in the proceedings.

'He had a big mouth. I wanted him at my feet where he belonged,' said Hagler, who also talked about retirement because his challengers were not strong enough to warrant excessive money. A million and a quarter dollars for only having to raise sweat against Scypion was a good rate for the job. Who's next? Take your pick. Hagler is simply too good for his own good.

Henry Cooper says . . .

Any fighter who's got fast hands is a good fighter. Hagler has. I think he's underrated. It was hard to judge him on film, but when I sat ringside doing a commentary on Hagler against Alan Minter I knew what a good fighter Hagler was even before the fight was over.

He throws punches in clusters. He's big; he's powerful with it. In full flight he takes the breath away. He demoralizes an opponent. He's so accurate. He doesn't need warming up. Going into print is not the time to stick a chin out – it's risky in our business – but I can't see anyone in the near future being good enough to beat Hagler. Pity that he never got the chance to fight Sugar Ray Leonard. That would have been the biggest gate of all. Weight for weight, I'd have to favour Hagler. It's happened so many times where the bigger guy beats the little one.

Archie Moore

He was undoubtedly the most fascinating character I've met and reported. Any man who could smile after twice being close to death, being on the breadline, in a reformatory, and after four wives, eight managers and nine rounds with Rocky Marciano (not to mention an appearance against Muhammad Ali) is something special.

Archie Moore was not seen by the worldwide television audiences in his prime. We cannot accurately judge how good he really was. He was the oldest of all champions, who had fought them all from cutie to clown, banger to runner, the holders, cowards and brave ones. He put together what he'd learned from the different styles and it made him a great fighter at an age when he should have been considering easier pastures, like convincingly playing the film role of Jim the Slave in *Huckleberry Finn*. He'd been a strolling player all his life.

He called himself Mongoose. He certainly never possessed any of the irritable habits of that ferocious little fighter, but he was sharp (and still is), agile and fearless, like a mongoose. He also had a hunter's patience gathering an opponent in his sights.

Although Moore's early record, which began being recorded in 1935 – the bootleg bouts are not listed – is littered with KO wins, he never considered himself a destructive puncher. But an incredible twenty-nine-year active ring span taught him marvellous timing. He knew not only *how*, but *when*, to unleash his chilling blows. Boxing to him was like a chess game. He could clear the board from the off or lure an unsuspecting opponent into a false sense of security, then explode.

Moore's blows came from more angles than Euclid dreamed

of, and he is credited with scoring the highest number of knock-outs in major competition by *Ring Encyclopedia* – 141 failing to finish in 229 recorded contests. 'They lost a few along the way, but who's counting?' says Archie.

Moore was chunkily built and designed for self-protection, with bulging shoulders, huge biceps and forearms which he used to block blows and often to cover his face in defiant criss-cross defence. He never wound up or signalled a knockout blow. He shot straight, often short, from the shoulder. Sometimes the blow looked a harmless clip, but the timing and use of the opponent's deadweight advance suddenly caused a cancellation of further interest in the proceedings.

His deliveries were perfect and anything but sweet, but most of the men of his size, 141 to be precise, got the message. Only when he fattened from lightheavy (12 st 7 lb) and took on full-blown heavies like Marciano or the younger, full of fight and speed, Floyd Patterson, did he falter. Archie was then old enough to be twenty-one-year-old Floyd's father. But he was fifty years old before bailing out.

Incredibly, Moore, at forty-two, was able to defeat huge Cuban Nino Valdes over fifteen rounds. Valdes wrecked Britain's Joe Erskine and was good enough to become world champion, but he never had a chance. He was a victim of boxing's oldest stratagem – the runaround.

But Valdes could not moan, because it took Moore, whom the trade had recognized as a super trouper for many years, more than twenty-seven years to get his first crack at the light-heavy title. He won, of course, decisioning a fine ring mechanic, Joey Maxim (who dethroned Freddie Mills), and the new champion took Maxim's manager, Doc Kearns, with him. Between them Moore and Kearns could knit a hot stove with a pound of wire wool. Incredibly generous, fascinating people, who both had surgeon's skill when it came to cutting up purse moneys.

There was an occasion when knocking out a fancied contender, Tony Anthony, that the loser's manager commented: 'Archie is a smart old guy; he talked his way to victory,' to which Moore countered: 'I should remind the gentleman that I also mixed a few punches with the conversation.'

Words, Archie insisted, were his only excess during the hectic ring years. His boxing was an exercise in calculated economy. Few punches were wasted. Each had to pay its way. When he mounted the criss-cross defence, he allowed an opponent to punch himself out while considering the counter-moves.

But not all the power that makes a champion is confined to techniques. Moore was brought up by foster parents – he was born Archibald Lee Wright – as a skinny kid who invented methods of developing unusual strength. For example, he would walk on his hands right round the block. His shoulders and biceps he developed by exercising on a chinning bar. As a teen-ager he could chin 355 times. He could also shadowbox with one of his auntie's flat irons in each hand. Subsequently, 6-oz professional gloves, by comparison, were made of weightless gossamer.

Moore fought the bulk of his career to maintain the 12 st 7 lb title poundage. Yet the drastic weight-shedding seldom affected his punch power. Often Archie's fondness for food would blow his frame to rotund proportions. It was as if he were trying to get even for all the meals he had missed as a kid. He defied all the rituals of dieting and had us believe that he learned the trick of instant slimming from an Australian aborigine. This was Down Under where he campaigned during 1940 (winning every fight by KO), because he was president of the Who-Needs-Him? Club along America's West Coast. He was too good for his own good.

Aboriginals carried meat while roaming the bush, asserted Moore, chewed the blood out, and then re-stored the meat without swallowing it. I have often seen Moore chew meat without swallowing. While making drastic efforts to come to scale at 12 st 7 lb to defend against Yoland Pompey at Harringay Arena in 1956, he dined daily at Isow's Restaurant in Soho. He infuriated waiters, carefully placing chewed meat in a napkin and whis-pering that it was too tough. Jack Isow, the rolypoly owner who could not punch his way out of a paper bag, threatened to throw Moore out. Every day the champion would heavily overtip waiters as a form of apology, until they tumbled his act. He also kept a small pharmacy of laxatives in his bathroom. One way or another he never failed to make the required weight.

He always aimed at weighing just 1 oz inside the limit. He almost missed becoming the Wizard of 1 oz fighting Pompey. Sniffing for an afternoon story for my paper, I waited for Moore outside a Turkish bath in Jermyn Street, Piccadilly, for the champion to finish sweating only half an hour before he reported for the weigh-in. Archie, apparently, admired my door-stepping (the blight of a chipmunk reporter's life), but tried to persuade me that he had merely been getting his pants pressed! 'I'm not a glutton,' he said, 'I'm an explorer of food.' He was particularly attracted to starch and fries. Fat, he reckoned was just a three-letter word invented to confuse people.

With Moore in his fortieth year, the strain of constant reducing had started to show. He had to conserve strength for a pace of fifteen rounds. He diced with his title. Pompey, from Trinidad, was heavily muscled and though he could box, relied chiefly on his excellent condition to win fights. (He finished the career of Randy Turpin with a KO.)

When Moore merely took stock in the first round, London referee, Jack Hart, who was also a licensed bookmaker, stopped the no-fight and insisted upon action. 'I thought the ref was very rude,' Moore said afterwards. For eight rounds Moore stalked, parried punches, conned Pompey, but was trailing. His cornermen became angry. 'Let's go to work or you'll blow the title,' I could hear them pleading. 'Don't worry, it'll be OK,' said Moore.

Moore was not carrying Pompey. He was afraid to put pressure on because he knew Pompey absorbed a good punch. The challenger, against the odds, was just ahead after seven rounds. But a cut above Pompey's left eye was the beginning of the end. 'I got something to work on,' I heard Moore assure his cornermen. Afterwards, Moore addressed his interviewers. 'Let's say, it was very unfortunate that my opponent should be injured.' Moore accepted several of the game Pompey's punches, and then decided it was time to go home. He put his punches together in short salvos, with an accuracy that distinguished artist from artisan.

Poor Pompey, such a nice guy, had difficulty leaving his corner for the tenth round because his injuries had become severe. Moore clubbed Pompey down three times – counts of eight, nine and eight – and he tried to cover up in a corner. No chance. Moore had him covered, and though referee Hart allowed Pompey a chance to recover, Moore was too professional. The referee dived in to halt the massacre.

Moore took his bow in a gold-lamé-trimmed black gown and leaned over the ropes to address the Boxing Board of Control president, J. Onslow Fane, an old Etonian. 'If you're a real lord,

you should have my robe'; and the champion presented him with
the garish gown. Moore left the ring with a towel draped over
his shoulders.

Pompey became a driver for the Trinidad Embassy officials
and returned to London – a town he loved – in 1979 for urgent
hospital treatment for cancer. I was on my way to visit him at
Bart's Hospital when he died, aged forty-nine.

The most elderly champion in history was still making a fast
buck, as they say in the States, in his twilight years. Cassius
Clay knows he knocked out a shadow of the real Archie Moore
in 1962. Archie, coming up fifty, could have been brash Cassius's
grandfather! He was hired, for a time, to teach the young dog a
few tricks, but it was probably a clash of personalities. Moore
switched allegiance, for a while, to heavyweight George
Foreman.

When sportswriters were milling around Kingston, Jamaica,
wrestling with the problem of picking a winner between Foreman
and Joe Frazier, unbeaten and seemingly indestructible, it was
Moore who sorted it out. 'My man, George,' he said 'is about
to knock him out, quick. It's a no-contest.' There was a
moment's silence and a pretentious listener questioned, 'But why
should you say that?' Moore fixed a firm eye, as though he were
measuring the shortest distance for a punch to the jaw, and
snapped, 'Because I'm an expert, sir, that's why.'

Archie was, and still is. Foreman did destroy Frazier in a
hurry. Both heavyweights were exciting, punishing and became
rich. But between them they did not possess even half the craft
and the secret of punch perfected by Archie Moore.

The measure of a champion's greatness, the ability to hit when
it matters, is to come from behind to win. To climb off the
canvas. Moore's first clash with a Canadian, Yvon Durelle, a
granite-jawed, immensely strong fighter, who twice fought in
England, was his most thrilling. Making a seventh defence of
the title he won from Joey Maxim, Moore had no qualms about
giving fifteen years to one of the roughest customers I have seen.

Moore took his bow, in a brocade gown, to 8848 Canadians
at the Montreal Forum and almost before the din of the crowd
and the opening bell had faded the old champ was flat on his
back! Durelle, a fisherman, had hooked the unsuspecting Moore,
who was still counting the house when Durelle exploded. It
seemed Moore would be counted out in twenty-eight seconds.

The champion was three days short of his birthday, somewhere between forty and fifty. He always claimed to be at least two years younger than listed, but Moore's mother, who was there at the time, reckoned the record books were right. Moore somehow managed to beat the count and, clasping his gloves in front of him like a darkened tortoise, he withstood swinging Durelle's next attack. But before the round ended Moore was down twice more. It was unthinkable. The crowd rose to cheer when Moore was standing at the bell. Ex-champion Jack Sharkey, who was referee, had given the old campaigner every chance.

Using every defensive cover in the book Moore survived until the fifth without being tagged again. But a right hook pierced Moore's defence and down he went again. The longer the fight lasted, it seemed, the greater advantage to the younger and stronger challenger.

But Moore defied traditions, baffled amateur tipsters, and could beat up any upstart who could not match his courage and skill. The fight suddenly switched when Moore decided Durelle had embarrassed him. Few championship fights have had such a thrilling turnabout. The virtually down-and-out champion, struggling in the other chap's backyard, picked punches with such power and precision that Durelle was knocked down four times!

By the eleventh round Durelle had been punished so severely he was counted out on his knees and unable to haul himself to the corner. Moore said, 'Every time I looked up Jack Sharkey seemed to be counting over me. I kept saying, "This can't be me down here." A voice inside me kept telling me to get up.' He claimed it was his 127th win inside the distance, which surpassed Young Stribling's record.

Give Moore the stage and canvas and ropes in place of grease-paint and footlights and he became a greater Moore than Othello. He extended the shocked Durelle the privilege of fighting him again. When the Canadian climbed into the ring Moore kept him waiting five minutes, shrivelling under the lights, as though he were a patient about to be painfully operated upon without the benefit of anaesthetic. When Moore arrived he took the ring over as though it were his workshop. This time Moore's punches were directed like guided missiles and bang on target. By the third round Durelle, hardly the same man who only eight months earlier had put Moore down five times, was a poor, diminished creature. After two minutes fifty-two seconds he was duly counted out. When the MC gave the formal result, instead of saying 'and *still* world champion' he said, 'The winner and *always* world champion.' It said it all.

It was a privilege to watch the old pro at work at a mere few of his remarkable 246 fights. Having knocked durable Rocky Marciano down, though he couldn't keep him down, also says it all. He was elected to boxing's Hall of Fame in 1966. I continue respectfully to doff my hat to him.

Henry Cooper says . . .

What a great old character, you've captured him just right. I called him old swivelhips because he just turned a fraction to avoid a punch. He believed, like we all do, in hitting without being hit. That's why he was around so long.

I watched him train at Windsor and saw him fight Pompey. He needed discipline to drag off something like a stone and a half for some of his fights. Incredible man. I loved the way he could wrap his arms around and take more punches on his arms than the rest of his body. He bridged the gap of fighting when one style of boxing seemed to change to another. A gifted technician. The average onlooker might not have understood his art, but the pros did. Must be one of the greats at his weight. But he suffered a bit in his old age moving up to heavy. It was the old thing about a good big 'un beating a good little 'un.

ghty Sugar Ray Robinson, on his way to
five world middleweight titles, has
men Basilio hurt

Here comes the punch that counts — Sugar
Ray Robinson aims the right. But Randolph
Turpin outsmarted Robinson to become
world middleweight champion in London

k McAvoy is beaten but unbowed, giving weight to Jack Petersen in 1936 for the British
t-heavy crown. Petersen won on points. Background is manager, Harry Levene. Front
t: second Dick Gutteridge

Randolph Turpin displaying the punch power that made him a world beater. The perfect right to the body against Hans Stretz

Marvin Hagler, announcing 'Marvelous' on his trunks, moves in to hammer Britain's Tony Sibson in a successful sixth defence of the world middleweight title he took from Alan Minter. Sibson was stopped in six

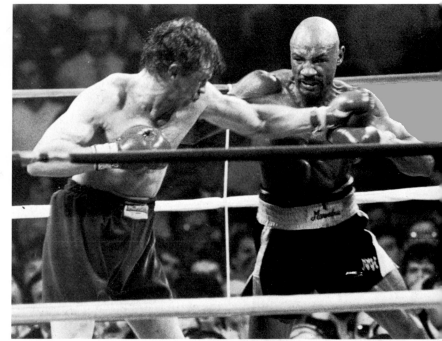

own Bomber Joe Louis doing his business — a left hook sends Billy Conn down and out in
eighth round

e author listens when three greats chat backstage — Joe Louis, Jersey Joe Walcott and
nes J. Braddock, former world heavyweight champions. Photo taken in 1965

Henry Cooper turns tiger, flooring
Welshman Dick Richardson. Cooper left
hooked Richardson in the fifth round to stay
British heavyweight kingpin

Ouch! Our 'Enery hit out of bounds by
Italian Tomasoni in Rome

The awesome power of Rocky Marciano landing a right against brave Don Cockell in San Francisco. Two punches later and Cockell was halted in the ninth round

Left: The left that made Henry Cooper a hero and then Cassius Clay hits the deck at Wembley, 1963

Above: The jaw-cruncher blow — a classic photo — of Rocky Marciano catching up with Jersey Joe Walcott to win the world heavyweight crown

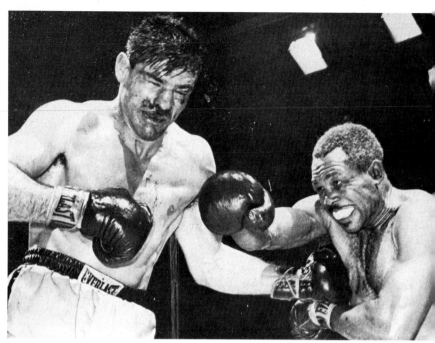

Baring a gumshield and getting down to business, Archie Moore, the master, batters Italian Rinaldi

Ingo's Bingo — the hammer blow of Sweden's Ingemar Johansson floors Floyd Patterson to win the world heavyweight championship

Joe Louis

When Joe Louis died, a month short of his sixty-seventh birthday, in Las Vegas in April 1981, I had politely nodded to him only hours before, when he sat in a wheelchair, sporting a yellow baseball cap, watching Larry Holmes fight Trevor Berbick. I pretend to myself that the great man nodded back. Anything to fatten my ego. But just being in the same arena as Joe Louis was enough.

We had chatted on many occasions, but Joe's health had sadly declined to warrant only a customary small-talk exchange. He had survived two strokes, a heart by-pass operation and was fitted with a pacemaker. Only a man of Louis's courage could have survived the previous five, or even ten, years.

The sport, or business, of boxing never produced a more loved person. A marvellous heavyweight champion; a decent person. An old colleague, Bob Waters of *Newsday*, New York, wrote: 'A team of arch-necked horses should be drawing the caisson upon which a flag-draped catafalque bearing the remains of Joe Louis rests. The procession should end at Arlington Cemetery where the brave and regal rest. Joe Louis was those things. He was as close to being king as any American ever was.'

The sad last years of Louis could not dim his lustre. I once suggested to him that if he had boxed in the seventies and eighties, he must have become a multi-millionaire. 'No,' he replied, 'I made about five million dollars and wound up broke, owing the government a million. If I'd been boxing today, I'd make at least ten million and wind up broke, owing the government two million.'

Born in a dirt farmer's shack in Alabama, and raised in a

ghetto of Detroit, he had no chance for courses in economics. He gambled heavily on golf matches, often a victim of diabolical hustlers, and generally spent money as though it were going out of fashion. A divorce settlement also made a hole in his income, but he was happy and always lived in style.

They built a statue inside Caesars Palace, Las Vegas, for Joe some years before he died. He described his job at the casino as 'walking about'. He had nothing left but his name. He attracted as many people as the roulette.

He had more ring style and incredibly 'correct' hitting power than any other heavyweight. He was, as they keep saying, years ahead of his time. His boxing, in many ways, was unspectacular, because he shuffled and cut down the area of a ring available for opponents to manoeuvre. He turned the destruction of an opponent almost into an art form. The power he packed, because of the accuracy and rapidity of his deliveries, was capable of making a man's head depart from his shoulders. When he sought a body shot, usually intending to make an opponent lower his guard, his blows were short, sharp and crushing.

The game of choosing the greatest ever is often narrowed to Louis (pronounced Lewis) – in England we still call him Louie – and Muhammad Ali. There is no convincing argument for either. Maybe the slight flaw in Louis's greatness was being put down by six opponents. Ali, I would debate, had the stronger chin, and his size, easily outweighing Louis, would have made him a winner. But there are fight-hardened old-timers horrified at the suggestion that Ali, just maybe, could have outsmarted a champion who made a record twenty-five defences – seven in one year – and was beaten only three times in seventy-one fights – one loss fewer than Ali. Two of these losses, like Ali, came when Louis was too old for fighting.

He demeaned himself trying to pay his debts. Eventually the Bureau of Internal Revenue threw in the towel and wiped out the deficit. Only Joe Louis could command such respect. Uncle Sam had taxed him for donating several purses to charity. They realized that Joe would have to live to 107 to clear a $1¼ million debt, at an agreed $20,000 a year.

I had seen Louis, in early post Second World War years, giving training exhibitions at Earl's Court in London. Even half-fit, the champion oozed class from every muscle. He had been taught by Jack Blackburn, an old pro, to use the left jab as the drilling blow, the one that began a drumroll of blows. It was the shortened version of the traditional English straight left. A chiller of a blow that had to be watched from close range rather than viewed on a deceptive, flickery film. Each landed with a thud. Apart from scoring and hurting an opponent, the blow also kept an opponent occupied while Joe was choosing a more formidable follow-up punch.

His hands were always held in a perfect position. He never dangled his arms or wasted footwork – the stuff that now excites the television viewer who is either ignorant or not interested in the science of the game. Louis was punch perfection and he cut down opponents with cold detachment, fighting with a deadpan expression both in victory or in defeat.

He was considered uncrowned heavyweight champion in 1935 when he thrashed giant Italian, Primo Carnera, whom I had known as a schoolboy because my father and uncle, twins Dick and Jack, taught him when first arriving in England in 1933. His size 16 ring boots adorned our kitchen.

Louis, the Brown Bomber, was pitted against Carnera to measure his progress. Carnera stood 6 ft 5¾ in and weighed 18 st 2 lb. It was Louis's first showing in the cynical Big Apple, New York, where 62,000 crammed into Yankee Stadium; the same year Louis had flattened eight out of ten opponents.

Louis massacred Carnera, a brave fighter, in six rounds. Having bided his time by pecking Carnera bloody with the famed left, Louis decided his softening-up process was over. The Louis shuffle moved closer to the Ambling Alp – Oh, those corny American tags! – and in a few awesome moments the seemingly indolent Louis, just twenty-one, sprang into action, reducing Carnera to a ruin. Paul Gallico, fight-writer–novelist, later to become a boxing abolitionist, wrote: 'Louis transformed a brawny, courageous man into a babbling, goggle-eyed jelly.' They were undoubtedly the hardest blows one man can land on another. Carnera's body quivered. It was as though Louis had undertaken to poleaxe a bull with his fists.

Soon after, Louis knocked out three more former world champions: Max Baer, King Levinsky and Jack Sharkey.

His was a remarkable achievement for a hungry black kid, without education, who discovered that boxing was his only outlet, helping him to overcome a shyness which had affected his speech. He began boxing, at sixteen, just to help a friend, Thurston McKinney, as an amateur sparmate.

The relaxed pose was natural, but the rough edges were smartly trimmed by Blackburn and experience. Power was also inbred, though Louis, like Jack Dempsey and Marciano, was not big as heavyweights go. In fifty-four amateur bouts, including AAU and Golden Gloves tournaments, the lithe Joseph Louis Barrow, part white and Cherokee, working at Ford's Plant, Detroit, lost only four decisions. Forty-one were stopped.

Joe swears he never hated an opponent. He could get angry, but never to the point of hate. He was so beautifully equipped for his craft that he never needed glib phrases planted in his mouth by publicists. Despite his humble background, Joe Louis had dignity.

Inevitably, the point came when even placid Joe was raised to anger. He was pitched, above his capacity at just twenty-two, against Max Schmeling, whom I consider vastly underrated and definitely worth a place in the all-time best top ten. My father had trained a tough South African, Ben Foord, to fight Schmeling in Hamburg.

In retrospect, I was aware of the German's true ability. He fought Louis two years earlier, in 1936, in New York. Schmeling, nine years his senior, had won the world heavyweight title in 1930 – the only time the crown was taken by a foul. This didn't detract from Schmeling's bravery and caginess. He knew that mobility, and using a raking left, might confuse the learning Louis, who normally slowed rivals down ready for the pay-off. (By knocking out twenty-two of twenty-five title challenges, his average kill was in six and a half rounds.)

Louis admitted watching Schmeling make mistakes and not countering. 'It was a lousy fight and I made it tough for myself. I'd dried out too much overnight, and my machine wasn't running. Make no mistake, the guy was a good fighter.'

In the twelfth round – the longest distance Louis had travelled – he walked into a long, fierce and accurate right. The young Bomber was brought down. No fluke, no argument. It was the only time Louis was humbled in his youth. It was fifteen years later, with Louis balding and portly, before he was clobbered again, by an ambitious young Rocky Marciano. It was Louis's last fight.

Losing to Schmeling hurt Joe's pride more than his pocket,

so the drum beaters began for the rematch. Adolph Hitler used Schmeling as an example of Aryan prowess. Max, who later served with Nazi paratroopers, was the petty Gauleiters' delight.

Americans became excessively nationalistic, and sportswriters, masters of the hype, encouraged by promoters and the circulation departments, whipped up a frenzy for Louis to gain revenge. Nobody was interested that Schmeling was not responsible for reported racial slurs and like Louis, he was a decent man making a living in the toughest trade of all. Facts, as they say, must not get in the way of a good story.

While words were bandied about and delaying tactics obvious, Louis was fed seven opponents of varying shapes and sizes to knock over, and so regain the confidence needed to whack the needling German. Louis once confided that knocking out an opponent of little consequence during this build-up, Al Ettore, in Philadelphia, was probably the peak performance of his career. The most important, of course, was defeating James J. Braddock, who had come off the breadline to defeat Max Baer, in eight rounds, to become world champion in 1936.

Braddock (dare I reveal that two years before he died Braddock admitted being born in Manchester, England, but nobody will confirm and his birth certificate cannot be traced) fought bravely and, he reckoned, at his best against Louis. But the challenger produced the classic kill. A left to the body brought Braddock's head forward, and a right-hander, still recalled for its velocity, knocked Braddock down. 'I couldn't have got up if they offered me a million dollars,' said Braddock.

It says much for the durability, ability and bravery of Britain's Tommy Farr that Louis was unable to stop him in his first defence of the title. This was not a condemnation of Louis's hitting power, but a tribute to Farr's ring generalship and, on the night, a marvellous devotion to duty. 'When they mention Joe's name, it still makes my nose bleed,' quips Farr.

Finally, Louis enticed Schmeling by offering him a title challenge. Louis resented the gloating by Germans over Schmeling's victory and declared his antagonism in burning personal terms. 'You wanna make a little money?' he asked reporters at the Pompton Lake training camp. 'Then bet I'll tear his head off in one round.' It was quite a speech by the least loquacious champion of all.

The fight took place in sultry weather at New York, 22 June

1938. The atmosphere was electric. When they came out for the first round Schmeling, who had turned thirty-three, was obviously not considering a long-distance war of attrition. He quickly sought to unleash the long right that had undone Louis two years before. He fractionally misjudged his distance and the mistake was uncorrectable. Louis pounced and hit the German with a controlled salvo of blows to the head. Pinned to the ropes, Schmeling's only effective resistance was to stoop and shelter between ropes. Louis put every ounce of 200 lb behind his right and drove it to Schmeling's jaw.

Schmeling's resistance was irrelevant. He tried to regain control of his legs turning into the ropes, and in doing so his left side was wide open. Louis, standing right over him, picked his spot for the next punch – a right to the ribs. The impact made Schmeling cry out involuntarily. Reporters preferred to call it a squeal. The 70,000 crowd was stirred. The impact could probably be felt by the spectators in the back of the stands – the bleachers at Yankee Stadium.

Instinctively, yet pathetically, Schmeling aimed a retaliatory right, but again Louis crashed his fists into the German's ribcage. A shorter blow to the jaw dropped Schmeling for a count of three. A Louis special, a left hook, sent him down again for two. Schmeling, to his credit, was still hauling himself up. He, too, was a proud pro. At that point I doubt if he was concerned about being Hitler's propagandist. When a right to the point of his jaw sent Schmeling down again, the towel of surrender – a rare sight from German warriors – fluttered into the ring. Referee Arthur Donovan ignored the towel, but abandoned his count at eight and flung his arms wide to signify that the massacre was over. 'I stopped it to prevent Schmeling being killed,' said Donovan. Time: two minutes four seconds.

It ranks as Louis's finest hour, and honour was restored. The perfect fighting machine at work.

Thirty-four years later, Schmeling visited Louis in hospital in Denver, and left quietly, donating money to pay hospital bills. He, too, admired Louis. So much for the famed hate campaign!

Henry Cooper says . . .

Like hundreds of other would-be boxers I was brought up on Louis. Tremendous man. If Muhammad Ali was the most expansive boxer, with all his moving and jumping around, Louis was the most economical. He wouldn't move an inch to get away from a punch if half an inch would do. I wouldn't attempt to pick a winner between Ali and Louis because nothing can be proved. It's a waste of time. If you pick Jack Johnson, Jack Dempsey, Joe Louis, Rocky Marciano and Ali as the greatest, you can sort out who would have beaten whom. I reckoned them all.

As a kid I aped being a Joe Louis – he was my makebelieve – because he was the best left-jabber. He could jab an opponent silly, then hook off the jab. His last years were very sad, being in a wheelchair. But it was probably because he was so strong and such an athlete in his heyday that he lived so long. How many 'normal' people could have survived two strokes, heart attacks, carrying a pacemaker? He earned the respect of the world – especially we people in the boxing game.

Rocky Marciano

We called him the Twentieth-Century Caveman, whose style was a preposterous, irresistible frontal assault. Rocky Marciano retired with a perfect record – unbeaten in forty-nine fights; forty-three knockouts or stoppages. He reigned supreme as world heavyweight champion from 1952 to 1956. Within three years the Rock was elected to boxing's Hall of Fame. Twenty years later, only Larry Holmes could come within a few fights of equalling Marciano's record.

I have long believed Marciano to be the best managed, best tutored, best conditioned heavyweight in history. When he brought out the bludgeon, things had a habit of happening. His fights were cut to the same pattern – the other guy lost. Apart from natural ability to hit hard, Marciano had every disadvantage except, of course, the complexion and connections that made him a box-office hero.

Under six foot, he also had the shortest reach in heavyweight history – 68 in. At about 184 lb (13 st 3 lb) he was a pigmy compared with the heavyweights of the eighties. He was easily hit and often bled profusely. Two fighters long past their prime – Archie Moore and Jersey Joe Walcott – put him down. Yet Marciano, despite his crudeness, was utterly dependable and immovable. His success was totally based on power and guts. The latent guile was slowly injected by little Charlie Goldman, an English-born trainer, who sported a bowler and had fought successfully as a bantamweight.

Jimmy Cannon, a New York wordsmith who loved to write about a heavyweight, any heavyweight, in his daily column, told me how Al Weill, then matchmaker at Madison Square Garden, persuaded him to visit the wilds of Massachusetts and take stock of a local ditch digger turned fighter. 'I saw this fat kid getting off the stool and thought he'd been kidnapped from waiting at an Italian restaurant. He threw a punch, missed and fell on his knees. He was grazed by resin crystals. Later he somehow belted the other guy. But I was looking for Weill to belt him. How could he do this to me? How the heck did I know the kid was Rocky Marciano?'

Goldman's tutoring, Marciano's dedication and Weill's obsessive management fashioned the Brockton Blockbuster into a formidable fighter, able to cut down the marvellous skills of Moore, Walcott, Ezzard Charles, and end-of-the-road Joe Louis.

Marciano is probably the only heavyweight champion whose power made a mockery of skills. His weight was compressed into brawny arms and biceps, where hitting power starts. His forearm hitting was estimated to be greater than most heavies can deliver by using the full force of their bodies. His right – nicknamed Suzie Q by Goldman – delivered the best one-blow finish to a world title fight. Marciano was being given the runaround by Jersey Joe Walcott who, having won the title at thirty-seven, was approaching his fortieth birthday when, for the best part of thirteen rounds, he taught Marciano a lesson.

There was a theory that Marciano's pummelling punches were landed deliberately on opponents' arms to cause instant tiredness. It sounded more like an anxious publicist feeding a yarn for columnists to eat up. In fact it was simply the way Marciano fought. Goldman would have preferred his charge to land every punch on more specific and vulnerable parts. There was always the danger that Marciano would damage his fists with wild blows, especially those landing on the elbows. None the less, it's an amusing myth which was certainly dispelled against Walcott, a true craftsman compared with the assortment Weill had previously chosen with excessive caution for Marciano to ply his trade upon.

Walcott was a smart mover, a beautiful technician, a stiff puncher who I believe would have given a peak Muhammad Ali his toughest match. He jabbed, countered and feinted Marciano into mistakes. It was a frustrating first title challenge for a man who had been accustomed to opponents crumbling.

There was no sign of tiredness from Walcott, who should have been seeking easier pastures at his age. How good was Walcott in his twenties? Obviously too good for his own good; avoided, as they say, like the plague. Twenty-three years of bread-and-butter campaigning were packed into Walcott's belated title fights. He was ahead on the three judges' cards when they came out for the thirteenth.

A big puncher is never beaten until the final bell – and Walcott lapsed. The God-fearing father of six had been able to read Marciano's punches coming. The hulk of granite was being chipped to pieces. But Walcott had underestimated Marciano's perseverance, despite being bloodied on scalp, eyes and lips.

Having left-hooked Marciano down for the first count of his career in the first round, Walcott began to lose defensive concentration. He was too much of a cold pro to display contempt. But Walcott still sought a repeat left hook to keep his rugged challenger down. He often used ring ropes in catapult fashion to gain leverage to land a punch. It came with years of practice. Walcott backed into the ropes awaiting a predicted face-first lunge from Marciano, who enjoyed having his prey standing stationary. Walcott cocked his glove for a planned left hook but was unable to pull his body back a few inches. At that second, Marciano unleashed his right and it reached the target just before Walcott's intended blow. It landed flush on Walcott's jaw. His face contorted and his body crumbled. A lifeless left arm hung entangled over the bottom rope and his head was twisted back as if looking down his own spine.

It was the perfect KO. Clout triumphed over class. From then on the sports-minded Americans, always yearning for a white hope, exploded into dollar-spinning ecstasies when Rocky came out fighting.

The inevitable return fight was arranged seven months later, and the ageing Walcott no longer had any resistance; or maybe he suffered stage fright having felt the stunning impact of Marciano's best punch. It was Walcott's last fight and he went out in just two minutes twenty-five seconds. It was also Marciano's only live television fight. Imagine the impact Marciano would have made in today's satellite-beamed as-it-happens world title fights around the world.

Marciano's head-down, punch-after-the-bell brawling would not have been tolerated in Europe. Teddy Waltham, then Boxing Board secretary and first-class referee, told Marciano so. The clubbing champion insisted that he never intentionally flouted the rules. He never complained when an opponent fought rough.

Don Cockell, who tasted Marciano's punches, summed up: 'He didn't foul deliberately, it was the way he fought. Mind you, he was a bit deaf when it came to hearing a bell. He whacked me when I was down and clearly after the bell. But he couldn't 'arf punch.' Cockell had fought bravely, and well, for nine rounds against the Rock in San Francisco. He was out on his feet, simply overwhelmed by sheer power.

Marciano did not fight in Europe. He would have fought anywhere, but Al Weill never had the slightest intention of turning his tiger loose outside the USA. Sugar Ray Robinson was disqualified in Germany (later reversed to no-contest) for alleged kidney punching. Imagine how Marciano would have been hounded by referees who ruled firmly that punches must land on permitted targets.

Marciano's career ended as it began – with a knockout. Archie Moore was the victim. Again it was Marciano's power that mocked the very concept of craft. He may have heaved punches like cobblestones, but he made them count. Marciano had been a slave to training and he became bored. He missed the enjoyment of family life, having to spend endless months at spartan training camps. He also became tired of Weill's eccentric ways and his constant berating in public.

Marciano was a gentle guy outside his brutal ring hours. He had a high, almost apologetic voice. He loved money – later to be translated as meanness to the point of burying cash in tins – but was not prepared to ruin his health and home life. His retirement was announced on 27 April 1956. He never came back. The perfect career.

There were two unofficial fights worth recording. The first was in South Wales when Rocky was ferrying supplies for GIs preparing for the Normandy invasion in 1944. He was embarrassed, repeating the tale about his apprentice effort at pugilism. Seems an Australian soldier (more likely a Cockney to an unsuspecting Yankee ear!) was spouting about the deficiencies of American troops within earshot of rookie Marciano – officially GI Rocco Francis Marchegiano. 'I wasn't really the troubleshooting type, but my pals elected me to take care of the matter. I was just a fat little Italian,' he told me. Having combated the rigours of warm beer, Marciano was wound up for action. He chose the left arm, not his greatest punch, but the offending soldier was hooked into oblivion.

The other engagement was the phoney, embarrassing computer fight in 1969 with Muhammad Ali, when Marciano, complete with toupee, had a privately filmed encounter with a carefully guarded ending, allegedly decided by facts fed into a computer. I found the gimmick totally unpalatable. But apparently millions enjoyed it, though I know that Ali, a charitable man, held back and acted beautifully, enabling the forty-five-year old Marciano to gain some more glory and earn more than a few bucks. Varying results were filmed, but the most liked (though certainly not acceptable) was a cut-up Rocky coming from behind to win by a knockout. Ali, to his credit, made the 'end' look realistic.

Marciano's tragic death on August Bank Holiday, 1969, was mourned around the world. He was killed, with two friends, in a private plane crash at Newton, Iowa, on his way from Florida. He hopped a lift instead of using a prepaid ticket for a regular airline to attend a function. He left a wife, a sixteen-year-old daughter, a seventeen-month-old son and millions of admirers.

Even in London, where Marciano never fought but visited in retirement, a memorial service was arranged. Henry Cooper, a converted Catholic, read the lesson. Don Cockell, the blacksmith nearly compressed by Marciano, was a church usher. Marciano commanded respect from the fraternity. There is no better tribute.

Henry Cooper says . . .

I can't make any secret of it. The two guys I would have tried to avoid were Marciano and Joe Frazier. They were such hard guys to fight. Boxing Ali was a lot different. At least he gave me moments to consider the next move. He clutched a bit and fooled around. In some respects Ali was easy to fight. But Rocky, who never threw a straight punch, could knock you bandy with any kind of punch. You never knew where they were coming from. He gave no respite, no time to consider. He just wanted to destroy. If you look again at Rocky's record none of the guys he fought were ever as good again. It was like being put through a mincing machine. If he missed a

*punch, and he often did, you had a good chance of copping an elbow
or forearm in the face. But he never complained if you did the same.*

*I met him twice. He brought a fellow called Tony Hughes here to
fight me. We beat him and I couldn't understand why Rocky fancied
Hughes might be a champion. Outside the ring he was so gentle and
unassuming, an absolute Jekyll and Hyde, considering he wanted to
clobber everyone without mercy when the bell sounded.*

Jock McAvoy

Jock McAvoy is the only fighter who regularly bit the hand that fed him. When he grunted and chewed the thumbs of his gloves, opponents were usually doomed. The habit presaged the pay-off. It was interpreted as bad temper in the most tigerish British middleweight champion and, arguably, the strongest puncher. Yes, McAvoy admitted being tetchy and would fight at the drop of a hat. Spiteful – but great. And nobody ever heard McAvoy squeal when he had to take it.

The strange mannerism was because McAvoy needed to bite his thumbs to loosen the joints, which had become stiffened after being broken working in Lancashire's cotton mills. This gave McAvoy a better grip of 6-oz gloves, and it is not an exaggeration that he was capable, and often proved it, of lifting an opponent clean off the canvas with punch power in either fist.

McAvoy shares with old foe Archie Sexton, whom he knocked out in 1933, the distinction of being the highest ranked Englishman in a world list of knockouts scored in major competition. He clobbered eighty-six – more than Dempsey, Louis or Marciano. Yet the Ironman from the North fought many times with bone-damaged hands and required pain-killing injections before a fight. McAvoy was never given sufficient praise for his ability, though nobody ever doubted his crushing power, even at an elderly age when his hands were buckled by arthritis. He reigned as a feared British champion from 1933 until relinquishing the 11 st 6 lb title in 1944, winning the first of the new Board of Control Lonsdale Belts outright and getting two notches on a second. Within four months he knocked out the reigning world *middle*weight champion, Eddie 'Babe' Risko, fought fifteen rounds for the world *light-heavy* title against John Henry Lewis, both in America, then returned home to battle fifteen rounds for the British *heavy*weight title against Jack Petersen.

McAvoy was never knocked out or stopped in 145 recorded fights – except for a freak first-round ending against Freddie Mills, who later became world light-heavy champion, at the Royal Albert Hall in 1942. McAvoy suffered a punctured lumbar muscle. I recall overstaying army leave and risked the punishment for the privilege of watching McAvoy at work. Mills, then on the lush rations of an RAF corporal, was also robust and aimed blows without bothering too much about hitting permitted parts. At thirty-four, McAvoy was picking up money – the purse was £750 – rather than seriously considering title fights during the Second World War years. Mills, as fearless as McAvoy and a lot younger, had outpointed him in Liverpool during Dunkirk days.

The rematch was a disaster. McAvoy clutched his back and muttered between clenched teeth, 'Hold it, Freddie, I've hurt my back.' Mills stood bewildered, ignoring pleas from manager, Ted Broadribb, to keep punching. Referee Ben Hardwicke moved in swiftly and McAvoy hopped on his right leg, gasping, 'It's my spine. I can't go on.' Backstage, two men held McAvoy down while Dr Phil Kaplan shot a pain-allaying injection between spine and kidney. He was borne away to hospital.

A mere five years later, McAvoy was stricken with infantile paralysis at thirty-nine; the brutal disease suffered at the same age by President F. D. Roosevelt. The Boxing Board's benevolent fund gave him £25 for a wheelchair, but McAvoy hated it.

I can verify that, even when sitting down and in his sixtieth year, McAvoy could whack hard. A young motorist who had cut up the old champ was reminded of his misbehaviour. The motorist swore at him. McAvoy's daughter was a passenger. Swearing in her presence was against the rules. 'I'm a bit deaf,' pretended McAvoy at the wheel. 'Come a bit closer and tell me.' He faked yet another 'opponent' – termed 'just a mug' by genuine ring men – into a mistake. A left hook somehow thrown out of the window flattened the rude young man. McAvoy said the magistrate threw the case out of court when he had to be helped to stand to offer a defence.

Nobody ever took liberties with McAvoy – in his prime or past it. He had a barrel chest, a powerful neck and blacksmith's sinews up his arms. A striking-looking man with black curly hair parted in the middle. Today, he would be a sensation. Hagler, Leonard, Sibson and others in that class would not have felt safe with McAvoy around; he would have fought Larry Holmes on stilts.

Promoter Harry Levene, who celebrated the arrival of 1983 as the elder statesman of world boxing, rarely finished a conversation without sighing, 'Oh, if only we had another McAvoy.' He was co-manager when Mac was magic. Charley Harvey, who managed Ted Kid Lewis, Peerless Jim Driscoll and Owen Moran, said of McAvoy, 'He's a throwback to the old timers. He feared nobody.'

They called McAvoy the Rochdale Thunderbolt, though he was born Joe Bamford in Burnley, Lancs and fight-raised in Manchester. His ring name came because he feared his mother would stop him fighting (with a licence, for a change) at seventeen. A promoter offered him 10s. 'Call me the real Jack McCoy,' he said. A typesetter printed Jock McAvoy on the programme. The name stuck and typesetters don't change either. 'They said ten bob but I only got seven shillings and sixpence,' said McAvoy. The fight game also doesn't change much.

In 1930 McAvoy, whom most of us called Joe, fell off a horse and broke his neck. He was a competent rider, the son of a horseman – 'Don't blame me, the girth broke.' Medical opinion was 'He might walk again, but he'll never box.' During Christmas week, 1935, McAvoy was fighting world middle champion Risko, in New York. A year later, ranked at No. 2 by *Ring* magazine – though I reckon he could have defeated the No. 1 Maxie Rosenbloom without coming to harm – McAvoy challenged Lewis for the world light-heavyweight crown.

Risko's handlers refused to accept a title match because McAvoy's deeds were unknown. He must prove himself in an overweight clash. McAvoy was midway between weights – 8 lb above middle. Being refused a title crack made McAvoy mad. (He once dangled a business partner outside a high-storey window until he was satisfied he was getting a square deal!) The Babe had to be spanked. McAvoy did not have time to bite his gloves. Risko was pounded so professionally he was up and down like a yo-yo – six times before he was counted out in 168 seconds. No other British fighter has since clobbered a reigning world champion with such ferocity. 'Not since Dempsey, has a fighter thrown so many devastating punches in so short a time,' wrote a New York critic.

It was logical that McAvoy should be offered a return fight with the title at stake. But there were no recognized ruling bodies and Risko's management were in charge of the logic. McAvoy was given a wide berth and had to be matched with Lewis (who fought Joe Louis) for the higher weight crown.

Sixteen days before the fight McAvoy again had painful, inflamed hands after hitting the solid head of Anson Green, of Philadelphia, for ten rounds. He had planned what now appears a ridiculous schedule of three fights in eight days as the build-up for Lewis. Jim Smith was knocked out in two rounds; in New York Mark Kiernan, from Massachusetts, suddenly went missing; and Green stayed the course.

While McAvoy, who preferred fighting to training, was resting at New York's Mayflower Hotel overlooking Central Park, the Madison Square Garden matchmaker Jimmy Johnston went beserk at the prospect of his seeking a postponement of the big fight. McAvoy agreed to train without sparring or bag-punching. Critics became sceptical. 'Where's the big punch?' they were asking. Finally, McAvoy was forced to spar, just for the publicity, and take his chance at the Pioneer Gym on 44th St. He sparred with Trader Horn and, attempting to impress, his hands were badly damaged. McAvoy could not pull a punch, even when practising. 'We can't postpone, the Garden is booked for every night of the year,' snapped Johnston. 'The punch is there, but Joe dare not deliver it,' said his faithful masseur, Bobby Dawson. 'If I don't fight I'll never get a second chance,' said McAvoy.

The word that the Englishman's hands were nearly useless filtered along Bruise Beach, Seventh Avenue, where the Garden stood, and Lewis's manager, John Greenlees, deliberately held up the start of the fight. This meant McAvoy's injected, doped hands had begun to come to life midway through the fight. They became a burning, pulsating agony. Yet the gritty challenger carried the fight, ignoring the share of foul blows, and when the points decision was given to the champion, the luckless McAvoy was cheered back to his dressing room.

'I never grumbled about the verdict,' McAvoy told me. 'Lewis deserved to win, but if my hands had been OK, I might have done him.' Dr Walker, at the ringside, diagnosed: 'No broken bones, but high synovial condition and inflammation. Don't box for several months.' Six weeks later McAvoy conceded parcels of poundage to challenge Jack Petersen for the British heavyweight crown. 'I couldn't break an egg,' shrugged McAvoy. But for £4000 he would try. Petersen, who fought as the topliner from start to finish of his career, won on points.

But the punch, as we repeatedly emphasize, was the last attribute McAvoy lost. Within months he knocked out the superbly built Cockney heavyweight, Eddie Phillips. Another Londoner, Jack Hyams, who knew every trick of the trade, could not overcome McAvoy. Neither could Archie Sexton, a graceful boxer with a big punch.

He essayed a comeback at thirty-seven, had three knockout wins against rank-and-file rivals, and retired.

My father seconded Cockney George Howard against the fading McAvoy, in support of Jack Solomons's championship fight afternoon, during war years at Tottenham FC ground in London. Howard, who lived nearby, was fit and able and had not been knocked out. Two bites of the glove, a grunt, and Howard was laid out like a wall-to-wall carpet. 'You've got to admit it was beautifully done,' said an unsympathetic second as he revived the shocked Howard.

McAvoy's dreadful handicap, since termed polio, brought him hardship. Proudly independent, he was market-hawking and weight-guessing for sixpences along Blackpool's Golden Mile. He sold a Lonsdale Belt for £450. He had sweated hard and taken his share of stick by defeating Len Harvey, Al Burke and Sexton to win it outright. He later tried, unsuccessfully, to buy it back.

In November 1967, Manchester members of the Anglo-American Sporting Club, which stages boxing, gave the ailing McAvoy the tonic he needed. I made a special journey to be there. A member had bought the belt for £750 and re-presented it to the admired ex-champion. Old rival, Jack Petersen, the first boxer to be appointed a Board of Control steward, made a fine speech proposing McAvoy's toast. Diners rose to sing 'For He's a Jolly Good Fellow'. The once ruthless fighter was KO'd for the first time by emotion. He wept.

I spent an afternoon with McAvoy, whose luck had changed, just after his sixtieth birthday. He lived with his third wife ('I've always been a bloody glutton for punishment') in a tastefully decorated, early-eighteenth-century cottage, in four acres at Timperley, near Manchester. He drove a specially adapted Mercedes. His home had stables for his daughter, Susan Bamford, who became a star show jumper. 'To see her win something big at the Wembley Horse Show would give me more pleasure than winning titles,' he said.

His upper body still possessed the strength of a fighter. He was restless. 'You know,' he confided in a whisper, 'my batteries haven't run down yet and it's hell being confined like this. And it's getting worse.'

Finally, and understandably, the fighting spirit burned out. On his sixty-third birthday, Joe Bamford was found dead after an overdose of drugs.

Henry Cooper says . . .

Jock was so ruthless it sends a chill up the spine reading about him. Imagine having to fight him! Babe Risko was no mug deliberately coming in over the title weight to fight him. In all but name McAvoy was a world champion. Totally fearless, didn't care who they were. I can never recall having a conversation with Harry Levene without him reminding me that McAvoy was a marvel. If Harry said so he must have been. My manager always said Levene was the best manager of his day.

Obviously the days have gone when men like McAvoy fought more or less at the drop of a hat in very hard times. Imagine McAvoy against Hagler. What a fight! But Jock's best must have been at light heavy. Not too much is written about McAvoy. I'm glad you have done so.

Ingemar Johansson

Ingo's Bingo was the most publicized blow of the fifties. Its owner, Ingemar Johansson, talked of his golden arm as though it had a separate life of its own. It was not a lucky punch; it was a well-timed poleaxe right, delivered straight as a lance, that abruptly ended proceedings. Its impact pulverized Floyd Patterson, the youngest heavyweight champion of the world, with the fastest fists of all, at Yankee Stadium, New York, on 27 June 1959.

The dimple-chinned Swede, ridiculed as an amateur playboy when he first appeared in America, knocked Patterson down seven times in eight minutes three seconds. What Johansson called his 'toonder' right matched the thunder that postponed the fight for twenty-four hours, creating a cauldron humidity at the stadium alongside the East River where Dempsey, Tunney, Marciano, Louis and our own Tommy Farr had laboured under the arc lights for hard currency.

The Americans laid 5–1 against the Swede's chances, and because he had shown so much sang-froid in his preparation, they regarded the absence of fire-eating threats as meekness.

I had watched Johansson at work in a spotless pine-built school gymnasium in his hometown of Göteborg, known as Little London, where he practised delivering the accurate right by picking off a sand-filled slungball the size of a coconut, which his trainer directed at him from all angles. In terms of world class, Johansson may not justify a place in this book compared with man-eaters like Joe Frazier or George Foreman. But though Ingo *did* wave his left, as a New Yorker put it, like a traffic cop gone bananas; though he *did* often move awkwardly; and though maybe his chin was not granite – his right was might.

He whacked all eight British-based opponents, one of them twice, and executed the perfect pay-off against Dick Richardson, the Welshman's first count-out. He also gave my chief second, Henry Cooper, a painful reminder. Whatever Johansson's deficiences, we know that he was not, in the jargon of the industry, a mug! Sometimes he'd demean his actions as though they were temporary flaws, but his boxing was sound, based on amateur teaching, and at 14 st plus, he was mobile, nicely proportioned, without bearing a ring trademark. He kept his own teeth and sported a Napoleon fashion hair-do that had the ladies staring at him with a hauteur generally reserved for actors.

With a penchant for ballroom dancing, and a quiet tuneful voice that produced a big selling record in Sweden, Johansson caused much amusement in America. Hard-bitten critics stared in disbelief when Johansson arrived with girlfriend Birgit Lundgren in tow. The heavyweight businessman who never had a managerial contract – promoter Eddie Alhqvist was adviser – modelled clothes, had a blonde secretary, a suite of offices, and did not require an accountant to certify that Miss Lundgren's statistics were perfectly arranged. It was a courtship that captured public attention, with photographers around Birgit like a herd of wild buffalo, in a way that was unique until Prince Charles and the then Lady Diana outshone them.

A retired Marciano remarked, 'This guy will ruin the American training methods. All I did was wake up to see manager Al Weill and trainer Charley Goldman looking mean and unshaven. It was enough to make a guy hate. But Ingemar has the beautiful doll to keep his eye sharpened.'

In Göteborg, I recall watching Johansson, clad in a trim scarlet outfit, learning to jab effectively, sparring with Londoner Albert Finch, an ex-British middleweight champion acting as coach. The lessons served the Swede well. The training drills were conducted with little fuss, and Johansson buttered his interviews with charm.

He had arrived in America, without the present-day obsession of being supported by bodyguards, with a family circle that shocked the fight traders, who are more accustomed to big-name fighters being surrounded by sharks and acolytes. The 5 ft 4 in Birgit was his private secretary. (She can type, but she can't cook, said Ingemar.) In tow was his father, Jens, a street paver who had boxed as an amateur and briefly held the post of his son's official manager, and mother Ebba. There was sister Eva, brother Rolf, cousin Ernest, second Nils Blomberg, with American Whitey Bimstein, who knew the scene, acting as adviser and, if needed, as cut man. The portly, polite Mr Alhqvist looking as though he had taken time out from a United Nations conference, added further dignity to the party. Sister-in-law Annette provided the eager news seekers with perfect copy – she had a baby girl, born at Johansson's Grossinger's training hostelry in upstate New York.

At home, Johansson would report to his spotless gymnasium carrying a holdhall and get down to serious drills without fuss. Often there would not even be an erected ring. It was all very ordinary. But Johansson actually worked hard, with fine reflex and movement for a big man. The Americans totally underestimated him because of his nonchalant air. In fact Johansson was laughing inside, and was happy to make the press help lead Floyd Patterson into a mistaken overconfidence. New Yorker Eddie Borden, a marvellous character who bet on everything that moved, was hired by the big-fight promoters to offer goodwill for Johansson at Grossinger's resort, and to request a suspicious press to say nice things about him.

While the family lounged around the swimming pool, Johansson worked out in an open-air ring, merely prodding punches and looking useless. The tradition of sweaty fight camps, with sparmates beaten up and the champion or challenger leading a hermit's life, had been created by managers and trainers. Ingemar was about to explode the myth.

He never shirked training, was athletic, and he knew that when his skill could not match that of the other guy, he always had the help of the hammer of Thor – the big right.

Odds-makers, however, remained unimpressed and offered 7–2 against his chances. 'The bum can't fight,' they were saying. 'Either he's a bum or an actor, or both.' The promoters rented a prime site along Broadway in order continuously to screen the Swede pulverizing No. 1 ranked Eddie Machen, in just two minutes sixteen seconds, at the Ullevi Stadium in Göteborg a year earlier.

Machen, a Californian with excellent ring technique, had twice beaten Joey Maxim, a world champion, and had twice hammered the Cuban Nino Valdes, whom Rocky Marciano's management had astutely avoided. He was on the brink of fighting Patterson and accepted a final eliminator against Johansson as an intended warm-up. Machen was then undefeated. So was Johansson, with twenty fights, but with only one American victim, Archie McBride.

Thirty-three thousand, eight hundred and sixty-four fans were barely seated when the local hero released his power punch and Machen was down. The imported Irish referee, Andrew Smyth, duly counted, and shocked Machen gained a wobbly perpendicular at eight. He grabbed instinctively as Johansson moved in. But the famed Bingo blow put paid to Machen, who slumped to the canvas, his head under the bottom rope, to be counted out.

Yet the vast majority of Americans remained disbelievers. Just a fluke in some foreign land! Experts, non-experts, bell boys, cops on the beat; they all thought Patterson (though he had been outpointed by Joey Maxim) was different class. My gut feeling, preparing a fight preview for my paper, was that Johansson could catch Patterson but maybe could not catch him quickly enough. Only four non-American heavyweights in eighty years had hit the top of the big-fight heap. By fight time the odds had lengthened to 5–1 against the Swede.

The humidity beneath the ring lights of the famous stadium was so stifling that I needed to douse my head with an iced soft drink as we waited for the arrival of the giants. I felt like fainting merely concentrating in order to write. Imagine the stress of having to fight!

The show had been put back an hour because of an earlier downpour, and being crammed shoulder to shoulder in nine press rows around the ring apron was like being witness to a surgeon about to work in an operating theatre with a leaky roof. Insects buzzed in the warm air beneath the arcs. White-coated vendors switched their ice creams for a brisk trade in plastic macs and cheap umbrellas. A crowd of 30,000 braved the elements, paying $425,000.

Patterson, at twenty-four, was outweighed by 14 lb. He was a pumped-up light heavy at 13 st, and was probably wrestling with his psychological problems during the drawnout preliminaries. Johansson's confidence had become contagious, but only the handful of Europeans bet on him. Despite the clinical, impressive flooring of Cooper and Richardson, and the boxing art displayed in outpunching the clever Joe Erskine, there were nagging doubts of Johansson's ability to cope with pressure away from home. The fight was virtually on Patterson's Brooklyn doorstep. Though Johansson had won a nondescript amateur bout in America, he had withdrawn from another, and was still living down the humiliation of being disqualified for allegedly 'not trying' in the 1952 Olympic final against American Ed Sanders in Helsinki. (Patterson won a gold medal at middle-weight in Helsinki.)

'Shame, Ingemar' Swedish papers had headlined. But before the first round had ended against Patterson, it was obvious why the Helsinki referee had been misled. It was Johansson's style to paw and plod, using a flicking left to keep an opponent occupied while he measured his right. The Swede stabbed at the white-trunked champion, and it was two minutes before a right was chanced. It was an arcing, fast, clubbing blow that did nothing more than clip Patterson's left ear. Patterson, gloves cupped around his face in the peek a boo style drilled by manager Cus D'Amato, attempted his unusual leap with a left hook, nicknamed a Gazelle punch. He missed, but attacked with body hooks, attempting to force Johansson's guard down.

Patterson's leaps in attempting to land a left hook left him vulnerable for a counter. His square-on stance was perfect for the Swede to pick his spot. We had no prior warning from the perfunctory first two rounds, which produced a few missionary left hooks and no more than watchful jabs, that Johansson was about to explode. He began to tuck his chin closer to his shoulder, negating Patterson's hooks, and by turning a left jab into a hook around Patterson's head, Johansson was given the opening he sought. Patterson was hit flush in the face by the first respectable and, it turned out, chilling right that Johansson had thrown. It shot straight through the champion's guard.

Patterson hit the deck while the baggy-trousered and bow-tied referee, Ruby Goldstein, counted, and also indicated with his fingers. Patterson propped himself up on his elbows, looking across the ring at Johansson jogging to a neutral corner, as though hoping to catch the number of the truck that had run him over.

He rolled over and hauled himself up at the count of nine, hands dropped to his thighs, and the referee dutifully dusted his gloves of resin before waving play on. But Patterson turned towards his corner, believing the round had ended, and the referee was wrongly positioned to prevent Johansson from landing a left as Patterson faced the wrong way. A following right landed on the back of Patterson's head – a blow that deserved at least a rebuke.

Patterson must have been oblivious, but a fighting instinct made him grab the middle rope, staring vacantly into the crowd as though searching for a friendly face. Again he regained a wobbly stance at a nine-count, glanced to his corner, then over his shoulder at Johansson. Goldstein pulled Patterson's hand off the top rope, again wiped both gloves on his shirt, and permitted the champion a chance to recover. No chance. The argument had been over from the first lance-like blow – the rest was merely a mopping-up operation.

After the third knockdown, the stadium lights were switched on as though a backstage electrician had decided the fight was over, despite Goldstein repeatedly delivering a hapless Patterson to Johansson for demolishing. At one stage, Whitey Bimstein was perched on the ring apron hollering for Johansson to hurry and finish the job, while Patterson's handlers, D'Amato and Dan Florio, were banging on the canvas for Patterson to keep getting up.

Trying to catalogue the massacre, with the crowd screaming, photographers jostling, broadcasters jumping up and down, was sheer bedlam. We sweated in the pressure-cooker atmosphere, but for poor Patterson, the thirty seconds he spent groping around the canvas from the first four knockdowns must have seemed a lifetime.

Between counts there were brave, but abortive, attempts to fight back by Patterson. But Johansson could afford to ignore the desperate charges. Patterson's body could not cope with the shocks inflicted on it, and his legs actually crossed and collapsed for yet another count. When the end came – and not before time – Patterson would have been blown over had there been any breeze. The final two blows were not on Patterson's chin. They were cursory clouts on top of his head.

Surprisingly, Patterson began to climb up quicker from the seventh knockdown than he did the first. But the referee clasped him around the waist and the slaughter was stopped.

I vividly recall Johansson being the last to realize he was the new champion. He was prancing away from the referee, reporting to a neutral corner, and was surprised when second Bimstein catapulted into the ring and hugged him in congratulation. The first Swede to become world heavyweight king. The first European to break the American stranglehold on the title since Italian Primo Carnera. The biggest upset since Max Schmeling had right-handed a youthful Joe Louis to defeat.

We had a softer path during the Normandy D-Day landings than we had trying to compel an urgent lane through a solid phalanx of ill-tempered cops guarding the dressing rooms beneath the blue bleacher seats of Yankee Stadium. But I felt less affronted at being pushed and prodded after I spotted a cop half strangling a solid-looking character by his neck tie. At least the cops did not only pick on us weaklings! The offended gentleman was Rocky Marciano, who was merely trying to console the loser and congratulate the winner.

'I was never worried,' assured Johansson. 'It was a matter of time before I hit him with my toonder right. He gave me a bad look as we went back to the corners after the second round. That was when I began going for him.'

For the next two years Johansson and Patterson played merry-go-round with the title. Nobody else had a look in. They broke the monopoly of the promoting IBC and managed their own. Sonny Liston, the ogre, was content to knock over other contenders and await the pleasure of the series winner.

Having witnessed two rematches, I became testy with the cynical opinion that the fights were fixed. Nobody throws away a world title, least of all Patterson, a man of immense pride, or Johansson with stout Viking stubbornness. In New York the rematch saw the Swede with his right-hand sword either rusted in the scabbard or stricken with indecision. Patterson had lived a hermit's existence, determined to prepare and plan for his revenge. When he leaped to land a left hook in the fifth round, Johansson, recovering from a knockdown, hit the deck so severely that his head banged on the boards, his left foot was trembling, signifying concussion. Out like a light. He was carted off to hospital. Some fix!

By the time the rubber meeting was arranged, we had written ourselves out trying to solve who would win. In Miami, Johansson boxed well enough, but Patterson was too mobile and wary. It lasted until the sixth round before Patterson again got his man. Patterson's pay-off punches were expertly executed, but nothing matched the drama of Johansson's stupefying right in that first fight.

With Swiss residence to ease taxes, with property and fishing boats bought, Johansson made no further serious effort to challenge again for the well-paid office of world champion. A dollar equivalent of £658,363 for three title fights was enough. But he proved undisputed boss of Europe by again defeating Jamaican Joe Bygraves, whom he regarded as his trickiest opponent, and regained the European crown with a copybook punch to knock out Dick Richardson, who was noted for his durability.

Having beaten Britain's best – Cooper, Richardson, Erskine and Brian London, surely the most formidable combination of any era – bully boy London was called to Stockholm for a non-title match. It was four years after the Swede's glory against Patterson who, only a month before he faced Johansson, had dispatched Blackpool's London in eleven rounds.

Eddie Alhqvist, promoting as a sideline to book publishing, still had thoughts of Ingo's last fling with a fight against Liston who, as we feared, easily relieved Patterson of his crown. A convincing win for his man over London might clinch it. To assure fair play, a British official, Andrew Smyth, was invited to referee. A good punch, they hoped, would bring a good pay day. 'I've trained nineteen rounds every day for six months,' said Johansson.

London had aroused an assortment of jeers and cheers from Milan to Vancouver, Wembley, Wales and Indianapolis. At thirty, Johansson was about to come apart at the seams, almost overnight, as heavyweights frequently do. For eleven rounds and fifty-two seconds the fight would have been booed at any baths hall in Britain. Johansson was slightly ahead in the final twelfth round when London, pepped by old Aldgate Tiger Al Phillips in his corner, clobbered the old champion. The bell interrupted timekeeper Bror Carlsson's count at what seemed nine seconds, to end the fight abruptly. Johansson was out on his feet. London raged; the crowd roared. Their hero was saved by the bell – and Smyth, having dispensed of the Swedish judges' system, hoisted Johansson's once famed arm. London was outpointed. The time-keeper showed me his stopwatch indicating the round had ended, and therefore the contest, when the count had reached four seconds.

'I don't remember the last punch,' shrugged Johansson. After only twenty-eight fights, he walked out of boxing a lot richer and wiser.

In 1982, Johansson, at fifty, kindly answered my request to attend a *National Advertisers'* charity boxing function between London and Sweden at a West End hotel. He flew from Florida, where he runs a motel, and his surprise entrance brought the house down – though he had not fought in Britain. He had married Birgit and was separated (after a previous unpublicized teenage marriage); has a daughter living in London; a son managing his Florida business; and continued interests in Geneva and Göteborg, whence he regularly commutes. He likes America, but will surely retire to Sweden.

His London visit coincided with his pride being restored when the International Olympic Committee submitted to years of protest by awarding Johansson a silver medal which was automatically withdrawn when he was disqualified in Helsinki. The present IOC president was a judge at that heavyweight final. 'They are arguing about who gives it and in which town,' laughed Johansson. But he was there when asked. He was so professional he almost took a cash register into the ring with him. None the less, it was nice to be exonerated as an amateur, after thirty years.

Johansson also ran, and finished, in the 1982 New York marathon. He was proud of that. So was another heavyweight fighter who finished ahead of him. Name of Floyd Patterson. Both are a credit to themselves – and the fight game.

Henry Cooper says . . .

Ingo's trick was being a super counter-puncher. When he was forced to go forward paving his way with a left hand he looked very ordinary. He was not an all-time great. But his one-punch power was something else. I know. He walloped me with it. I fought him in the open-air in Stockholm. Of course, we had to be given the corner with the sun in our eyes. My cornermen kept saying, 'Let him come to you,' and I managed a few rounds of backing off, finding my way, but I could hear a buzz from the crowd. They were bored stiff. Still, I couldn't get Ingo to come forward. He had a lot of patience. In the fourth round I started marching in. Right chump I must have been. But I felt I had to make a go of it.

In the fifth he caught me, wallop – with the right hand they say it was, because I never saw it – and down I went. I got up, but the fight was over. Must have been a peach of a punch. I don't think there was a film of that fight. Just as well. Jim Wicks, doing his usual good job, talked about the sun being in our eyes. Trust you to have said, 'Don't you mean Mrs Johansson's son?' All I needed after hitting the deck.

Henry Cooper

Henry Cooper stole the affection of the public for a longer period than any other sportsman. He had an indestructible dignity. Eleven years British heavyweight champion; outright holder of three Lonsdale Belts; awarded the OBE. It proves that nice guys don't always finish second, though Our 'Enery just missed the world title boat even though he slogged for fifteen years.

It was eleven years after retiring that Cooper revealed his greatest fear – he had suffered gout for the best part of his career. It caused a fight postponement, using a feigned injury as an excuse. Worry of being stricken by the pheasant-and-wine disease while rigorously training for a championship was concealed by Cooper.

For one of Cooper's most important fights – knocking out Piero Tomasoni in Rome for the European title – his Cockney character manager, Jim Wicks, had to be propped in an upright chair against the ring apron because he suffered from sciatica. For a couple of crocks the old firm were a bit special.

While Wicks was the undoubted champion of the Word, Cooper carried out instructions with the finest left-hook delivery of any heavyweight – and I mean *any* heavyweight. It was a superbly timed anaesthetic blow, the kind that boxing tutors consider the most difficult to block. Cooper's right hand was carried mostly as a passenger, and though the occasional right induced its share of discomfort, the left hook always finished the job.

The most memorable hook Cooper landed, though not necessarily the best, was against the then Cassius Clay, an arrogant twenty-one-year old, the Louisville Lip, later to become marvellous Muhammad Ali, world heavyweight champion. It was thirty-nine days after Ali's twenty-second birthday in 1964. (Floyd Patterson was ten months younger when he became world kingpin in 1956 – the youngest to win the title. Ali twice defeated Patterson.)

Cooper's single blow, which floored the seemingly indestructible Clay, must be the most celebrated blow in British boxing history, although it did not win the fight. He has been hailed and hoorayed ever since. The nation was charged with gripping emotion on 18 June 1963, when boxing's Mr Nice Guy met the loudmouth at Wembley Stadium. The winner had the unenviable task of fighting the then fearsome Sonny Liston, holder of the world crown.

Promoter Jack Solomons, master of hype, made the most of a Goodie *v.* Baddie match. It was, of course, sucker soap, and we loved it. Clay, gold-medallist at light heavyweight (12 st 11 lb) in the Rome 1960 Olympics, weighed only 14 st 11 lb compared with the 16½ st at the sad end of his career eighteen years later.

We all realized later, although some of us knew at the time, that Clay was merely acting his arrogant part. His egotistical excesses were quoted by the hour. His sour words sweetened the gate take. For years his sweet and sour worked wonders but, like Cooper, he was, and is, a nice human being. None of his opponents ever hated him – afterwards. Backstage he rarely spoke above a whisper, and he was warm and charitable to the point of foolishness. Clay–Ali fed off people. He never really understood why his boasting, at that time, had angered a nation. When he came into the ring wearing a stage crown, in a long scarlet and white robe, he was booed and hissed by a high paying public who reacted as a pantomime audience.

It was not an overplayed publicity stunt. The seats had all been sold. Clay had just spotted the crown on a shelf backstage when the weigh-in ceremony was held, as only Solomons could dream up, on stage at the London Palladium. Two thousand people queued to gaze. He couldn't resist hamming it up. He walked off insolently, signalling five fingers as a prediction for a fifth-round finish. 'It ain't no jive, ole Henry will fall in five,' he yelled. The crowd jeered. Clay struck a defiant Charles Atlas pose.

Cooper was not the slightest flustered by the by-play. He too was amused and plucked a hair from Clay's chest. No doubt he was wondering, maybe worrying, because he had become a symbol for fair play and honesty. Cooper embodied the virtues that Englishmen consider peculiarly their own; modest to a fault and fairly brimming with love of family and country. A gentle, courteous man who could turn gunfighter when required.

'I have trained to go the distance. We take it as it comes. It's him or me,' was the closest Cooper came to bragging. It must have been a burden bearing the weight of British hopes on his back.

At twenty-nine, Cooper had reigned resplendent as British and Empire champion for four years. Hard-nut heavies Dick Richardson and Brian London had been humbled by his punches. He was at his peak, 13 st 3½ lb, just a cruiserweight by the heavyweight standards of the eighties.

Bookies, and most boxing writers including me, had favoured Clay to win because Cooper was prone to cut eyebrows. His craggy brows were encrusted with scar tissue, and American writers termed him 'a notorious bleeder'. In fact, Cooper had lost only two contests, against Italian Bacilleri in his tenth fight, and Briton Peter Bates, because of blood flow. After fifty-five fights he had lost only four by injury, so the bleeder tag seems a bit harsh. Regrettably, the two that counted most, both against the same man, Clay then Ali, were blood-flow endings that brought worldwide exposure.

Mr Wicks, as Henry fondly called him, made his pride and joy rinse his face three times a day in a foul-smelling solution that the old sorcerer claimed to have brewed from exotic herbs. It was an old-fashioned mixture of brine, alum and other ingredients intended to toughen the skin. A famous dermatologist dismissed the solution as 'literal and metaphorical eyewash', but Wicks insisted, 'I got the recipe from an old sailor. So what does the other fellow know?' Many of Wicks's words were mixed with 'the other fellow' and 'what's is name'.

It was a typical British summer evening, wet and breezy, when 35,000 people arrived in the stands and on the boarded famous turf of Wembley. For the first and last time I sported a waterproof American stetson trilby, sitting in the first press row against the ring apron, two seats away from the timekeeper. You could have cut the tension with a knife. Coldstream Guards played rousing music. Flag-draped trumpeters heralded the gladiators into the ring, following the shouting and shoving entrance of Elizabeth Taylor in turquoise ensemble, accompanied by Richard Burton in rosy flush.

The spotlight glittered on Clay's purple and gold crown as he strutted from the stadium tunnel to the ring which was pitched near the soccer centre spot. Cooper was able to swagger modestly. He obviously possessed a fine sense of purpose because Clay, surprisingly, backed off in the first round. Cooper shaped up in old lithograph style, taught textbook fashion at Eltham Amateur Club, and later as an army boxer, but unloaded his punches quickly. He was riled, I suspect, by having been written off by critics. He confounded Clay and jabbed effectively, clearly winning the opening round.

Retreating against Cooper was the worst possible move for any man having to contend with his left hook. It was also dangerous coming out of clinches unprepared, because Cooper was a master at hitting on the break, which was then legal by British ruling. ('Defend yourselves at all times,' boxers were instructed by referees.) Clay appealed to London referee, Tommy Little, ex-boxer turned newsagent, when Cooper neatly and painfully clipped him when dropping his hands on the break. Dreams of glory seemed to rise from the onlookers on this 148th anniversary of the Battle of Waterloo.

In the corner I heard Angelo Dundee scolding Clay for too much movement, not enough countering, and he was inflamed by the blood dripping from Clay's nose. In the second, Clay was forced to stop show-boating and offer precise punch combinations. The first sign of blood on Cooper we thought had been smudged from Clay's nose, but it was a small cut around Cooper's left eye. For him a cut was comparable to a snag in a silk stocking; the unravelling was inevitable.

Cornermen are like cosmeticians; their handiwork is often unavailing in the hot light of reality. But Cooper's worked feverishly, and he came out for the third looking as good as new.

We were staggered when tufts of horse hair were seen coming out of Clay's right glove in the third. Board of Control secretary, Teddy Waltham, and chief inspector, Andy Cunningham, were debating alongside me as to where they could quickly find a replacement glove. Cunningham left the ringside for the dressing rooms, which dispels the belief that trainer Dundee (they come no smarter) had deliberately cut the glove following the drama to come. Clay jutted out his chin, defying Cooper to hit him, made foolish faces and dropped his arms down by his thighs. Cooper liked that. 'If this keeps up I'll tag him proper,' he assured manager Wicks.

Bill Faversham, a Louisville lawyer who headed Clay's pro-launching, all-white syndicate, raced to the corner between rounds, angrily roaring at Dundee to make Clay stop the nonsense. Seemingly chastened, Clay came out for the fourth with hands up and ready for business. He jabbed casually with a right, a risky and unorthodox procedure.

Cooper was like a radar scanner, he could spot openings coming. Just five seconds from the end of the round, Cooper caught Clay with the prime punch, a rising left hook, and the cocky one crumbled in a heap a few feet from my seat. He was propped on the bottom rope. His eyes glared like organ stops. There seemed no hope of his rising. But at that time a count did not continue when a round ended with a boxer on the canvas. When the timekeeper reached four, he also struck the bell (hardly audible in the roar of the crowd), but amazingly Clay hauled himself up and rolled unsteadily back to his corner.

Had the punch landed earlier in the round, it must have been odds-on that Cooper, the ferocious finisher, would nail Clay again and put him down for the ten-count. In conversation, Clay contended that his recovery rate was exceptional – which it was – and that he could 'have waited and hung on to Cooper' to clear his head. We shall never know.

The between-rounds drama unfolded with Dundee able to make a meal of Clay's torn glove – damaged along the seam of the thumb – hollering to officials that it must be changed. The sixty seconds' respite was stretched, it seemed, to infinity. The crowd were tense and restless. Cooper's cornermen were appealing to Board officials. Dick Reekie, a personal friend of mine, was among those working in Clay's corner. 'We couldn't find a replacement glove quick enough. Angelo was untying Clay's glove, then had to lace it up again when referee Little demanded that Clay could not take any more time. The glove would have to be changed at the end of the next round.' Presumably Clay's torn glove had become dangerously thinner with the padding coming out. The extra time certainly permitted Clay to recover his senses and even utter one of his classical lines: 'I'm OK. Cooper's getting tired.'

In fact, Cooper was standing, despite being cut, and his seconds yanked his left hand tighter into his gloves – then 6 oz each, now an obligatory 8 oz and often 10 oz – for the intended repeat punch. Clay flung himself at Cooper and with remarkable accuracy peppered sufficient punches to make Cooper's scars reopen like zip fasteners. After one minute fifteen seconds referee Little spread his arms. 'It's all over,' he apologized to Cooper, whose blood literally fountained down his face.

Clay's prediction had come true, but with a nice streak of dignity he consoled Cooper and refused to put on the stage crown that had rested on a pillow during the fight. He had woefully underestimated Cooper.

Clay then took the world crown, the genuine one, from Sonny Liston, and returned to Britain as Muslim Ali, defending against Cooper, after having again defeated Liston and having staved off brave challenges from Floyd Patterson and George Chuvalo. This time the new champion showed due respect. He didn't make a single clowning gesture during the fight. He feared being floored again. It was not the cocksure Ali we saw in many subsequent fights.

Again the atmosphere was electric on the Arsenal FC ground at Highbury in May 1966. This big match was not screened on home television for over two years, despite government discussions that it could be considered a national event with Viewsport, who controlled the closed-circuit and pay-television in London's Southwark and Sheffield, and the Postmaster General, who was then the up-and-coming Anthony Wedgwood-Benn, a disciple of the political left.

The gate take – £212,000, a pittance by today's American standards – was larger than the World Cup final two months later between England and West Germany. Promoter Harry Levene, matchmaker Micky Duff – who had paid ten bob to watch the first Clay-Cooper fight! – and Viewsport had a field day. Ali was paid £148,000.09 – his accurate share of the receipts.

It ended, regrettably, with Cooper again cut up, this time in six rounds. From my battered notebooks I had totalled the combined fights even on completed rounds, and Cooper was not off his feet. As he told an American scribe on the way back to the dressing room, 'We didn't do so bad for a bum and a cripple.'

There were still sweeter moments to come for Cooper – seven wins that not only displayed his hooking power, but restored some faith in his consummate ringcraft and strategy. But the hook always kept the crowds hooked. An American, Chip Johnson, made the mistake of defeating Henry's twin brother, George, who boxed as Jim. It was Cooper II's last fight. Big brother was engaged to settle the family honour, though George at one time threatened to be the big hitter of the pair – brittle hands and thin skin handicapped him. It could be argued that too many British boxers still shape up like gentlemen about to chastise a ruffian. Cooper was not prepared to display leniency with Chip Johnson at Wolverhampton. The big American neglected to raise his right hand in defence from the region of his bosom at the belligerent approach of Cooper's left hook. With an accompanying shriek – 'Whoomph' – the blow landed on the button, and poor Johnson made a resounding thud on the canvas. Count out in two minutes twenty-four seconds. Cowboy Jeff Davis, from the USA, suffered a similar indignity in the same ring a year later – also out in the first, by the left.

In Rome in 1969, Cooper came off the canvas several times – all diabolically low punches – to land a finishing blow that I swear lifted the offending Piero Tomasoni clean off his feet in the fifth round. Our hero won the European title amid scenes familiar to Roman rings. Backstage we were shown Cooper's battered foul-proof protector: it resembled a discarded sardine tin.

Cooper relinquished his tenure as champion in an out-of-character form of protest, by returning the Lonsdale Belt to the Board's offices when the ruling body refused to recognize a match between Cooper and Jimmy Ellis for the World Boxing Association version of the title. For Cooper it was not only the fact of losing money, but a protest of principle. The Board were not members of the WBA. They joined ten years later, though at the time of writing no solo WBA title match has taken place in Britain.

Cooper's career ending was the now much debated 'defeat' on points, over fifteen rounds, by rising blond Joe Bugner in 1971, when a mere quarter point (a scoring decimal now abandoned) robbed him of regaining the British title. 'Well, gentlemen,' he said in the dressing room, 'that's me lot.' He had come a long way, as puncher and person, since losing his first three amateur bouts.

I had reported him from amateur (he fought for Britain at the 1952 Helsinki Olympics) to Lance-corporal Cooper, H., 22698686, from Walworth near his London birthplace (at Westminster hospital) to Wolverhampton, Wembley, Dortmund and Rome: big fights, little fights, wins and losses. You could scrape the bottom of boxing's barrel and never hear a bad word spoken about him.

Cooper left the ring at thirty-seven, not seeking a licence as a promoter or a manager, but to grow in stature, become a national figure and continue to shore up the fight game through many times of degradation.

Henry Cooper says . . .

What do you expect me to say? Very nice, thank you. I'm flattered. You've done a right 'This Is Your Life' on me and it's all accurate. The knockdown of Ali will live with me for ever and you've certainly made me live it again. Who knows whether or not I could have kept him down if the bell hadn't sounded in the middle of the count? Nowadays the count would have continued. That's the rule, and a good one, too. Yeah, he'd have no doubt got up, but I had a lot going for me. But the right time to have knocked him over was in the return fight for the title. He played it a lot cooler and cautious. That's what made him a good 'un.

I hadn't realized you knew I'd lost my first three amateur bouts, though I remember you writing an amateur boxing column after J. T. Hulls on the London Evening News. *It was dear old Mr Hulls, who loved his amateur boxing, who introduced me to Jim Wicks when he knew I wanted to become a pro. He guided me right. I did the contract signing on television.*

I can only say that if I had it all to do over again I'd do the same thing. Well, maybe a little change here and there. But I honestly enjoyed my ring years. The game was good to me.

PS: Mind if I make a reasonable excuse about losing those first three fights? Brother George and I could eat like vultures and Mum used to fill us up with chunks of bread pudding. 'You can't box on an empty stomach,' she said. I remember rushing home from school and having a right bellyful before going off to box. Used to think it was good for me.

Teofilo Stevenson

He made pro promoters eat their hearts out. The picture heavyweight. Height, weight, handsome and, undoubtedly, the hardest punch of all amateur heavyweights. But Teofilo Stevenson preferred to be red than rich. Britain might have called him the one that got away. Had Teo's poor stevedore father followed the customary West Indian emigrant's route to England from St Vincent instead of seeking work in Havana's dockyards, we could have boasted the first 'British' world heavyweight champion since Bob Fitzsimmons left Cornwall in 1897, emigrated to New Zealand, and became champion.

Stevenson's grandfather was English – hence the name. Teo became Fidel Castro's 'pillar of the Revolution' in the western hemisphere's first Communist regime, and was duly voted a seat in the Cuba National Assembly for his home state of Orientes, where the marvellous professional welterweight champion, Jose Napoles, was born.

Bachelor Stevenson is boxing's best record big fellow. Three times Olympic champion, twice world amateur champion, twice Pan-Am Games champion. At thirty-two, the Belafonte in boxing gloves is being pressured into producing the unthinkable by winning a fourth Olympic crown – a span of twelve years – in Los Angeles in 1984. ('About twenty-eight is the best age for heavyweights,' he says.)

Six feet four inches, nearly 16 st, upright with a sporting-print stance, slightly knock-kneed, a pose with palms down, Stevenson has the most devastating delayed-action power I have seen. At long range he seemed invincible. He boxed with a patient arrogance, seemingly bored by the proceedings, pawed often with a reconnaissance left and was able to drop a right hand on an opponent's chin with time-bomb effect. Sometimes the shocked receiver would turn away, then collapse as though wondering how the bolt from the blue had landed without warning.

I reported all Stevenson's Olympic bouts, not all epic, but comparable to watching a man weaving his way through a minefield and waiting for the blast. I know a bit about that. In Munich in 1972, the games wrecked by the appalling murder of some Israeli competitors and coaches, Stevenson, at twenty, was superb. Inevitable comparisons were made with Muhammad Ali, Olympic champion in Rome twelve years earlier. But Ali weighed inside the light-heavy maximum of 12 st 10 lb, was eighteen, and three of his four wins (all against the best opposition) were settled on points.

Stevenson simply poleaxed rivals. Team-mates called him the Doc because he operated with a surgeon's care. Rarely a rash move. He began at sixteen, coached by a Russian imported for Cuba's ring challenge in the medal-chasing world. Castro had banned professionalism as a decadent West's commercial enterprise, despite the outstanding success in America of Napoles, Kid Gavilan and Sugar Ramos. Stevenson was, and presumably still is, a totally dedicated disciple of the regime which believes in sport, realizes its importance and fêtes its champions.

'I don't believe in professionalism,' said Stevenson, 'only in revolution. I tell these men from America, the promoters, that money means nothing to me. What is eight million dollars against eight million Cubans who love me? All they care about is dollars. The boxer does not matter.' A party line, incidentally, that would not be supported by many champions who climbed out of poverty with the only qualification they had – a punch.

Stevenson paraded around the Olympic village in Munich (it was easier to obtain press visits to Dachau camp than entry into the athletes' pen) reminiscent of Ali in Rome. Ali had lost in his unpaid days, including to Louisville friend Jimmy Ellis, and Stevenson's pride was stunned losing a debatable 3–2 judges' vote to red-haired Duane Bobick, an American sailor, in the Pan-Am Games.

The scene was set for Stevenson's revenge. Big-heart Bobick, who led the US team in training with commendable enthusiasm, began by eliminating a Russian. The Cuban countered, dropping his right-hand anaesthetizer on the chin of a Pole. Regrettably, the big rivals were drawn in the same section. They clashed in the quarter final. I recall Bobick telling me, 'He couldn't have improved that much. I beat him once, I can do it again.'

Stevenson and his coaching counsel had done their homework well. He speared the US quartermaster with a series of destructive left hands, often ripped weakening blows to the body, and bided his time releasing the right. In the third round, when Stevenson considered Bobick ripe for picking, he fired the deadly weapon. Bobick took two counts and the crowd yelled for a stoppage. He was bruised, bleeding and reduced to a walk. After one minute forty seconds the referee moved in and the new star was born.

In the semifinal Stevenson clobbered a strong and capable West German, Peter Hussing, breaking his nose with his bolt fists. He then became the first Olympic heavyweight to collect his gold medal with a walkover final. He kissed the medal, gave it to his trainer and was the winner of the Games' Val Barker best-style trophy. Ion Alexe, of Rumania, had broken a thumb winning his semifinal.

Hereby hangs a tale. ABC TV decided to move a commentary position at extra cost from the television row in the first section of the stand (press and television are not normally seated close to the ring at Olympic events). It cut them off from some information. I heard ABC's announcer, Howard Cosell, previewing the appearance of the Cuban wonder boy. There was a surprise when I informed him that Alexe had withdrawn. The Rumanian's hand had a plaster cast. An X-ray of his broken thumb was available for inspection in the medical room. There were ridiculous slurs from the American crew, obviously upset that viewer-puller Stevenson would make only a formal appearance in the ring, that Alexe had faked an injury. Having frequently watched Alexe on the amateur international circuit, I was equally angered by the insinuation. Alexe had certainly not shown fear fighting Herculean George Foreman in the Mexico Games four years earlier.

He who laughs last. . . . Alexe went to South America to box Stevenson in a club event. And he won! 'I was not myself for the contest. I am not complaining,' said the golden boy. The result was the biggest turn-up of the time and many newspapers did not publish it because they thought the result had been wrongly wired by the news agencies.

It was defeat by Alexe, Bobick, a clobbering by Cuban compatriot Angel Milan, a novice at the time, plus a KO by Russian Igor Vyssotsky, who did not appear at the Olympics, that created doubts when considering the pro potential of Stevenson. Frankly, I doubted if he could have hit a peak Ali on the backside with a bag of rice. He frequently lacked the desire which gameness demands. He seemed a looking-glass boxer. None the less, he more than matched Frazier, Foreman, Ali and Holmes for lethal hitting. The punch could have overcome deficiences.

The first World championships were invented for Cuba, 1974. (Britain has not competed.) The sunshine punch-ups were the stage for Stevenson, with television monitors hung on street corners in Havana, the traffic halted when the hero was in action. Alexe, the branded runaway, turned up again. But he was eliminated by German Hussing who, in turn, was duly thrashed in the first round by Stevenson. In the final, America's Marvin Stinson, a solid journeyman later to become a sparmate for Frank Bruno, forced Stevenson to fight a full three rounds.

In Montreal in 1976, maturing Stevenson reached peak. A Senegalese, who did not belong in the same event as the Cuban, was KO'd. Again the right proved might. A Finn could not last a round. Then Stevenson showed the world, via the inquisitive television lens, the power that proved him the amateur game's greatest. Big John Tate, from Tennessee, staggered like a bull taking a few seconds to feel the pain of the matador's sword as he reeled back to a corner, slumping slowly to the canvas, when the Cuban clobbered him with one punch. Tate's chin subsequently proved susceptible to big hitters, like Mike Weaver and Trevor Berbick, but he also won the WBA heavyweight title. It showed that Stevenson had the form to become a king in the commercial world.

In Belgrade, Yugoslavia, in 1978, Stevenson yawned his way to a second World series gold with three of four bouts failing to finish. Then Moscow, in 1980, and cracks finally appearing in the Cuban's make-up. He had been injured when a stove blew up. Training had always been a chore, but the double medallist had sufficient skill from memory, backed by the reliable chiller punch, to come good again.

The Games that propagandists tried to convince us were designed to display Soviet mastery were certainly wrong at the boxing arena. The Cubans were the stars and Stevenson was virtually a bit player among them. Russia won only one gold medal, at light flyweight, and that by a 3–2 verdict. We sadly missed the competition of the Americans in Moscow. (The refusal to compete by many countries because of the Russian invasion of Afghanistan is an issue of personal opinion. I disagree with politics influencing sport; Games have taken place when other nations, including Britain and America, were 'in conflict' – the modern soft-pedal words for war. The protest made no visible mark on Russia's conflict with her neighbours and while sport was barred there was no stoppage of commercial trading. Total hypocrisy. Perhaps actor Peter Ustinov is right when he says Russia is always regarded as the enemy of the West, but history has never shown it.)

Stevenson, as expected, starred in the final bout of a well-organized event when, for a change, there were few controversial decisions. I witnessed every blow of 262 bouts. It was left to a Nicaraguan judge, now probably holding a ticket to obscurity, to vote against Stevenson in his bid for a third gold against rolypoly Zaev, of Russia, chosen for his strength and awkward-ness to compete against the Cuban. The Soviet squad surely had sharper boxers, but Zaev was designed to give the Cuban a hard workout. He did. Three judges marked the Cuban a winner by only 1 point. Much of his golden glory was tarnished. But you can't knock success.

It was time for Stevenson to retire. I was convinced Moscow was his last stand. Instead, they wheeled the great man out for the World championships in Munich in 1982, and he was humbled by so-so Italian Francesco Damiani, outpointed 5–0. The bout, expected to be shown in continual rerun on British television was, in fact, blacked out because the ring was plastered with advertising. So a limited world audience saw the downfall of Stevenson. It was a face-saver. If Stevenson is pushed to compete in Los Angeles he can genuinely be compared with Ali, who was sadly encouraged to fight when he became an embarrassing shadow of himself. The slide continued in June 1983, losing in Santiago, Cuba, to the Soviet's Alex Krupkin.

Henry Cooper says . . .

If Ali was worth a million to become a pro after the Rome Olympics, Stevenson was worth two million after he won in Munich. The thing he could do better than Ali was knock 'em out with one punch. I say he could do because it seems he's way past it now. Be silly of him to go for the fourth Olympics in Los Angeles. You could never tell if Stevenson had the temperament to become a world champion pro. He was keen to get out of the way of punches, though I couldn't blame him. But had he improved, like Ali, there is no telling how good he could have been. Yeah, terrific one-punch hitter.

I bet old Angelo Dundee would have swum from Miami to Havana if he thought Stevenson would sign with him.

Career Records

Compiled by *Ring/Boxing News*

Abbreviations
D   Drew
Dis   Disqualified
DNC   Declared no contest
Exh   Exhibition
KO   Knockout
L   Lost
LF   Lost on foul
ND   No decision
Pts   Points
RSF   Referee stopped fight
Rtd   Retired
W   Won
WD   Won on disqualification
WF   Won on foul

Eric Boon

Born: 28 December 1919, Chatteris, Cambridgeshire, England

1935

17 Jan. Young Snowball, Peterborough	W	RSF	6
7 Feb. Teddy Royal, St Ives	W	Pts	6
10 Mar. Young Higgins, Hackney	D		6
7 Apr. Teddy Softley, Hackney	W	Pts	6
21 Apr. Yorkie Perkins, Hackney	W	KO	5
2 June Young Higgins, Hackney	W	Pts	6
23 June Boy Bessell, Hackney	W	Pts	6
28 Aug. Kid Savage, Hackney	L	Pts	6
21 Oct. Charlie Smith, Cambridge	W	Pts	6
25 Nov. Ginger Daniels, Cambridge	W	RSF	2
4 Dec. Charlie Smith, Watford	W	RSF	2

1936

3 Feb. Terry Ellis, Cambridge	W	KO	1
2 Mar. Young Hawes, Norwich	W	KO	1
16 Mar. Young Griffo, Norwich	W	KO	1

30 Mar. Charlie Smith, Cambridge	W	Pts	10
15 Apr. Jack Roberts, Hackney	W	KO	2
21 Aug. Len Ash, Hackney	W	Pts	8
4 Sept. Charlie Wise, Hackney	W	Pts	8
1 Oct. Bert Whall, Norwich	W	RSF	2
4 Oct. Teddy Larkham, Hackney	W	KO	1
18 Oct. Len Ash, Hackney	W	Pts	8
1 Nov. Jack Watkins, Hackney	W	Pts	8
5 Nov. Fred Dyer, Norwich	D		8
12 Nov. Bobby Lyons, Norwich	W	RSF	6
16 Nov. Jackie Kershaw, Earl's Court	D		6
22 Nov. Joe Page, Hackney	W	KO	1
26 Nov. Jack Watkins, Hackney	W	Pts	8
30 Nov. Nat Williams, Earl's Court	W	KO	5
10 Dec. George Cunningham, Holborn	W	Pts	4
13 Dec. Nick Lucas, Hackney	W	RSF	6

1937

3 Jan. Al Church, Hackney	W	RSF	6
11 Jan. Bert Chambers, Earl's Court	D		6
14 Jan. Billy Bennett, Holborn	W	KO	2
24 Jan. Billy Sheldon, Hackney	W	Pts	10
27 Jan. Billy Griffiths, Hackney	W	KO	1
7 Feb. Mike Sullivan, Hackney	W	KO	4
16 Feb. Dave James, Reading	W	Pts	8
23 Feb. Chalky Robinson, Norwich	W	Pts	10
1 Mar. Spin Anson, Bury St Edmunds	W	KO	5
7 Mar. Terry Butcher, Hackney	W	Rtd	3
21 Mar. Harry Brooks, Hackney	L	Rtd	4
12 Apr. Jocker Johnson, Bury St Edmunds	W	RSF	5
15 Apr. Angus McGregor, Harringay	D		4
29 Apr. Bob Barlow, Norwich	W	Pts	10
7 May George Kelly, Hackney	W	Pts	12
9 May Bobby Lyons, Bury St Edmunds	W	KO	1
16 May Ron Porter, Hackney	W	Rtd	5
28 May Jack Lilley, Hackney	W	Pts	12
2 July Johnny Softley, Hackney	L	Rtd	7
16 July Bryn Morris, Hackney	W	Pts	10
3 Aug. Albert Heasman, Hackney	W	KO	3
3 Sept. Wilf Dexter, Hackney	W	RSF	7
15 Sept. Charlie Wise, Hackney	W	RSF	3
16 Oct. Bryn Morris, Hackney	W	Pts	10
5 Nov. Harry Mackenzie, Hackney	W	KO	2
29 Nov. Bob Rowlands, Cambridge	W	KO	2
10 Dec. Con Flynn, Hackney	W	Dis	3
13 Dec. Llew Thomas, Bury St Edmunds.	W	KO	3

1938

13 Jan. Alex Jackson, Ipswich	W	Pts	8
21 Jan. George Reynolds, Hackney	W	KO	2
28 Jan. Tommy Dowlais, Hackney	W	KO	1
2 Feb. Jack Hardiman, Hackney	W	KO	3
18 Feb. Dodo Williams, Hackney	W	KO	1
3 Mar. Johnny Softley, Albert Hall	W	Pts	8
7 Apr. Johnny Ward, Harringay	W	RSF	1

17 Apr. Matt Moran, Hackney	W	RSF	7
2 May Boyo Rees, Holborn	W	KO	1
28 May Jimmy Walsh, Chatteris	W	Pts	10
21 June Len Lemaux, Harringay	W	KO	1
16 July Raymond Renard, Chatteris	W	Rtd	1
24 July Billy Masters, Mile End	W	KO	2
2 Sept. Eric Dolby, Manchester	W	RSF	3
27 Sept. Mitsos Grispos, Harringay	W	Pts	8
20 Oct. George Reynolds, Marylebone	W	KO	2
31 Oct. Mac Perez, Earl's Court	WD		7
15 Dec. Dave Crowley, Harringay	W	KO	13
(British lightweight title)			

1939

30 Jan. Boyo Rees, Mountain Ash	W	RSF	2
23 Feb. Arthur Danahar, Harringay	W	RSF	14
(British lightweight title)			
28 June Johnny McGrory, Peterborough	W	KO	9
17 July Len Wickwar, Leicester	W	KO	9
9 Dec. Dave Crowley, Harringay	W	KO	7
(British lightweight title)			

1940

21 Sept. Ernie Roderick, Liverpool	L	Pts	10

1941

20 Feb. Dave Finn, London Odeon Theatre	W	Pts	6
21 Apr. Kid Berg, London Coliseum	L	Dis	2

1942

2 Feb. Norman Snow, Marylebone	W	KO	4
26 Aug. Dick Wheller, Watford	W	KO	3
12 Sept. Frank Duffy, Bristol	L	Dis	6
21 Oct. Jake Kilrain, London Casino	W	KO	2
11 Nov. Jake Kilrain, London Casino	W	Pts	10

1943

13 July Tommy Armour, Belfast	L	KO	5
23 Aug. Harry Mizler, Albert Hall	L	Pts	8
24 Sept. Billy Jones, Blackburn	W	Pts	8

1944

26 Apr. Jimmy Molloy, Albert Hall	W	Pts	8
12 Aug. Ronnie James, Cardiff	L	KO	10
(British lightweight title)			

1945

17 July Henry Hall, Tottenham	L	RSF	5

1946

8 Jan. Cyril Wills, Marylebone	W	KO	1
22 Jan. Paddy Burgin, Albert Hall	W	RSF	2
5 Feb. Jean Wanes, Marylebone	W	Rtd	5
19 Feb. Mick Magee, Albert Hall	W	KO	2
5 Mar. Maurice Ouezmann, Marylebone	W	RSF	7

19 Mar. Billy Stevens, Albert Hall	W	KO	7
14 May Arthur Danahar, Harringay	L	RSF	5
(British welterweight title eliminator)			
27 July Laurie Stevens, Johannesburg	W	KO	3
7 Sept. Tiger Burns, Johannesburg	W	KO	2

1947

3 Mar. Alf James, Johannesburg	W	KO	7
29 Apr. Maurice Ouezmann, Johannesburg	W	RSF	8
10 May Alf James, Nkhana	W	KO	5
22 Aug. Maurice Ouezmann, Pretoria	W	Pts	10
8 Sept. Giel de Roode, Johannesburg	L	Pts	10
9 Dec. Ernie Roderick, Harringay	L	Pts	15
(British welterweight title)			

1948

1 Mar. Omar Kouidri, Albert Hall	W	RSF	2
20 Apr. Robert Villemain, Harringay	L	KO	10
31 May Gwyn Williams	DNC		6
(British welterweight title eliminator)			
5 Aug. Johnny Greco, Montreal	L	KO	3
28 Oct. Beau Jack, Washington	L	RSF	3
14 Dec. Robert Takeshita, Honolulu	L	KO	3

1949

22 Mar. Fernando Jannilli, Albert Hall	L	Dis	7

Marcel Cerdan
Born: 22 July 1916, Sidi Bel-Abbes, Algeria

1934

4 Nov. Marcel Bucchianeri, Meknes	W		6
12 Nov. Benazra, Meknes		KO	5

1935

16 Feb. Perez Ill, Casablanca	W		10
20 Mar. Privat, Casablanca		KO	5
13 Apr. Benazra, Casablanca	W		10
5 July Mac Perez, Casablanca		KO	2
19 July Joseph Sarfati, Casablanca	W		10
8 Aug. Mestre, Casablanca	W		10
23 Nov. Mac Perez, Casablanca	W		10
14 Dec. Mac Perez, Casablanca	W		10

1936

4 Mar. Antoine Abad, Casablanca	W		10
7 Apr. M. Hergane, Casablanca	W		10
11 Apr. Joseph Martinez, Taza		KO	9
23 May M. Ricardo, Casablanca		KO	5
27 May Kid Abadie, Casablanca		KO	3
6 June M. Castillanos, Casablanca	W		10
19 July Joseph Sarfati, Casablanca	W		10
2 Aug. Al Francis, Oran		KO	6

17 Oct. Primo Rubio, Casablanca	W		10
2 Nov. Aissa Attaf, Casablanca		KO	1
21 Nov. Jean Debeaumont, Casablanca	W		10

1937

16 Jan. Aissa Attaf, Algiers		KO	8
30 Jan. Maurice Naudin, Algiers		KO	3
2 Mar. Omar Kouidri, Rabat	W		10
3 Apr. Omar Kouidri, Algiers	W		10
3 July Ali Omar, Algiers		KO	5
2 Aug. Kid Marcel, Oran	W		10
13 Sept. Eddy Rabak, Casablanca		KO	6
7 Oct. Louis Jampton, Paris	W		10
21 Oct. Jean Morin, Paris	W		10
18 Dec. Ifergane, Rabat	W		10

1938

6 Jan. Charles Feodorowich, Paris		KO	2
13 Jan. Eddie Ran, Paris		KO	2
20 Jan. Jean Zides, Paris		KO	9
21 Feb. Omar Kouidri, Casablanca	W		12
(Won French welterweight title)			
12 Mar. Charles Pernot, Algiers	W		10
13 Apr. Eddy Rabak, Paris	W		10
5 May Anacleto Locatelli, Paris	W		12
20 May Gustave Humery, Paris		KO	6
4 June Jean Morin, Algiers	W		10
3 July Victor Deckmer, Oran	W		10
15 Sept. Al Baker, Paris	W		10
27 Oct. Amedeo Devaine, Paris	W		10
10 Nov. Alfredo Kattiq, Paris		KO	4
24 Nov. Omar Kouidri, Paris	W		12
(Retained French welterweight title)			

1939

9 Jan. Harry Craster, London	LF		5
21 Jan. Ercole Buratti, Algiers	W		10
4 Feb. Al Baker, Brussels		KO	7
20 Feb. Saverio Turiello, Paris	W		12
22 Mar. Felix Wouters, Brussels	W		12
21 May Roger Cadot, Marseilles		KO	6
3 June Saverio Turiello, Milan	W		15
(Won European welterweight title)			
18 June Anacleto Locatelli, Marseilles	W		10

1940
(Inactive)

1941

19 Jan. Young Raymond, Algiers		KO	1
26 Jan. Young Raymond, Casablanca		KO	6
2 Feb. Victor Fortes, Algiers		KO	7
9 Mar. Victor (Kid) Janas, Casablanca	W		10
13 Apr. Victor Fortes, Oran		KO	2
4 May Omar Kouidri, Oran		KO	6

22 June Francois Blanchard, Marseilles		KO	6
20 July Joe Brun, Oran		KO	2
13 Sept. Roland Coureau, Algiers		KO	9
31 Dec. Robert Seidel, Vichy		KO	3

1942

21 Feb. Fred Flury, Nice		KO	7
26 Apr. Gustave Humery, Paris		KO	1
17 May Fernand Viez, Paris	W		10
28 June Gaspard de Ridder, Paris		KO	1
25 July Victor (Kid) Janas, Algiers		KO	2
2 Aug. Ben Frely, Marseilles		KO	3
15 Aug. Victor Buttin, Algiers	LF		8
30 Sept. Jose Ferrer, Paris		KO	1
(Retained European welterweight title)			

1943

8 Aug. John McCoy, Oran		KO	2
12 Sept. Omar Kouidri, Algiers	W		10
13 Oct. Larry Cisneros, Oran		KO	6
31 Oct. Bulldog Milano, Casablanca		KO	2
26 Dec. James Toney, Oran		KO	2
29 Dec. Larry Cisneros, Algiers		KO	2

1944

30 Jan. Willie Sampson, Casablanca		KO	2
15 Feb. Eugene Drouhin, Algiers		KO	1
17 Feb. Sammy Adragna, Algiers	W		3
20 Feb. Joe DiMartino, Algiers		KO	2
(Won Inter-Allied welterweight tournament)			
21 Oct. Bouaya, Casablanca		KO	1
12 Dec. Clinton Perry, Rome		KO	1
14 Dec. Floyd Gibson, Rome		KO	1
16 Dec. Fred Burney, Rome		KO	2
(Won Inter-Allied welterweight tournament)			

1945

9 Mar. Joe Brun, Paris		KO	7
13 May Jean Despeaux, Paris		KO	5
3 June Oscar Menozzi, Marseilles		KO	3
24 June Edouard Tenet, Croix de Berny	W		10
19 Oct. Tommy Davies, Paris		KO	1
30 Nov. Assane Diouf, Paris		KO	3
(Won French middleweight title)			
8 Dec. Victor Buttin, St Etienne		KO	3

1946

13 Jan. Agustin Guedes, Lisbon		KO	1
18 Jan. Edouard Tenet, Paris	W		12
(Retained French middleweight title)			
24 Feb. Jose Ferrer, Barcelona		KO	4
14 Apr. Joe Brun, Nice		KO	2
25 May Robert Charron, Paris	W		12
(Retained French middleweight title)			
7 July Holman Williams, Paris	W		10

20 Oct. Jean Pankowiak, Paris		KO	5
6 Dec. Georgie Abrams, New York	W		10

1947

2 Feb. Leon Foquet, Paris		KO	1
(Won Vacant Europe middleweight title)			
11 Feb. Bert Gilroy, London		KO	4
28 Mar. Harold Green, New York		KO	2
7 Oct. Billy Walker, Montreal		KO	1
31 Oct. Anton Raadik, Chicago	W		10

1948

26 Jan. Giovanni Manca, Paris		KO	2
(Retained European middleweight title)			
9 Feb. Jean Walzack, Paris		KO	4
(Retained European middleweight title)			
12 Mar. Lavern Roach, New York		KO	8
25 Mar. Lucien Krawsyck, Paris	W		10
23 May Cyrille Delannoit, Brussels	L		15
(Lost European middleweight title)			
10 July Cyrille Delannoit, Brussels	W		15
(Regained European middleweight title)			
21 Sept. Tony Zale, Jersey City		KO	12
(Won World middleweight title)			
2 Dec. Dave Andrews, Lewiston, Maine	Exh		4
10 Dec. Cosby Linson, New Orleans	Exh		4

1949

29 Mar. Dick Turpin, London		KO	7
8 May Lucien Krawsyck, Casablanca		KO	4
16 June Jake LaMotta, Detroit		KO by	10
(Lost World middleweight title)			

Dave Charnley
Born: 10 October 1935, Dartford, Kent, England

1954

19 Oct. Malcolm Ames, London	W	RSF	3
12 Nov. Percy James, Blackpool	W	KO	2
23 Nov. Roy Paine, London	W	Pts	6
7 Dec. Pat McCoy, London	W	RSF	6

1955

7 Jan. Andy Monahan, Blackpool	W	KO	1
27 Jan. Nye Ankrah, London	W	KO	1
8 Feb. Neville Tetlow, London	W	KO	2
17 Feb. Willie Lloyd, Liverpool	D		8
22 Mar. Denny Dawson, London	W	Dis	7
24 May Jeff Walters, London	W	Dis	6
9 June Johnny Mann, Birmingham	W	Pts	8
26 July Teddy Best, Birmingham	W	Pts	8
3 Oct. Stan Skinkiss, Nottingham	W	RSF	4
13 Oct. Jackie Butler, London	W	RSF	4

1 Nov. Leo Molloy, London	W	Pts	8
15 Nov. Guy Gracia, London	L	Pts	10
28 Nov. Kurt Ernest, Nottingham	W	RSF	6

1956

6 Mar. Johnny Butterworth, London	W	RSF	5
3 Apr. Sammy McCarthy, London	W	Pts	10
19 June Fernand Coppens, London	W	RSF	2
24 July Johnny Miller, Dartford	W	Rtd	6
27 Aug. Willie Lloyd, Cardiff	L	Pts	10
16 Nov. Alby Tissong, Manchester	W	Pts	8

1957

22 Jan. Willie Lloyd, London (Eliminator for British lightweight title)	W	RSF	12
9 Apr. Joe Lucy, London (British lightweight title)	W	Pts	15
4 June Johnny Gonsalves, London	W	RSF	8
9 July Willie Toweel, London (British Empire lightweight title)	L	Pts	15
30 Sept. Joe Woussem, Southampton	W	RSF	10
19 Nov. Ron Hinson, London	W	Pts	10

1958

28 Jan. Don Jordan, London	W	Pts	10
11 Mar. Tony Garcia, London	W	RSF	5
15 Apr. Peter Waterman, London	W	RSF	5
3 Jun. Joe Lopes, London	W	Pts	10
18 Sept. Jimmy Croll, Liverpool	W	Ret	4
28 Oct. Carlos Ortiz, London	L	Pts	10

1959

10 Mar. Guy Gracia, Wembley	L	Pts	10
12 May Willie Toweel, Wembley (British Empire lightweight title)	W	KO	10
17 June Billy Kelly, Glasgow	W	Dis	6
4 Sept. Jimmy Brown, London	W	RSF	8
2 Dec. Joe Brown, Houston (World lightweight title)	L	Ret	5

1960

23 Feb. Saveur Benamou, Wembley	W	Pts	10
29 May Mario Vecchiatto, Wembley (European lightweight title)	W	Ret	10
31 May Paul Armstead, Wembley	W	KO	9

1961

17 Jan. Gene Gresham, London	W	Pts	10
21 Feb. Fernand Nollett, London (European lightweight title)	W	Pts	15
18 Apr. Joe Brown, London (World lightweight title)	L	Pts	15
5 July Raymondo Nobile, Rome (European lightweight title)	W	Ret	4
5 Sept. Lenny Matthews, Wembley	W	Pts	10

20 Nov. David (Darkie) Hughes, Nottingham (European, British and Empire lightweight titles)	W	KO	1
27 Nov. L. C. Morgan, Manchester	W	KO	3

1962

30 Jan. Jose Stable, Liverpool	W	Pts	10
5 June Doug Vaillant, Wembley	L	Pts	10
4 Aug. Bunny Grant, Kingston, Jamaica (British Empire lightweight title)	L	Pts	15
11 Dec. J. D. Ellis, London	W	RSF	6

1963

15 Jan. Jethro Cason, Wembley	W	Pts	10
25 Feb. Joe Brown, Manchester	W	KO	6
20 May Maurice Cullen, Manchester (British lightweight title)	W	Pts	15
25 Nov. Tito Marshall, Manchester	L	Pts	10

1964

24 Mar. Brian Curvis, Wembley	L	Pts	10
2 June Kenny Lane, Wembley	W	Pts	10
1 Dec. Emile Griffith, Wembley	L	RSF	9

Henry Cooper
Born: 3 May 1934, Westminster, London, England

1954

14 Sept. Harry Painter, Harringay	W	KO	1
19 Oct. Dinny Powell, Harringay	W	RSF	4
23 Nov. Eddie Keith, Manor Place Baths	W	RSF	1
7 Dec. Denny Ball, Harringay	W	KO	3

1955

27 Jan. Colin Strauch, Royal Albert Hall	W	RSF	1
8 Feb. Cliff Purnell, Harringay	W	Pts	6
8 Mar. Hugh Ferns, Earl's Court	W	Dis	2
29 Mar. Joe Crickmar, Empress Hall	W	Rtd	5
18 Apr. Joe Bygraves, Manor Place Baths	W	Pts	8
26 Apr. Uber Bacilieri, Harringay	L	RSF	2
6 June Ron Harman, Nottingham	W	RSF	7
13 Sept. Uber Bacilieri, White City	W	KO	7
15 Nov. Joe Erskine, Harringay (British heavyweight title eliminator)	L	Pts	10

1956

28 Feb. Maurice Mols, Royal Albert Hall	W	RSF	4
1 May Brian London, Empress Hall	W	RSF	1
26 June Giannino Luise, Wembley	W	RSF	7
7 Sept. Peter Bates, Manchester	L	Rtd	5

1957

19 Feb. Joe Bygraves, Earl's Court (British Empire heavyweight title)	L	KO	9

19 May Ingemar Johansson, Stockholm	L	KO	5
(European heavyweight title)			
17 Sept Joe Erskine, Harringay	L	Pts	15
(British heavyweight title)			
16 Nov. Hans Kalbfell, Dortmund	W	Pts	10

1958

11 Jan. Heinz Neuhaus, Dortmund	D		10
19 Apr. Erich Schoeppner, Frankfurt	L	Dis	6
3 Sept. Dick Richardson, Porthcawl	W	RSF	5
14 Oct. Zora Folley, Wembley	W	Pts	10

1959

12 Jan. Brian London, Earl's Court	W	Pts	15
(British and Empire heavyweight titles)			
26 Aug. Gawie de Klerk, Porthcawl	W	RSF	15
(British Empire heavyweight title)			
17 Nov. Joe Erskine, Earl's Court	W	RSF	12
(British and Empire heavyweight titles)			

1960

13 Sept. Roy Harris, Wembley	W	Pts	10
6 Dec. Alex Miteff, Wembley	W	Pts	10

1961

21 Mar. Joe Erskine, Wembley	W	Rtd	5
(British and Empire heavyweight titles)			
5 Dec. Zora Folley, Wembley	L	KO	2

1962

23 Jan. Tony Hughes, Wembley	W	Rtd	5
26 Feb. Wayne Bethea, Manchester	W	Pts	10
2 Apr. Joe Erskine, Nottingham	W	RSF	9
(British and Empire heavyweight titles)			

1963

26 Mar. Dick Richardson, Wembley	W	KO	5
(British and Empire heavyweight titles)			
18 June Cassius Clay, Wembley	L	RSF	5

1964

24 Feb. Brian London, Manchester	W	Pts	15
(British Empire and vacant European heavyweight titles)			
9 Sept. European heavyweight title declared vacant because of Cooper's inability, through injury, to defend it against Karl Mildenberger			
16 Nov. Roger Rischer, Royal Albert Hall	L	Pts	10

1965

12 Jan. Dick Wipperman, Royal Albert Hall	W	RSF	5
20 Apr. Chip Johnson, Wolverhampton	W	KO	1
15 June Johnny Prescott, Birmingham	W	Rtd	10
(British and Empire heavyweight titles)			
19 Oct. Amos Johnson, Wembley	L	Pts	10

1966

25 Jan. Hubert Hilton, Olympia	W	RSF	2
16 Feb. Jefferson Davis, Wolverhampton	W	KO	1
21 May Muhammad Ali (Cassius Clay), Arsenal Stadium	L	RSF	6
(World heavyweight title)			
20 Sept. Floyd Patterson, Wembley	L	KO	4

1967

17 Apr. Boston Jacobs, Leicester	W	Pts	10
13 June Jack Bodell, Wolverhampton	W	RSF	2
(British and Empire heavyweight titles)			
7 Nov. Billy Walker, Wembley	W	RSF	6
(British and Empire heavyweight titles)			

1968

18 Sept. Karl Mildenberger, Wembley	W	Dis	8
(European heavyweight title)			

1969

13 Mar. Piero Tomasoni, Rome	W	KO	5
(European heavyweight title)			
28 May Gave up British and Empire heavyweight titles in protest			
9 Oct. Gave up European heavyweight title because of injury			

1970

24 Mar. Jack Bodell, Wembley	W	Pts	15
(British and Commonwealth heavyweight titles)			
10 Nov. José Urtain, Wembley	W	RSF	9
(European heavyweight title)			

1971

16 Mar. Joe Bugner, Wembley	L	Pts	15
(British, European and Commonwealth heavyweight titles)			

Roberto Duran
Born: 16 June 1951, Guarare, Panama

1967

8 Mar. Carlos Mendoza, Colon	W		4
4 Apr. Manuel Jimenez, Colon		KO	1
14 May Juan Gondola, Colon		KO	1
30 May Eduardo Morales, Panama City		KO	1
10 Aug. Enrique Jacobo, Panama City		KO	1

1968

12 Jan. Uche De Leon, Panama City		KO	2
8 Feb. Leroy Cargill, Panama City		KO	2
16 Mar. Cafe Howard, Panama City		KO	1
2 Apr. Alberto Brands, Panama City		KO	4
4 Sept. Eduardo Pruto, Panama City	W		8

1969

12 Mar. Jacinto Garcia, Panama City		KO	5
3 May Adolfo Osses, Panama City		KO	7
16 July Serafin Garcia, Panama City		KO	5
15 Aug. Luis Patino, Panama City		KO	7

1970

5 Apr. Felipe Torres, Mexico City	W		10
16 May Ernesto Marcel, Panama City		KO	10
10 July Clemente Mucino, Colon		KO	6
5 Sept. Marvin Castanedas, Puerto Armuelles		KO	1

1971

10 Jan. Nacho Castanedas, Panama City		KO	4
5 Mar. Jose Angel Herrera, Mexico City		KO	6
4 Apr. Jose Acosta, Panama City		KO	1
29 May, Lloyd Marshall, Panama City		KO	6
18 July Fermin Soto, Monterrey		KO	3
13 Sept. Benny Huertas, New York		KO	1
1 Oct. Hiroshi Kokayashi, Panama City		KO	7

1972

15 Jan. Angel Robinson Garcia, Panama City	W		10
10 Mar. Francisco Munoz, Panama City		KO	1
26 June Ken Buchanan, New York		KO	13
(Won World lightweight title)			
2 Sept. Greg Potter, Panama City		KO	1
29 Oct. Lupe Ramirez, Panama City		KO	1
17 Nov. Esteban DeJesus, New York	L		10

1973

20 Jan. Jimmy Robertson, Panama City		KO	5
(Retained World lightweight title)			
23 Feb. Juan Medina, Los Angeles		KO	7
17 Mar. Javier Ayala, Los Angeles	W		10
14 Apr. Gerardo Ferrat, Panama City		KO	2
2 June Hector Thompson, Panama City		KO	8
(Retained World lightweight title)			
4 Aug. Doc McClendon, San Juan	W		10
8 Sept. Ishimatsu Suzuki, Panama City		KO	10
(Retained World lightweight title)			
1 Dec. Tony Garcia, Santiago		KO	2

1974

21 Jan. Leonard Tavarez, Paris		KO	4
16 Feb. Armando Mendoza, Panama City		KO	3
16 Mar. Esteban DeJesus, Panama City		KO	11
(Retained World lightweight title)			
6 July Flash Gallego, Panama City		KO	5
2 Sept. Hector Matta, San Juan	W		10
10 Oct. Alberto Vanegas, Panama City		KO	1
31 Oct. Jose Vasquez, San Jose		KO	2
21 Dec. Masataka Takavama, San Jose		KO	1
(Retained World lightweight title)			

1975

15 Feb. Andres Salgado, Panama City		KO	1
2 Mar. Ray Lampkin, Panama City		KO	14
(Retained World lightweight title)			
3 June Jose Peterson, Miami Beach		KO	1
2 Aug. Pedro Mendoza, Managua		KO	1
13 Sept. Alirio Acuna, Chitre		KO	3
30 Sept. Edwin Viruet, Uniondale	W		10
14 Dec. Leonico Ortiz, San Juan		KO	15
(Retained World lightweight title)			

1976

4 May Saoul Mamby, Miami Beach	W		10
22 May Lou Bizzaro, Erie		KO	14
(Retained World lightweight title)			
31 July Emilliano Villa, Panama City		KO	9
15 Oct. Alvaro Rojas, Hollywood, Florida		KO	1
(Retained World lightweight title)			

1977

29 Jan. Vilomar Fernandez, Miami Beach		KO	13
(Retained World lightweight title)			
16 May Javier Muniz, Landover	W		10
6 Aug. Bernandro Diaz, Panama City		KO	1
17 Sept. Edwin Viruet, Philadelphia	W		15
(Retained World lightweight title)			

1978

21 Jan. Esteban DeJesus, Las Vegas		KO	12
(Retained World lightweight title)			
27 Apr. Adolph Viruet, New York	W		10
1 Sept. Ezequiel Obando, Panama City		KO	2
8 Dec. Monroe Brooke, New York		KO	8

1979

1 Feb. Relinquished World lightweight title			
8 Apr. Jimmy Heair, Las Vegas	W		10
22 June Carlos Palomino, New York	W		10
28 Sept. Zeferino Gonzalez, Las Vegas	W		10

1980

13 Jan. Josef Nsubuga, Las Vegas		KO	4
24 Feb. Wellington Wheatley, Las Vegas		KO	6
20 June Ray Leonard, Montreal	W		15
(Won World welterweight title)			
25 Nov. Ray Leonard, New Orleans		KO	8
(Lost World welterweight title)			

1981

10 June Simon Smith, New York	Exh		3
9 Aug. Nino Gonzalez, Cleveland	W		10
26 Sept. Luigi Minchillo, Las Vegas	W		10

1982

30 Jan. Wilf Benitez, Las Vegas	L	15
(WBA light-middleweight title)		
4 Sept. Kirkland Laing, Detroit	L	10
12 Nov. Jimmy Batten, Miami	W	10

1983

29 Jan. Pipino Ceuvas, Las Vegas	KO	4
16 June. Davey Moore, New York	KO	8
(WBA junior middleweight title)		

Terry Downes
Born: 9 May 1936, Paddington, London, England

1957

9 Apr. Tony Longo, London		KO	1
30 Apr. Jimmy Lynas, London		KO	3
14 May Dick Tiger, London		KO by	5
4 June Alan Dean, London		KO	4
18 June Sammy Hamilton, London		KO	3
25 June John Woolard, London		KO	7
17 Sept. Lew Lazar, London	W		8
1 Oct. Derek Liversidge, London		KO	2
28 Oct. Eddie Phillips, London		KO	3
19 Nov. Les Allen, London	L		8
10 Dec. George Lavery, London		KO	5
19 Dec. Hamouda Bouraoui, London		KO	8

1958

7 Jan. Serge Leveque, London		KO	4
28 Jan. Freddie Cross, London		KO by	6
25 Feb. Dennis Booty, London		KO	3
17 Mar. Ben Salah Fahrat, London		KO	5
16 Apr. Tuzo Portuguez, London	W		8
3 June Pat McAteer, London	W		8
15 July Constant Alcantara, London		KO	3
30 Sept. Phil Edwards, London		KO	13
(Won vacant British middleweight title)			
4 Nov. Mohamed Taibi, London		KO	3
9 Dec. Spider Webb, London		KO by	8

1959

24 Feb. Michel Diouf, London		KO by	5
7 July Andre Davier, London		KO	7
15 Sept. John McCormack, London	LF		8
(Lost British middleweight title)			
2 Nov. John McCormack, London		KO	8
(Retained British middleweight title)			

1960

8 Mar. Carlos Van Neste, London		KO	4
24 Mar. Orlando DePietro, Liverpool		KO	4

9 June Richard Bouchez, Manchester		KO	2
5 July Phil Edwards, London		KO	12
(Retained British middleweight title)			
11 Oct. Joey Giardello, London	W		10

1961

14 Jan. Paul Pender, Boston		KO by	7
(For World middleweight title)			
7 Mar. Willie Green, London		KO	3
2 May Tony Montano, London		KO	5
11 July Paul Pender, London		KO	9
(Won World middleweight title)			

1962

7 Apr. Paul Pender, Boston	L		15
(Lost World middleweight title)			
22 May Don Fullmer, London	W		10
25 Sept. Ray Robinson, London	W		10
13 Nov. Phil Moyer, London		KO	9

1963

5 Mar. Jimmy Beecham, London		KO	9
8 Oct. Rudi Nehring, London		KO	
25 Nov. Mike Pusateri, Manchester		KO	5

1964

28 May Ed Zaremba, Glasgow	W		10
30 Nov. Willie Pastrano, Manchester		KO by	11
(For World light-heavyweight title)			

Marvin Hagler
Born: 23 May 1954, Newark, New Jersey, USA

1973

18 May Terry Ryan, Brockton		KO	2
25 July Sonny Williams, Boston	W		6
8 Aug. Muhammad Smith, Boston		KO	2
6 Oct. Don Wigall, Brockton	W		8
26 Oct. Cove Green, Brockton		KO	4
18 Nov. Cocoa Kid, Brockton		KO	2
7 Dec. Manny Freitas, Portland, Maine		KO	1
18 Dec. James Redford, Boston		KO	4

1974

5 Feb. Bob Harrington, Boston		KO	5
5 Apr. Tracy Morrison, Boston		KO	8
14 May James Redford, Brockton		KO	2
30 May Curtis Phillips, Portland, Maine		KO	5
16 July Robert Williams, Boston		KO	3
13 Aug. Peachy Davis, New Bedford		KO	1
30 Aug. Ray Seales, Boston	W		10
29 Oct. Morris Jordan, New Bedford		KO	4
16 Nov. George Green, Brockton		KO	1

26 Nov. Ray Seales, Seattle	D		10
20 Dec. D. C. Walker, Boston		KO	2

1975

15 Feb. Don Wigfall, Brockton		KO	5
31 Mar. Joey Blair, Boston		KO	2
14 Apr. Jimmy Owens, Boston	W		10
24 May Jimmy Owens, Brockton	WD		6
7 Aug. Jesse Bender, Portland, Maine		KO	1
30 Sept. Lamont Lovelady, Boston		KO	7
20 Dec. Johnny Baldwin, Boston	W		10

1976

13 Jan. Bobby Watts, Philadelphia	L		10
7 Feb. Matt Donovan, Boston		KO	2
9 Mar. Willie Monroe, Philadelphia	L		10
2 June Bob Smith, Taunton		KO	5
3 Aug. D. C. Walker, Providence		KO	6
14 Sept. Eugene Hart, Philadelphia		KO	8
21 Dec. George Davis, Boston		KO	6

1977

15 Feb. Willie Monroe, Boston		KO	12
16 Mar. Reginald Ford, Boston		KO	3
10 June Roy Jones, Hartford		KO	3
23 Aug. Willie Monroe, Philadelphia		KO	2
24 Sept. Ray Phillips, Boston		KO	7
15 Oct. Jim Henry, Providence	W		10
26 Nov. Mike Colbert, Boston		KO	12

1978

4 Mar. Kevin Finnegan, Boston		KO	9
7 Apr. Doug Demmings, Los Angeles (US middleweight title)		KO	8
13 May Kevin Finnegan, Boston		KO	7
24 Aug. Bennie Briscoe, Philadelphia (US middleweight title)	W		10
11 Nov. Willie Warren, Boston		KO	7

1979

2 Feb. Ray Seales, Boston		KO	1
12 Mar. Bob Patterson, Providence		KO	3
25 May Jamie Thomas, Portland, Maine		KO	3
30 June Norberto Cabrera, Monte Carlo		KO	8
30 Nov. Vito Antuofermo, Las Vegas (For middleweight title)	D		15

1980

16 Feb. Loucif Hamani, Portland, Maine		KO	2
20 Apr. Bobby Watts, Portland, Maine		KO	2
17 May Marcos Geraldo, Las Vegas	W		10
27 Sept. Alan Minter, London (WBA/WBC middleweight title)		KO	3

1981

17 Jan. Fulgencio Obelmejias, Boston (WBA/WBC middleweight title)	KO	8
13 June Vito Antuofermo, Boston (WBA/WBC middleweight title)	KO	5
3 Oct. Mustafa Hamsho, Rosemont, Illinois (WBA/WBC middleweight title)	KO	11

1982

7 Mar. Caveman Lee, Atlantic City (WBA/WBC middleweight title)	KO	1
31 Oct. Fulgencio Obelmeijas, San Remo (WBA/WBC middleweight title)	KO	5

1983

11 Feb. Tony Sibson, Worcester (WBA/WBC middleweight title)	KO	6
27 May Wilford Scypion, Providence (Recognized USA title)	KO	4

Eder Jofre
Born: 26 March 1936, São Paulo, Brazil

1957

26 Mar. Raul Lopez, São Paulo	KO	5
23 Apr. Raul Lopez, São Paulo	KO	3
5 May Osvaldo Perez, São Paulo	KO	1
7 June Osvaldo Perez, São Paulo	KO	2
14 June J. C. Gonzalez, São Paulo	KO	5
5 July Raul Jamie, São Paulo	W	10
19 July Raul Jamie, São Paulo	W	10
16 Aug. Ernesto Mirando, São Paulo	D	10
6 Sept. Ernesto Miranda, São Paulo	D	10
31 Oct. Luis Jimenez, São Paulo	KO	8
13 Dec. Adolfo Pendas, São Paulo	W	10
22 Dec. Carlos Galisans, Rio de Janeiro	W	8

1958

24 Jan. Avelino Romero, São Paulo	KO	2
7 Mar. Cristobal Galisans, São Paulo	KO	6
14 May Ruben Caceres, Montevideo	D	10
20 June German Escudero, São Paulo	KO	2
29 June German Escudero, Rio de Janeiro	KO	2
18 July Juan C. Acebal, São Paulo	KO	2
9 Aug. Roberto Olmedo, São Paulo	KO	5
12 Sept. Jose Casas, São Paulo	W	10
9 Oct. Jose Casas, São Paulo	KO	5
14 Nov. Jose Smecca, São Paulo	KO	7
12 Dec. Roberto Castro, São Paulo	KO	2

1959

23 Mar. Aniceto Pereyra, São Paulo	W	10
20 Apr. Salustiano Suarez, São Paulo	KO	4

4 June Leo Espinosa, São Paulo	W	10
28 June Angel Bustos, São Paulo	KO	1
19 July Salustiano Suarez, São Paulo	KO	4
31 July Ruben Caceres, São Paulo	KO	7
9 Oct. Angel Bustos, Rio de Janeiro	KO	3
30 Oct. Gianni Zuddas, São Paulo	W	10
12 Dec. Danny Kid, São Paulo	W	10

1960

19 Feb. Ernesto Miranda, São Paulo	W	15
(Won South American bantamweight title)		
10 June Ernesto Miranda, São Paulo	KO	3
(Retained South American bantamweight title)		
15 July Claudio Barrientos, São Paulo	KO	8
18 Aug. Jose Medel, Los Angeles	KO	10
30 Sept. Ricardo Moreno, São Paulo	KO	6
18 Nov. Eloy Sanchez, Los Angeles	KO	6
(Won vacant NBA bantamweight title)		
16 Dec. Billy Peacock, São Paulo	KO	2

1961

25 Mar. Piero Rollo, Rio de Janeiro	KO	10
(Won vacant World bantamweight title)		
18 Apr. Sugar Ray, São Paulo	KO	2
26 July Sadao Yaoita, São Paulo	KO	10
19 Aug. Ramon Arias, Caracas	KO	7
(Retained World bantamweight title)		
6 Dec. Fernando Soto, São Paulo	KO	8

1962

18 Jan. Johnny Caldwell, São Paulo	KO	10
(Retained World bantamweight title)		
4 May Herman Marquez, San Francisco	KO	10
(Retained World bantamweight title)		
11 Sept. Jose Medel, São Paulo	KO	6
(Retained World bantamweight title)		

1963

4 Apr. Katsutoshi Aoki, Tokyo	KO	3
(Retained World bantamweight title)		
18 May Johnny Jamito, Manila	KO	12
(Retained World bantamweight title)		

1964

27 Nov. Bernardo Caraballo, Bogota	KO	7

1965

17 May Fighting Harada, Nagoya	L	15
(Lost World bantamweight title)		
5 Nov. Manny Elias, São Paulo	D	10

1966

1 June Fighting Harada, Tokyo	L	15
(For World bantamweight title)		

1976
2 Jan. Announced retirement.

1968
(Inactive)

1969

27 Aug. Rudy Corona, São Paulo	KO	6

1970

30 Jan. Nevio Carbi, São Paulo	W	10
29 May Manny Elias, São Paulo	W	10
25 Sept. Roberto Wong, São Paulo	KO	3
7 Nov. Giovanni Girgenti, São Paulo	W	10

1971

26 Mar. Jerry Stokes, São Paulo	KO	2
9 June Domenico Chiloiro, São Paulo	W	10
10 Sept. Terry Jurnao, São Paulo	W	10
29 Oct. Robert Porcel, São Paulo	KO	2

1972

24 Mar. Guillermo Morales, São Paulo	KO	6
28 Apr. Felix Figueroa, São Paulo	W	10
30 June Jose Bisbal, São Paulo	KO	2
18 Aug. Shig Fukuyama, São Paulo	KO	9
29 Sept. Djiemei Belhadf, São Paulo	KO	3

1973

5 May Jose Legra, Brasilia	W	15
(Won World featherweight title)		
21 July Godfrey Stevens, São Paulo	KO	4
25 Aug. Frankie Crawford, Bauru	W	10
21 Oct. Vicente Saldivar, Salvador	KO	4
(Retained World featherweight title)		

1974
Stripped of World featherweight title.

1975

3 Jan. Filiberto Herrera, Jundiai	W	10

1976

24 Feb. Enzo Farinelli, Porto Alegre	KO	4
1 May Michael Lefebvre, Brasilia	KO	3
29 May Pasquale Morbitelli, São Paulo	KO	4
2 June Gitanio Jimenez, São Paulo	W	10
14 Aug. Juan A. Lopez, São Paulo	W	10

5 Oct. Famoso Gomez, São Paulo	W	12

Ingemar Johansson
Born: 16 October 1932, Gothenburg, Sweden

1952

5 Dec. Robert Masson, Gothenburg	KO	4

1953

7 Feb. Emil Bentz, Gothenburg	KO	2
6 Mar. Lloyd Barnett, Gothenburg	W	6
12 Mar. Erik Jensen, Copenhagen	W	6
8 Dec. Ray degli Innocenti, Gothenburg	KO	2

1954

5 Nov. Werner Wiegand, Stockholm	KO	5

1955

5 Jan. Ansel Adams, Gothenburg	W	8
13 Feb. Kurt Schiegl, Stockholm	KO	5
5 Mar. Aldo Pellegrini, Gothenburg	WF	5
3 Apr. Uber Baccilieri, Stockholm	W	8
12 June Gunter Nurnberg, Dortmund	KO	7
28 Aug. Hein Ten Hoff, Gothenburg	KO	1

1956

24 Feb. Joe Bygraves, Gothenburg	W	10
15 Apr. Hans Friedrich, Stockholm	W	10
30 Sept. Francesco Cavicchi, Bologna	KO	13
(Won European heavyweight title)		
28 Dec. Peter Bates, Gothenburg	KO	2

1957

19 May Henry Cooper, Stockholm	KO	5
(Retained European heavyweight title)		
13 Dec. Archie McBride, Gothenburg	W	10

1958

21 Feb. Joe Erskine, Gothenburg	KO	13
(Retained European heavyweight title)		
13 July Heinz Neuhaus, Gothenburg	KO	4
14 Sept. Eddie Machen, Gothenburg	KO	1

1959

26 June Floyd Patterson, New York	KO	3
(Won World heavyweight title)		

1960

20 June Floyd Patterson, New York	KO by	5
(Lost World heavyweight title)		

1961

13 Mar. Floyd Patterson, Miami Beach	KO by	6
(For World heavyweight title)		

1962

9 Feb. Joe Bygraves, Gothenburg	KO	7
15 Apr. Wim Snoek, Stockholm	KO	5
17 June Dick Richardson, Gothenburg	KO	8
(Regained European heavyweight title)		

1963

21 Apr. Brian London, Stockholm	W		12

Sugar Ray Leonard
Born: 17 May 1956, Wilmington, North Carolina, USA

1977

5 Feb. Luis Vega, Baltimore	W	6
14 May Willie Rodriguez, Baltimore	W	6
10 June Vinnie DeBarros, Hartford	KO	3
24 Sept. Frank Santore, Baltimore	KO	5
5 Nov. Augustin Estrada, Las Vegas	KO	5
17 Dec. Hector Diaz, Washington DC	KO	2

1978

4 Feb. Rocky Ramon, Baltimore	W	8
1 Mar. Art McKnight, Dayton	KO	7
19 Mar. Javier Muniz, New Haven	KO	1
13 Apr. Bobby Haymon, Landover	KO	3
13 May Randy Milton, Utica	KO	8
3 June Rafael Rodriguez, Baltimore	W	10
18 July Dick Eckland, Boston	W	10
9 Sept Floyd Mayweather, Providence	KO	9
6 Oct. Randy Shields, Baltimore	W	10
3 Nov. Bernardo Prada, Portland, Maine	W	10
9 Dec. Armando Muniz, Springfield	KO	6

1979

11 Jan. Johnny Gant, Landover	KO	8
11 Feb. Fernand Marcotte, Miami Beach	KO	8
24 Mar. Daniel Gonzales, Tucson	KO	1
21 Apr. Adolfo Viruet, Las Vegas	W	10
20 May Marcos Geraldo, New Orleans	W	10
24 June Tony Chiaverini, Las Vegas	KO	4
12 Aug. Pete Ranzany, Las Vegas	KO	4
(Won NABF welterweight title)		
28 Sept. Andy Price, Las Vegas	KO	1
(Retained NABF welterweight title)		
30 Nov. Wilfred Benitez, Las Vegas	KO	15
(Won World welterweight title)		

1980

31 Mar. Dave (Boy) Green, Landover	KO	4
(Retained World welterweight title)		
20 June Roberto Duran, Montreal	L	15
(Lost World welterweight title)		
25 Nov. Roberto Duran, New Orleans	KO	8
(Regained World welterweight title)		

1981

28 Mar. Larry Bonds, Syracuse	KO	10
(Retained World welterweight title)		
25 June Avub Kalule, Houston	KO	9
(Won World junior middleweight title)		
16 Sept. Thomas Hearns, Las Vegas	KO	14
(Retained World welterweight title)		

1982

15 Feb. Bruce Finch, Reno	KO	3

Ted Kid Lewis
Born: 24 October 1894, London, England

1909

13 Sept. Johnny Sharpe, London	L	6
19 Sept. Joe Lipman, London	W	6
9 Oct. Alf Cohen, London	W	6
30 Oct. George Thomas, London	KO by	1
27 Nov. Pte. Joe Marks, London	W	6
6 Dec. Dick Hart, London	D	6
18 Dec. Jack (Kid) Levene, London	KO	3

1910

8 Jan. Bill Marsh, London	W	6
16 Jan. Alf Jacobs, London	W	6
31 Jan. Jim Brown, London	L	6
13 Feb. George Powell, London	KO	1
27 Feb. Piper Holmes, London	W	6
28 Feb. Gus Marks, London	W	6
15 May Jack (Kid) Levene, London	W	6
22 May Young Morris, London	W	6
29 May Young Sullivan, London	W	6
5 June Joe Madden, London	KO	3
17 July Jack Greenstock, London	D	6
24 July Alf Jacobs, London	W	6
31 July Joe Madden, London	D	6
Sid Venner, London	W	6
Young Smith, London	KO	3
20 Nov. Hughie Doyle, Liverpool	KO by	3

1911

Dick Murray, London	W	6
Bill Marsh, London	W	6
Jack Marks, London	W	6
Alf Jacobs, London	W	6
Joe Jacobs, London	W	6
12 Feb. Young Sullivan, London	L	6
19 Feb. Joe Madden, London	D	6
20 Feb. Jack (Kid) Levene, London	W	6
29 Mar. Charlie Smith, London	KO	4
5 Apr. Jack Ginnion, London	KO	3
9 Apr. Joe Ross, London	W	6

9 Apr. Nat Brooks, London	W		10
(Won 116 lb competition)			
22 Apr. Jack Fisher, London	L		6
23 Apr. Pte. Joe Marks, London		KO	7
24 Apr. Young Hyams, London	W		6
26 Apr. Tom Chinnery, London	W		6
30 Apr. Nat Brooks, London	L		15
1 May Sid Venner, London	W		6
24 May Jack English, London		KO	3
Young Klein, London		KO	3
18 June Dick Murray, London	W		6
Joe Madden, London	W		10
Alf Small, London		KO	12
23 July George Marks, London	W		6
13 Aug. Curley Hume, London	W		6
27 Aug. Jack Harbour, London	WF		3
2 Sept. Fred Halsband, London	D		6
4 Sept. Walter Marshall, London		KO	3
10 Sept. Tom Perkins, London	D		6
17 Sept. Billy Smith, London		KO	4
20 Sept. Ted O'Neill, London		KO	5
30 Sept. Tom Perkins, London	W		6
7 Oct. Lew Cohen, London	Exh		3
9 Oct. Harry Ray, London	W		6
10 Oct. Tom Perkins, London	D		6
18 Oct. Tom Perkins, London	W		6
21 Oct. Alf Small, London	W		6
23 Oct. Jack Bunner, London	W		10
28 Oct. Tom Perkins, London	W		10
9 Nov. Jim Hales, London	W		6
18 Nov. Kid Olds, London	W		6
27 Nov. Billy Griggs, London		KO	1
2 Dec. Frank Warner, London	W		6
4 Dec. Jimmy Butler, London		KO	2
9 Dec. Billy Taylor, London	W		6
16 Dec. Jim Shires, London	W		10
17 Dec. Frank Fay, London	W		6
24 Dec. Eddie Foy, London	W		6

1912

6 Jan. Jewey Murray, London		KO	1
20 Jan. Harry Wilson, London	W		10
10 Feb. Tom Mack, London	W		6
17 Feb. Duke Lynch, London	W		10
24 Feb. Alf Mitchell, London	W		10
2 Mar. George Buswell, London	W		10
16 Mar. Alan Porter, London	W		10
1 Apr. Duke Lynch, London		KO by	1
3 Apr. Leon Truffler, Paris	W		10
6 Apr. Gus Venn, London		KO	7
27 Apr. Gus Venn, London	W		10
18 May Jim Shires, London		KO	2
25 May Leon Truffler, London	W		10
10 June Darkey Haley, London	W		6
22 June George Ruddick, London	W		10

6 July Seaman Arthur Hayes, London	W		10
10 Aug. Young Brooks, London	L		10
31 Aug. Fred Halsband, London	L		10
14 Sept. Sam Russell, London	W		10
Tom Clifford	W		6
Fred Blake	W		6
5 Oct. Con Houghton, London	LF		6
Tom Allen	W		10
Jim Lloyd		KO	5
24 Oct. Jim Campbell, London	W		6
Jack Chinnery		KO	3
9 Nov. Fred Halsband, London	W		10
Alf Small		KO	5
30 Nov. George Ruddick, London	W		12
2 Dec. Jack Harrison, London		KO	3
Darkey Harris		KO	3
Jack Chinnery	W		6
22 Dec. Harry Berry, London	W		15

1913

2 Jan. Jim Lloyd, Liverpool	W		10
4 Jan. George Buswell, Liverpool		KO	14
16 Jan. Nat Williams, Liverpool	D		15
27 Jan. Johnny Condon, London	W		20
3 Mar. Johnny Condon, London	W		20
7 Apr. Young Brooks, London	W		15
2 June Joe Starmer, London	W		15
19 July Harry Stirling, London		KO	7
26 July Duke Lynch, London	W		20
23 Aug. Harry Stirling, London	W		20
15 Sept. Bernard Quendreaux, London		KO	10
6 Oct. Alec Lambert, London		KO	17
(Won British featherweight title)			

1914

14 Jan. George Buswell, London		KO	2
2 Feb. Paul Til, London	WF		12
(Won vacant European featherweight title)			
14 Mar. Harry Berry, London		KO	3
18 Mar. Ted Saunders, Coventry		KO	6
30 May Herb McCoy, Sydney	W		20
12 June Hughie Mehegan, Sydney	W		20
26 June Young Shugrue, Sydney	W		20
11 July Herb McCoy, Melbourne	L		20
1 Aug. Bobby Moore, Melbourne	W		20
9 Nov. Phil Bloom, New York	ND		10
25 Dec. Young Jack O'Brien, Philadelphia	ND		6

1915

1 Jan. Willie Moore, Philadelphia	ND		6
10 Mar. Frankie Mack, Havana	W		20
26 Mar. Jack Britton, New York	ND		10
6 Apr. Harry Lenny, New York	ND		10
16 Apr. Johnny Lore, Montreal	ND		10
30 Apr. Johnny Lustig, Montreal	ND		10

9 June Kid Graves, New York	ND		10
23 June Johnny Marto, New York	ND		10
25 June Mike Mazie, New York	ND		10
21 July Charley White, New York	ND		10
3 Aug. Mike Glover, Boston	W		12
11 Aug. Kid Curley, Buffalo	ND		10
17 Aug. Fighting Zunner, Buffalo	ND		10
31 Aug. Jack Britton, Boston	W		12
(Won World welterweight title)			
27 Sept. Jack Britton, Boston	W		12
(Retained World welterweight title)			
18 Oct. Willie Moore, Philadelphia	ND		6
26 Oct. Joe Mandot, Boston	W		12
2 Nov. Milburn Saylor, Boston	W		12
23 Nov. Jimmy Duffy, Boston		KO	1
30 Nov. Mike Glover, Boston	L		12
28 Dec. Willie Ritchie, New York	ND		10

1916

1 Jan. Kayo Brennan, Buffalo	ND		10
17 Jan. Kid Graves, Milwaukee	ND		10
26 Jan. Jack Britton, Buffalo	ND		10
5 Feb. Marty Farrell, Philadelphia	ND		6
15 Feb. Jack Britton, Brooklyn	ND		10
21 Feb. Jimmy Duffy, Buffalo	ND		10
24 Feb. Harry Trendall, St Louis		KO	7
1 Mar. Harry Stone, New Orleans	W		20
19 Apr. Jake Abel, Chattanooga	W		8
24 Apr. Jack Britton, New Orleans	L		20
(Lost World welterweight title)			
18 May Mike Gibbons, New York	ND		10
24 May Eddie Moha, Dayton, Ohio		KO	13
13 June Mike Glover, Boston	W		12
17 Oct. Jack Britton, Boston	L		12
24 Oct. Young Denny, St Louis	ND		12
14 Nov. Jack Britton, Boston	D		12
23 Nov. Johnny Griffiths, Cleveland	ND		10
21 Dec. Johnny Griffiths, Cleveland	ND		10

1917

29 Jan. Willie Beecher, New York	ND		10
31 Jan. Sam Robideaux, Providence	W		15
6 Feb. Kid Graves, New York		KO	9
26 Feb. Johnny Griffiths, Akron	ND		12
19 Mar. Willie Moore, New York		KO	1
26 Mar. Jack Britton, Cincinnati	ND		10
4 Apr. Jim Coffey, New York		KO	1
12 Apr. Billy Weeks, Springfield, Ohio		KO	12
28 Apr. Johnny Griffiths, Columbus	ND		12
4 May Jimmy O'Hagen, New York		KO	2
19 May Jack Britton, Toronto	ND		10
22 May Joe Egan, Boston	W		12
24 May Mike O'Dowd, New York	ND		10
6 June Jack Britton, St Louis	ND		10
14 June Jack Britton, New York	ND		10

25 June, Jack Britton, Dayton	W		20
(Regained World welterweight title)			
4 July Johnny Griffiths, Akron	ND		15
(Retained World welterweight title)			
7 Aug. Jimmy O'Hagen, Saratoga	ND		10
17 Aug. Mike O'Dowd, New York	ND		10
28 Aug. Mike O'Dowd, Boston	L		12
31 Aug. Albert Badoud, New York		KO	1
3 Sept. Soldier Bartfield, Buffalo	ND		10
11 Sept. Soldier Bartfield, Rochester	ND		10
14 Sept. Jimmy O'Hagen, New York	ND		10
15 Sept. Italian Joe Gans, Brooklyn	ND		10
22 Sept. Frank Carbone, Brooklyn	ND		10
24 Oct. Battling Ortega, Emeryville	D		4
13 Nov. Johnny McCarthy, San Francisco	W		4
17 Dec. Bryan Downey, Columbus	ND		12

1918

14 Jan. Soldier Bartfield, Columbus	ND		12
23 Jan. Soldier Bartfield, Toronto	ND		10
4 Feb. Johnny Tillman, Philadelphia	ND		6
18 Feb. Jimmy Duffy, Toledo, Ohio		KO	1
25 Feb. Soldier Bartfield, Philadelphia	ND		6
26 Feb. Willie Langford, Buffalo	ND		10
6 Mar. Jack Britton, Atlanta	ND		10
16 Apr. Joe Egan, Milwaukee	ND		10
2 May Jack Britton, Scranton	ND		10
17 May Johnny Tillman, Denver	W		20
(Retained World welterweight title)			
24 May Jack Britton, New York	ND		6
20 June Jack Britton, New York	ND		6
25 June Tommy Robson, Boston	W		12
4 July Johnny Griffiths, Akron	ND		20
(Retained World welterweight title)			
3 Aug. Tommy Robson, Boston	W		12
17 Aug. Walter Mohr, Jersey City	ND		8
25 Sept. Benny Leonard, Newark	ND		8

1919

1 Jan. Bryan Downey, Columbus	ND		12
15 Jan. George Rivet, Montreal	ND		10
10 Mar. Johnny Griffiths, Memphis	ND		8
17 Mar. Jack Britton, Canton		KO by	9
(Lost World welterweight title)			
14 July Steve Latzo, Philadelphia	ND		6
28 July Jack Britton, Jersey City	ND		8
4 Aug. Steve Latzo, Philadelphia	ND		6
1 Sept. Mike O'Dowd, Syracuse	ND		10
11 Oct. K. O'Laughlin, Portland, Maine		KO	1
16 Oct. Jimmy McCabe, Atlantic City		KO	1
29 Oct. Jake Abel, Atlanta, Georgia	ND		10
26 Dec. Matt Wells, London		KO	12

1920

13 Jan. Frank Moody, Manchester	KO	1
14 Feb. Maurice Prunter, Paris	KO	9
28 Feb. Jerry Shea, Mountain Ash	KO	1
4 Mar. Gus Platts, Sheffield	KO	18
11 Mar. Johnny Bee, London	KO	4
(Won British welterweight title)		
5 Apr. Kid Doyle, Liverpool	KO	11
30 Apr. Kid Doyle, London	KO	5
9 June Johnny Basham, London	KO	9
(Retained British welterweight title)		
(Won European welterweight title)		
23 Sept. Mike O'Dowd, Jersey City	ND	12
12 Oct. Marcel Thomas, Jersey City	ND	8
19 Nov. Johnny Basham, London	KO	19
(Retained British and European welterweight titles)		
Dec. Relinquished European welterweight title		

1921

7 Feb. Jack Britton, New York	L	15
(For World welterweight title)		
14 Mar. Jack Perry, Detroit	ND	10
8 Apr. Nate Siegal, Boston	L	10
13 Apr. Augie Ratner, New York	L	15
27 June Jack Bloomfield, London	W	20
(Won British middleweight title)		
21 Sept. Ernie Barrieau, Toronto	KO	10
14 Oct. Johnny Basham, London	KO	12
(Retained British middleweight title)		
(Won European middleweight title)		
17 Nov. Noel (Boy) McCormick, London	KO	14
(Claimed British light-heavyweight title)		

1922

16 Feb. Tom Gummer, Brighton	KO	1
11 May Georges Carpentier, London	KO by	1
(For World light-heavyweight title)		
19 June Frankie Burns, London	KO	11
(Won British Empire middleweight title)		
4 Sept. Marcel Thomas, London	KO	4
20 Nov. Roland Todd, London	W	20
(Retained British Empire and European middleweight titles)		

1923

15 Feb. Roland Todd, London	L	20
(Lost British Empire and European middleweight titles)		
30 July Augie Ratner, London	L	20
4 Oct. Frankie Burns, London	W	20
8 Nov. Fred Archer, London	W	20
26 Dec. Fred Davies, London	W	20

1924

28 Jan. Sid Pape, Bradford	KO	2
12 Feb. Bruno Frattini, Milan	KO	17
18 Mar. Francis Charles, Paris	W	15
5 Apr. Chic Nelson, Hamburg	D	15
12 Apr. Eric Milenz, Berlin	KO	8
1 June Piet Hobin, Paris	D	20
3 July Johnny Brown, London	W	20
(Retained British welterweight title)		
(Won British Empire welterweight title)		
26 Nov. Tommy Milligan, Edinburgh	L	20
(Lost British and Empire welterweight title)		

1925

22 Jan. Francis Charles, London	W	20
19 Mar. Tommy Milligan, London	LF	5
10 July Bob Sage, Hollywood, California	W	10
8 Oct. Marcel Thuru, London	LF	1
8 Nov. Simon Rosman, London	LF	8
27 Nov. Len Johnson, Manchester	KO by	9

1926

7 Mar. Billy Pritchard, London	KO	10
21 Mar. Billy Mattick, London	WF	5

1927

4 Aug. Joe Green, London	KO	4
14 Aug. Jim Carr, London	KO	3
28 Aug. Nol Steenhorst, London	KO	9
11 Sept. Ted Coveney, London	KO	6
2 Oct. Ansemes, London	KO	1
16 Oct. Joe Rolfe, London	KO	11
3 Dec. Alec Storbeck, Johannesburg	KO	1

1928

7 Jan. Johnny Squires, Johannesburg	D	15
23 July Maxie Rosenbloom, Long Island City	LF	6
17 Dec. Charley Belanger, Toronto	KO by	1

1929

13 Dec. Johnny Basham, London	KO	3

Joe Louis
Born: 13 May 1914, Lafayette, Alabama, USA

1934

4 July Jack Kracken, Chicago	KO	1
11 July Willie Davis, Chicago	KO	3
29 July Larry Udell, Chicago	KO	2
13 Aug. Jack Kranz, Chicago	W	8
27 Aug. Buck Everett, Chicago	KO	2
11 Sept. Alex Borchuk, Detroit	KO	4
25 Sept. Adolph Wiater, Chicago	W	10
24 Oct. Art Sykes, Chicago	KO	8

30 Oct. Jack O'Dowd, Detroit		KO	2
14 Nov. Stanley Poreda, Chicago		KO	1
30 Nov. Charley Massera, Chicago		KO	3
14 Dec. Lee Ramage, Chicago		KO	8

1935

4 Jan. Patsy Perroni, Detroit	W		10
11 Jan Hans Birkie, Pittsburgh		KO	10
21 Feb. Lee Ramage, Los Angeles		KO	2
8 Mar. Donald (Reds) Barry, San Francisco		KO	3
29 Mar. Natie Brown, Detroit	W		10
12 Apr. Roy Lazer, Chicago		KO	3
22 Apr. Biff Benton, Dayton		KO	2
27 Apr. Roscoe Toles, Flint		KO	6
3 May Willie Davis, Peoria		KO	2
7 May Gene Stanton, Kalamazoo		KO	3
25 June Primo Carnera, New York		KO	6
7 Aug. King Levinsky, Chicago		KO	1
24 Sept. Max Baer, New York		KO	4
14 Dec. Paulino Uzcudun, New York		KO	4

1936

17 Jan. Charley Retzlaff, Chicago		KO	1
19 June Max Schmeling, New York		KO by	12
18 Aug. Jack Sharkey, New York		KO	3
22 Sept. Al Ettore, Philadelphia		KO	5
9 Oct. Jorge Brescia, New York		KO	3
14 Oct. Willie Davis, South Bend	Exh	KO	3
14 Oct. K. O. Brown, South Bend	Exh	KO	3
20 Nov. Paul Williams, New Orleans	Exh	KO	2
20 Nov. Tom Jones, New Orleans	Exh	KO	3
14 Dec. Eddie Simms, Cleveland		KO	1

1937

11 Jan. Stanley Ketchell, Buffalo	Exh	KO	2
29 Jan. Bob Pastor, New York	W		10
17 Feb. Natie Brown, Kansas City		KO	4
22 June James J. Braddock, Chicago		KO	8
(Won World heavyweight title)			
30 Aug. Tommy Farr, New York	W		15
(Retained World heavyweight title)			

1938

23 Feb. Nathan Mann, New York		KO	3
(Retained World heavyweight title)			
1 Apr. Harry Thomas, Chicago		KO	5
(Retained World heavyweight title)			
22 June Max Schmeling, New York		KO	1
(Retained World heavyweight title)			

1939

25 Jan. John Henry Lewis, New York		KO	1
(Retained World heavyweight title)			
17 Apr. Jack Roper, Los Angeles		KO	1
(Retained World heavyweight title)			

"Two hour tone"

28 June Tony Galento, New York		KO	4
(Retained World heavyweight title)			
20 Sept. Bob Pastor, Detroit		KO	11
(Retained World heavyweight title)			

1940
9 Feb. Arturo Godoy, New York	W		15
(Retained World heavyweight title)			
29 Mar. Johnny Paychek, New York		KO	2
(Retained World heavyweight title)			
20 June Arturo Godoy, New York		KO	8
(Retained World heavyweight title)			
16 Dec. Al McCoy, Boston		KO	6
(Retained World heavyweight title)			

1941
31 Jan. Red Burman, New York		KO	5
(Retained World heavyweight title)			
17 Feb. Gus Dorazio, Philadelphia		KO	2
(Retained World heavyweight title)			
21 Mar. Abe Simon, Detroit		KO	13
(Retained World heavyweight title)			
8 Apr. Tony Musto, St Louis		KO	9
(Retained World heavyweight title)			
23 May Buddy Baer, Washington DC	WD		7
(Retained World heavyweight title)			
18 June Billy Conn, New York		KO	13
(Retained World heavyweight title)			
11 July Jim Robinson, Minneapolis	Exh	KO	1
29 Sept. Lou Nova, New York		KO	6
(Retained World heavyweight title)			
25 Nov. George Giambastiani, Los Angeles	Exh		4

1942
9 Jan. Buddy Baer, New York		KO	1
(Retained World heavyweight title)			
27 Mar. Abe Simon, New York		KO	6
(Retained World heavyweight title)			
5 June George Nicholson, Fort Hamilton	Exh		3

1943
(Inactive)

1944
3 Nov. Johnny Demson, Detroit	Exh	KO	2
6 Nov. Charley Crump, Baltimore	Exh		3
9 Nov. Dee Amos, Hartford	Exh		3
13 Nov. Jimmy Bell, Washington DC	Exh		3
14 Nov. Johnny Davis, Buffalo	Exh	KO	1
15 Nov Dee Amos, Elizabeth	Exh		3
17 Nov. Dee Amos, Camden	Exh		3
24 Nov. Dan Merritt, Chicago	Exh		3

1945

15 Nov. Sugar Lip Anderson, San Francisco	Exh	2
15 Nov. Big Boy Brown, San Francisco	Exh	2
29 Nov. Big Boy Brown, Sacramento	Exh	2
29 Nov. Bobby Lee, Sacramento	Exh	2
10 Dec. Bob Frazier, Victoria	Exh	3
11 Dec. Big Boy Brown, Portland	Exh	2
11 Dec. Dave Johnson, Portland	Exh	2
12 Dec. Big Boy Brown, Eugene	Exh	3
13 Dec. Big Boy Brown, Vancouver	Exh	3

1946

19 June, Billy Conn, New York		KO	8
(Retained World heavyweight title)			
18 Sept. Tami Mauriello, New York		KO	1
(Retained World heavyweight title)			
11 Nov. Cleo Everett, Honolulu	Exh		4
11 Nov. Wayne Powell, Honolulu	Exh		2
25 Nov. Perk Daniels, Mexicali	Exh		4

1947

7 Feb. Arturo Godoy, Mexico City	Exh		10
5 Dec. Jersey Joe Walcott, New York	W		15
(Retained World heavyweight title)			

1948

25 June Jersey Joe Walcott, New York		KO	11
(Retained World heavyweight title)			

1949

1 Mar. Announced retirement

1950

27 Sept. Ezzard Charles, New York	L	15
(World heavyweight title)		
29 Nov. Cesar Brion, New York	W	10

1951

3 Jan. Freddie Beshore, Detroit		KO	4
7 Feb. Omelio Agramonte, Miami	W		10
23 Feb. Andy Walker, San Francisco		KO	10
2 May Omelio Agramonte, Detroit	W		10
15 June Lee Savold, New York		KO	6
1 Aug. Cesar Brion, San Francisco	W		10
15 Aug. Jimmy Bivins, Baltimore	W		10
26 Oct. Rocky Marciano, New York		KO by	8

Jock McAvoy
Born: 1908, Burnley, Lancashire, England

1928

Knockouts: Billy Longworth, 2; Bert Hildich, 6; Tommy Walsh, 3

1929

Knockouts: Teddy Hay, 9; Teddy Cox, 7; Frank Ormond, 1; Jack Ogden, 10; Bob Ennis, 1; Basher Bargh, 3; Lud Gresvig, 2; Seaman Douglas, 6; Jack Jukes, 4; Billy Lee, 2; J. L. Jones, 2; Jack Ogden, 3; Billy Horner, 4; Andy Ross, 5; Marine Davis, 5; Dia Beynon, 3. Won: Shocker Bowman, 10; Griff Williams, 10

1930

Knockouts: Jack Wilkinson, 2; Jim Johnston, 1; Sid Aldridge, 4; Jack Harrison, 4; Patsy Flynn, 3; Fred Oldfield, 8; Shocker Bowman, 3; Johnny Seamarks, 2; Jim Pearson, 7; Bill Green, 13; Billy Delahaye, 2; Eddie Strawer, 6. Won: Fred Oldfield, 12; Framer Jackson, 12; Fred Blything, 15; Eddie Strawer, 10; Joe Rostron, 15; Billy Chew, 10; George Porter, 15. Lost: Jim Pearson, 12; Joe Rostron, 12

1931

Knockouts: Jack Bottomley, 1; Charlie Keeling, 2; Con Van Lewen, 4; Tate Evans, 14; Jack O'Brien, 3; Dick Burt, 7; Sonny Doke, 3. Won: Sonny Doke, 15; Jim Cox, 10; Charlie McDonald, 15; Fred Shaw, 15; Joe Lowther, 15; Jim Cox, 12; Jack Ogden, 10; Jim Cox, 15

1932

2 Feb. Seaman Harvey, Manchester	W		15
1 Mar. Jack Etienne, Manchester	W		15
21 Mar. Len Harvey, Manchester	L		15
9 May Edwin John, Manchester		KO	6
21 May Bill Hood, Royton		KO	2
14 June Sandy McKenzie, Royton		KO	1
22 June Billy Thomas, Blackpool		KO	3
4 July Carmelo Candel, London	W		10
18 July Jack Casey, Manchester	LF		14
1 Aug. Tom Benjamin, Blackpool		KO	5
31 Aug. Geo. Brown, Morecambe	W		15
9 Sept. Billy Roberts, Royton		KO	3
22 Sept. Phil Green, Rawenstall		KO	2
12 Oct. Tommy Moore, Morecambe		KO	3
28 Oct. Ted Coveney, Blackburn		KO	4
26 Nov. Mihail Fulea, Manchester		KO	4
7 Dec. Hans Seifried, London	W		10

Knockouts: Billy Adair, 2; Jack Marshall, 2; Alf Pagazzano, 3; Jerry Daley, 3; Joe Lowther, 9; Red Pullen, 1. Won: Joe Lowther, 15; Jack Hyams, 7 (Dis). Lost: Paul Baguire, 5 (foul)

1933

30 Jan. Glen Moody, Manchester		KO	6
13 Feb. Les Ward, Royton		KO	6
20 Feb. Red Pullen, Blackburn		KO	3
27 Feb. Leonard Steyaert, Manchester		KO	8
10 Apr. Len Harvey, Manchester	W		15
14 May Jack Hyams, London	W		15
12 June Oddone Piazza, London	W		10
21 Aug. Geo. Brown, Manchester	W		15
9 Oct. Archie Sexton, Manchester		KO	10

18 Nov. Jack Forster, Royton	W		12

1934

29 Jan. Eddie Pierce, Manchester	W		12
28 Feb. Al Burke, London		KO	5
17 Mar. Eddie Maguire, Manchester		KO	2
30 Apr. Ernie Simmons, Manchester	W		12
18 June Teddy Philips, Manchester		KO	8
13 Aug. Charlie Parkin, Manchester		KO	1
8 Oct. Jack Etienne, Manchester		KO	1
9 Oct. Sid Parkens, London		KO	1
3 Dec. Kid Tunero, Manchester		KO	7

1935

14 Jan. Marcel Thil, Paris	L		15
8 Apr. Garcia Luch, Manchester	W		12
4 June Al Burke, Mancheser (title)	W		15
7 Oct. Marcel Lauriot, Manchester	W		12
29 Nov. Al McCoy, New York	W		10
20 Dec. Babe Risko, New York		KO	1

1936

17 Feb. Jimmy Smith, New York City		KO	2
24 Feb. Anson Green, Philadelphia	W		10
13 Mar. John Henry Lewis, New York City	L		15
(Light heavyweight title)			
23 Apr. Jack Petersen, London	L		15
14 Sept. Albert Barjolin, Manchester		KO	2
26 Oct. Bill Wainwright, Manchester		KO	3
23 Nov. Bob Simkins, Manchester		KO	3
1 Dec. Arenus de Boer, Sheffield	W		12

1937

8 Mar. Cheo Morejon, Manchester	W		12
27 Apr. Eddie Phillips, London		KO	14
3 May Dai Jones, Bristol	W		10
25 Oct. Jack Hyams, Manchester		KO	11
23 Nov. Alban Mulrooney, Hanley		KO	3
6 Dec. Vasile Serbanesco, Manchester		KO	4

1938

24 Jan. Bill Hardy, Leicester		KO	6
28 Feb. Jack Strongbow, Manchester		KO	6
7 Apr. Len Harvey, London	L		15
6 May Marcel Lauriot, Dublin		KO	2
2 Nov. Jack Strongbow, Birmingham		KO	5
21 Nov. Joe Quigley, Derby	W		10
28 Nov. Frank Hough, Manchester		KO	6
6 Dec. Jack Robinson, Leicester		KO	2

1939

20 Feb. Emile Lebriza, Manchester		KO	1
9 Mar. Tino Rolando, Liverpool		KO	9
22 May Ginger Sadd, Manchester	W		15
10 July Len Harvey, London	L		15

5 Aug. Jack Hyams, Manchester   W   10

1940
29 Apr. Jim Berry, Manchester   KO   6
8 Aug. Freddie Mills, Liverpool   L   10
7 Oct. Charley Parkin, Nottingham   KO   6
28 Oct. Eddie Maguire, Nottingham   L   10

1941
        Jack Hyams, Marylebone   W   10
18 Dec. Jim Berry, London   KO   6

1942
23 Feb. Freddie Mills, London   KO by   1

1945
17 July George Howard, London   KO   2
7 Aug. Johnny Clements, Portsmouth   KO   6
15 Sept. Tom Davies, Swansea, Wales   W   8

Rocky Marciano
Born: 1 September 1923, Brockton, Massachusetts, USA

1947
17 Mar. Lee Epperson, Holyoke, Massachusetts   KO   3

1948
12 July Harry Bilazarian, Providence   KO   1
19 July John Edwards, Providence   KO   1
9 Aug. Bobby Quinn, Providence   KO   3
23 Aug. Eddie Ross, Providence   KO   1
30 Aug. Jimmy Weeks, Providence   KO   1
13 Sept. Jerry Jackson, Providence   KO   1
20 Sept. Bill Hardeman, Providence   KO   1
30 Sept. Gil Cardione, Washington, DC   KO   1
4 Oct. Bob Jefferson, Providence   KO   2
29 Nov. Pat Connolly, Providence   KO   1
14 Dec. Gilley Ferron, Philadelphia   KO   2

1949
21 Mar. Johnny Pretzie, Providence   KO   5
28 Mar. Artie Donato, Providence   KO   1
11 Apr. James Walls, Providence   KO   3
2 May Jimmy Evans, Providence   KO   3
23 May Don Mogard, Providence   W   10
18 July Harry Haft, Providence   KO   3
16 Aug. Peter Louthis, New Bedford   KO   3
26 Sept. Tommy DiGiorgio, Providence   KO   4
10 Oct. Ted Lowry, Providence   W   10
7 Nov. Joe Dominic, Providence   KO   2
2 Dec. Pat Richards, New York   KO   2
19 Dec. Phil Muscato, Providence   KO   5

30 Dec. Carmine Vingo, New York   KO   6

1950
24 Mar. Roland LaStarza, New York   W   10
 5 June Eldridge Eatman, Providence   KO   3
10 July Gino Buonvino, Boston   KO   10
18 Sept. Johnny Shkor, Providence   KO   6
13 Nov. Ted Lowry, Providence   W   10
18 Dec. Bill Wilson, Providence   KO   1

1951
29 Jan. Keene Simmons, Providence   KO   8
20 Mar. Harold Mitchell, Hartford   KO   2
26 Mar. Art Henri, Providence   KO   9
30 Apr. Red Applegate, Providence   W   10
12 July Red Layne, New York   KO   6
27 Aug. Freddie Beshore, Boston   KO   4
26 Oct. Joe Louis, New York   KO   8

1952
13 Feb. Lee Savold, Philadelphia   KO   6
21 Apr. Gino Buonvino, Providence   KO   2
12 May Bernie Reynolds, Providence   KO   3
28 July Harry (Kid) Matthews, New York   KO   2
23 Sept. Jersey Joe Walcott, Philadelphia   KO   13
   (Won World heavyweight title)

1953
15 May Jersey Joe Walcott, Chicago   KO   1
   (Retained World heavyweight title)
24 Sept. Roland LaStarza, New York   KO   11
   (Retained World heavyweight title)

1954
17 June Ezzard Charles, New York   W   15
   (Retained world heavyweight title)
17 Sept. Ezzard Charles, New York   KO   8
   (Retained World heavyweight title)

1955
16 May Don Cockell, San Francisco   KO   9
   (Retained World heavyweight title)
21 Sept. Archie Moore, New York   KO   9
   (Retained World heavyweight title)

Archie Moore
Born: 13 December 1913, Benoit, Mississippi, USA

1935
        Piano Man Jones, Hot Springs   KO   2

1936
31 Jan. Pocohontas Kid, Hot Springs   KO   2
 7 Feb. Dale Richards, Poplar Bluffs   KO   1

18 Feb. Ray Halford, St Louis	KO	3
20 Feb. Willie Harper, St Louis	KO	3
21 Feb. Courtland Sheppard, St Louis	L	6
Kneibert Davidson	KO	2
Ray Brewster	KO	3
Billy Simms	KO	2
Johnny Leggs	KO	1
15 Apr. Peter Urban, Cleveland	KO	6
16 Apr. Frankie Nelson, Cleveland	L	6
4 May Tiger Brown, St Louis	L	6
18 May Thurman Martin, St Louis	W	5
Ferman Burton	KO	1
Billy Simms	KO	1
14 July Murray Allen, Quincy, Illinois	KO	6
Julius Kemp	KO	3
Four H. Posey	KO	6
9 Oct. Sammy Jackson, St Louis	W	6
Dick Putnam	KO	3
8 Dec. Sammy Jackson, St Louis	D	6
Sammy Christin, St Louis	KO	6

1937

5 Jan. Dynamite Payne, St Louis	KO	1
18 Jan. Johnny Davis, Quincy, Illinois	KO	3
2 Feb. Joe Huff, St Louis	KO	2
Murray Allen, Keokuk, Iowa	KO	2
9 Apr. Charley Dawson, Indianapolis	KO	5
23 Apr. Karl Martin, Indianapolis	KO	1
Frank Hatfield	KO	1
Al Dublinsky	KO	1
19 Aug. Deacon Logan, St Louis	KO	3
9 Sept. Sammy Slaughter, Indianapolis	W	10
Sammy Slaughter, Jenkins	W	10
Billy Adams, Cincinnati	L	10
16 Nov. Sammy Christian, St Louis	W	5
Sammy Jackson	KO	8

1938

7 Jan. Carl Lautenschlager, St Louis	KO	2
20 May Jimmy Brent, San Diego	KO	1
27 May Ray Vargas, San Diego	KO	3
24 June Johnny Romero, San Diego	L	10
22 July Johnny Sykes, San Diego	KO	1
5 Aug. Lorenzo Pedro, San Diego	W	10
2 Sept. Johnny Romero, San Diego	KO	8
16 Sept. Frank Rowsey, San Diego	KO	3
27 Sept. Tom Henry, Los Angeles	KO	4
Bobby Yannes	KO	2
22 Nov. Ray Lyle, St Louis	KO	2
8 Dec. 'Irish' Bob Turner, St Louis	KO	2

1939

20 Jan. Jack Moran, St Louis	KO	1
2 Mar. Domenic Ceccarelli, St Louis	KO	1
16 Mar. Marty Simmons, St Louis	W	10

20 Apr. Teddy Yarosz, St Louis	L		10
21 July Jack Coggins, San Diego	NC		8
1 Sept. Jack Coggins, San Diego	W		10
22 Sept. Bobby Seaman, San Diego		KO	7
7 Dec. Honeyboy Jones, St Louis	W		10
29 Dec. Shorty Hogue, San Diego	L		6

1940

30 Mar. Jack McNamee, Melbourne		KO	4
18 Apr. Ron Richards, Sydney		KO	10
9 May Atilio Sabatino, Sydney		KO	5
12 May Joe Delaney, Adelaide		KO	7
2 June Frank Lindsay, Tasmania		KO	4
27 June Fred Henneberry, Sydney		KO	7
11 July Ron Richards, Sydney	W		12
18 Oct. Pancho Ramirez, San Diego		KO	5

1941

17 Jan. Clay Rowan, San Diego		KO	1
31 Jan. Shorty Hogue, San Diego	L		10
21 Feb. Eddie Booker, San Diego	D		10
Freddie Dixon, Phoenix		KO	5

1942

28 Jan. Bobby Britton, Phoenix		KO	3
27 Feb. Guero Martinez, San Diego		KO	2
17 Mar. Jimmy Casino, Oakland		KO	5
30 Oct. Shorty Hogue, San Diego		KO	2
6 Nov. Tabby Romero, San Diego		KO	2
27 Nov. Jack Chase, San Diego	W		10
11 Dec. Eddie Booker, San Diego	D		12

1943

8 May Jack Chase, San Diego	W		15
(Won California middleweight title)			
22 July Big Boy Hogue, San Diego		KO	5
28 July Eddie Cerda, San Diego		KO	3
2 Aug. Jack Chase, San Francisco	L		15
(Lost California middleweight title)			
16 Aug. Aaran (Tiger) Wade San Francisco	L		10
5 Nov. Kid Hermosillo, San Diego		KO	5
26 Nov. Jack Chase, Hollywood	W		10

1944

7 Jan. Amado Rodriguez, San Diego		KO	1
21 Jan. Eddie Booker, Hollywood		KO by	8
24 Mar. Roman Starr, Hollywood		KO	2
21 Apr. Charley Burley, Hollwyood	L		10
19 May Kenny LaSalle, San Diego	W		10
11 Aug. Louie Mays, San Diego		KO	3
18 Aug. Jimmy Hayden, San Diego		KO	5
1 Sept. Battling Monroe, San Diego		KO	6

18 Dec. Nate Bolden, New York   W   10

1945

11 Jan. Joey Jones, Boston		KO	1
29 Jan. Bob Jacobs, New York		KO	9
12 Feb. Nap Mitchell, Boston		KO	6
2 Apr. Nate Bolden, Baltimore	W		10
23 Apr. Teddy Randolph, Baltimore		KO	9
21 May Lloyd Marshall, Baltimore	W		10
18 June George Kochan, Baltimore		KO	6
26 June Lloyd Marshall, Cleveland		KO	10
22 Aug. Jimmy Bivins, Cleveland		KO by	6
17 Sept. Cocoa Kid, Baltimore		KO	8
22 Oct. Holman Williams, Baltimore	L		10
12 Nov. Odell Riley, Detroit		KO	6
26 Nov. Holman Williams, Baltimore		KO	11
13 Dec. Colion Chaney, St Louis		KO	5

1946

28 Jan. Curtis Sheppard, Baltimore	W		12
5 Feb. Georgie Parks, Washington DC		KO	1
2 May Verne Escoe, Orange, New Jersey		KO	7
20 May Ezzard Charles, Pittsburgh	L		10
19 Aug. Buddy Walker, Baltimore		KO	4
9 Sept. Shamus O'Brien, Baltimore		KO	2
23 Oct. Billy Smith, Oakland	D		12
6 Nov. Jack Chase, Oakland	D		10

1947

18 Mar. Jack Chase, Los Angeles		KO	9
11 Apr. Rusty Payne, San Diego	W		10
5 May Ezzard Charles, Cincinnati	L		10
16 June Curtis Sheppard, Washington DC	W		10
14 July Bert Lytell, Baltimore	W		10
30 July Bobby Zander, Oakland	W		12
8 Sept. Jimmy Bivins, Baltimore		KO	9
10 Nov. George Fitch, Baltimore		KO	6

1948

13 Jan. Ezzard Charles, Cleveland		KO by	8
12 Apr. Dusty Wilkerson, Baltimore		KO	7
19 Apr. Doc Williams, Newark		KO	7
5 May Billy Smith, Cincinnati	W		10
2 June Leonard Morrow, Oakland		KO by	1
28 June Jimmy Bivins, Baltimore	W		10
2 Aug. Ted Lowry, Baltimore	W		10
20 Sept. Billy Smith, Baltimore		KO	4
15 Oct. Henry Hall, New Orleans	L		10
1 Nov. Lloyd Gibson, Washington, DC	LF		4
15 Nov. Henry Hall, Baltimore	W		10
6 Dec. Bob Amos, Washington, DC	W		10
27 Dec. Charley Williams, Baltimore		KO	7

1949

10 Jan. Alabama Kid, Toledo		KO	4
31 Jan. Bob Satterfield, Toledo	KO		3

4 Mar. Alabama Kid, Columbus		KO	3
23 Mar. Dusty Wilkerson, Philadelphia		KO	6
11 Apr. Jimmy Bivins, Toledo		KO	8
26 Apr. Harold Johnson, Philadelphia	W		10
13 June Bob Sikes, Indianapolis		KO	3
27 June Clinton Bacon, Indianapolis	LF		6
29 July Esco Greenwood, North Adams		KO	2
4 Oct. Bob Amos, Toledo	W		10
24 Oct. Phil Muscato, Toledo		KO	6
6 Dec. Doc Williams, Hartford		KO	8
13 Dec. Leonard Morrow, Toledo		KO	10

1950

31 Jan. Bert Lytell, Toledo	W		10
31 July Vernon Williams, Chicago		KO	2

1951

2 Jan. Billy Smith, Portland		KO	8
28 Jan. John Thomas, Panama City		KO	1
21 Feb. Jimmy Bivins, New York		KO	9
13 Mar. Abel Cestac, Toledo	W		10
26 Apr. Herman Harris, Flint		KO	4
14 May Art Henri, Baltimore		KO	4
9 June Abel Cestac, Buenos Aires		KO	10
23 June Karel Sys, Buenos Aires	D		10
8 July Alberto Lovell, Buenos Aires		KO	1
15 July Vicente Quiroz, Montevideo		KO	6
26 July Victor Carabajal, Cordoba		KO	3
28 July Americo Capitanelli, Tucuman		KO	3
5 Aug. Rafael Miranda, Argentina		KO	4
17 Aug. Alfredo Lagay, Bahia Bianca		KO	3
5 Sept. Embrell Davison, Detroit		KO	1
24 Sept. Harold Johnson, Philadelphia	W		10
29 Oct. Chubby Wright, St Louis		KO	7
10 Dec. Harold Johnson, Milwaukee	L		10

1952

29 Jan. Harold Johnson, Toledo	W		10
27 Feb. Jimmy Slade, St Louis	W		10
19 May Bob Dunlap, San Francisco		KO	6
26 June Clarence Henry, Baltimore	W		10
25 July Clint Bacon, Denver		KO	4
17 Dec. Joey Maxim, St Louis	W		15
(Won World light heavyweight title)			

1953

27 Jan. Toxie Hall, Toledo		KO	4
16 Feb. Leonard Dugan, San Francisco		KO	8
3 Mar. Sonny Andrews, Sacramento		KO	5
11 Mar. Nino Valdes, St Louis	W		10
17 Mar. Al Spaulding, Spokane		KO	3
30 Mar. Frank Buford, San Diego		KO	9
24 June Joey Maxim, Ogden, Utah	W		15
(Retained World light-heavyweight title)			
22 Aug. Reinaldo Ansaloni, Buenos Aires		KO	4

12 Sept. Dogomar Martinez, Buenos Aires	W	10

1954

27 Jan. Joey Maxim, Miami	W	15
(Retained World light-heavyweight title)		
9 Mar. Bob Baker, Miami Beach	KO	9
7 June Bert Whitehurst, New York	KO	6
11 Aug. Harold Johnson, New York	KO	14
(Retained World light-heavyweight title)		

1955

2 May Nino Valdes, Las Vegas	W	15
22 June Bobo Olson, New York	KO	3
(Retained World light-heavyweight title)		
21 Sept. Rocky Marciano, New York	KO by	9
(For World heavyweight title)		
22 Oct. Dale Hall, Philadelphia	Exh	4

1956

2 Feb. Dale Hall, Fresno, Califnornia	Exh	4
20 Feb. Howard King, San Francisco	W	10
27 Feb. Bob Dunlap, San Diego	KO	1
17 Mar. Frankie Daniels, Hollywood	W	10
27 Mar. Howard King, Sacramento	W	10
10 Apr. Willie Bean, Richmond, California	KO	5
16 Apr. George Parmentier, Seattle	KO	3
26 Apr. Sonny Andrews, Edmonton	KO	4
30 Apr. Gene Thompson, Tucson	KO	3
5 June Yolande Pompey, London	KO	10
(Retained World light-heavyweight title)		
25 July James J. Parker, Toronto	KO	9
8 Sept. Roy Shire, Ogden, Utah	KO	3
30 Nov. Floyd Patterson, Chicago	KO by	5
(For vacant World heavyweight title)		

1957

1 May Hans Kalbfell, Essen, Germany	W	10
2 June Alain Cherville, Stuttgart	KO	6
20 Sept. Tony Anthony, Los Angeles	KO	7
(Retained World light-heavyweight title)		
31 Oct. Bob Mitchell, Vancouver	KO	5
5 Nov. Eddie Cotton, Seattle	W	10
29 Nov. Roger Rischer, Portland	KO	4

1958

18 Jan. Luis Ignacio, São Paulo	W	10
1 Feb. Julio Neves, Rio de Janeiro	KO	3
4 Mar. Bert Whitehurst, San Bernardino	KO	10
10 Mar. Bob Albright, Vancouver	KO	7
2 May Willi Besmanoff, Louisville	W	10
17 May Howard King, San Diego	W	10
26 May Charlie Norkus, San Francisco	W	10
9 June Howard King, Sacramento	W	10
4 Aug. Howard King, Reno, Nevada	D	10
10 Dec. Yvon Durelle, Montreal	KO	11
(Retained World light-heavyweight title)		

1959

5 Feb. Eddie Cotton, Victoria, BC	Exh		5
9 Mar. Sterling Davis, Odessa, Texas		KO	3
12 Aug. Yvon Durelle, Montreal		KO	3
(Retained World light-heavyweight title)			

1960

25 May Willi Besmanoff, Indianapolis		KO	10
13 Sept. George Abinet, Dallas		KO	4
25 Oct. NBA withdrew recognition as world light-heavyweight champion from Moore			
29 Oct. Giulio Rinaldi, Rome, Italy	L		10
28 Nov. Buddy Turman, Dallas	W		10

1961

25 Mar. Buddy Turman, Manila	W		10
8 May Dave Furch, Tucson	Exh		4
12 May Cliff Gray, Nogales, Arizona		KO	4
10 June Giulio Rinaldi, New York	W		15
(Retained World light-heavyweight title)			
23 Oct. Pete Rademacher, Baltimore		KO	6

1962

10 Feb. NYSAC and EBU withdrew recognition as world light-heavyweight champion from Moore			
30 Mar. Alejandro Lavorante, Los Angeles		KO	10
7 May Howard King, Tijuana		KO	1
28 May Willie Pastrano, Los Angeles	D		10
15 Nov. Cassius Clay, Los Angeles		KO by	4

1963

15 Mar. Mike DiBiase, Phoenix		KO	3

1964
(Inactive)

1965

27 Aug. Nap Mitchell, Michigan City	Exh	KO	3

Sugar Ray Robinson
Born: 3 May 1921, Detroit, Michigan

1940

4 Oct. Joe Escheverria, New York		KO	2
8 Oct. Silent Stefford, Savannah		KO	2
22 Oct. Mistos Grispos, New York	W		6
11 Nov. Bobby Woods, Philadelphia		KO	1
9 Dec. Norment Quarles, Philadelphia		KO	4
12 Dec. Oliver White, New York		KO	3

1941

4 Jan. Henry LaBarba, Brooklyn		KO	1
13 Jan. Frankie Wallace, Philadelphia		KO	1

31 Jan. George Zengaras, New York	W		6
8 Feb. Benny Cartegena, Brooklyn		KO	1
21 Feb. Bobby McIntire, New York	W		6
27 Feb. Gene Spencer, Detroit		KO	5
3 Mar. Jimmy Tygh, Philadelphia		KO	8
14 Apr. Jimmy Tygh, Philadelphia		KO	1
24 Apr. Charley Burns, Atlantic City		KO	1
30 Apr. Joe Ghnouly, Washington DC		KO	3
10 May Vic Troise, Brooklyn		KO	1
19 May Nick Castiglione, Philadelphia		KO	1
16 June Mike Evans, Philadelphia		KO	2
2 July Pete Lello, New York		KO	4
21 July Sammy Angott, Philadelphia	W		10
27 Aug. Carl (Red) Guggino, Long Island City		KO	3
29 Aug. Maurice Arnault, Atlantic City		KO	1
19 Sept. Maxie Shapiro, New York		KO	3
25 Sept. Marty Servo, Philadelphia	W		10
31 Oct. Fritzie Zivic, New York	W		10

1942

16 Jan. Fritzie Zivic, New York		KO	10
20 Feb. Maxie Berger, New York		KO	2
20 Mar. Norman Rubio, New York		KO	7
17 Apr. Harvey Dubs, Detroit		KO	6
30 Apr. Dick Banner, Minneapolis	W		10
28 May Marty Servo, New York	W		10
31 July Sammy Angott, New York	W		10
21 Aug. Ruben Shank, New York		KO	2
27 Aug. Tony Motisi, Chicago		KO	1
2 Oct. Jake LaMotta, New York	W		10
19 Oct. Izzy Jannazzo, Philadelphia	W		10
6 Nov. Vic Dellicurti, New York	W		10
1 Dec. Izzy Jannazzo, Cleveland		KO	8
14 Dec. Al Nettlow, Philadelphia		KO	3

1943

5 Feb. Jake LaMotta, Detroit	L		10
19 Feb. Jackie Wilson, New York	W		10
26 Feb. Jake LaMotta, Detroit	W		10
30 Apr. Freddie Cabral, Boston		KO	1
1 July Ralph Zannelli, Boston	W		10
27 Aug. Henry Armstrong, New York	W		10

1944

13 Oct. Izzy Jannazzo, Boston		KO	2
27 Oct. Sgt. Lou Woods, Chicago		KO	9
17 Nov. Vic Dellicurti, Detroit	W		10
12 Dec. Sheik Rangel, Philadelphia		KO	2
22 Dec. Georgie Martin, Boston		KO	7

1945

10 Jan. Billy Furrone, Washington DC		KO	2
16 Jan. Tommy Bell, Cleveland	W		10
14 Feb. George Costner, Chicago		KO	1
24 Feb. Jake LaMotta, New York	W		10

14 May Jose Basora, Philadelphia	D		10
15 June Jimmy McDaniels, New York		KO	2
18 Sept. Jimmy Mandell, Buffalo		KO	5
26 Sept. Jake LaMotta, Chicago	W		12
4 Dec. Vic Dellicurti, Boston	W		10

1946

14 Jan. Dave Clark, Pittsburgh		KO	2
5 Feb. Tony Riccio, Elizabeth		KO	4
15 Feb. O'Neill Bell, Detroit		KO	2
26 Feb. Cliff Beckett, St Louis		KO	4
4 Mar. Sammy Angott, Pittsburgh	W		10
14 Mar. Izzy Jannazzo, Baltimore	W		10
21 Mar. Freddy Flores, New York		KO	5
12 June Norman Rubio, Union City	W		10
12 July Joe Curcio, New York		KO	2
15 Aug. Vinnie Vines, Albany		KO	6
25 Sept. Sidney Miller, Elizabeth		KO	3
7 Oct. Ossie Harris, Pittsburgh	W		10
1 Nov. Cecil Hudson, Detroit		KO	6
6 Nov. Artie Levine, Cleveland		KO	10
20 Dec. Tommy Bell, New York	W		15
(Won vacant World welterweight title)			

1947

27 Mar. Bernie Miller, Miami		KO	s3
3 Apr. Fred Wilson, Akron		KO	3
8 Apr. Eddie Finazzo, Kansas City		KO	4
16 May Georgie Abrams, New York	W		10
24 June Jimmy Doyle, Cleveland		KO	8
(Retained World welterweight title)			
21 Aug. Sammy Secreet, Akron		KO	1
29 Aug. Flashy Sebastian, New York		KO	1
28 Oct. Jackie Wilson, Los Angeles		KO	7
10 Dec. Billy Nixon, Elizabeth		KO	6
19 Dec. Chuck Taylor, Detroit		KO	6
(Retained World welterweight title)			

1948

4 Mar. Ossie Harris, Toledo	W		10
16 Mar. Henry Brimm, Buffalo	W		10
28 June Bernard Docusen, Chicago	W		15
(Retained World welterweight title)			
23 Sept. Kid Gavilan, New York	W		10
15 Nov. Bobby Lee, Philadelphia	W		10

1949

10 Feb. Gene Buffalo, Wilkes-Barre		KO	1
15 Feb. Henry Brimm, Buffalo	D		10
25 Mar. Bobby Lee, Chicago	W		10
11 Apr. Don Lee, Omaha	W		10
20 Apr. Earl Turner, Oakland		KO	8
16 May Al Tribuani, Wilmington	Exh		4
7 June Freddie Flores, New Bedford		KO	3
20 June Cecil Hudson, Providence		KO	5

11 July Kid Gavilan, Philadelphia	W	15
(Retained World welterweight title)		
24 Aug. Steve Belloise, New York	KO	7
2 Sept. Al Mobley, Chicago	Exh	4
9 Sept. Benny Evans, Omaha	KO	5
12 Sept. Charley Dotson, Houston	KO	3
9 Nov. Don Lee, Denver	W	10
13 Nov. Vern Lester, New Orleans	KO	5
15 Nov. Gene Burton, Shreveport	Exh.	6
16 Nov. Gene Burton, Dallas	Exh	6

1950

30 Jan. George LaRover, New Haven	KO	4
13 Feb. Al Mobley, Miami	KO	6
22 Feb. Aaron Wade, Savannah	KO	3
27 Feb. Jean Walzack, St. Louis	W	10
22 Mar. George Costner, Philadelphia	KO	1
21 Apr. Cliff Beckett, Columbus	KO	3
28 Apr. Ray Barnes, Detroit	W	10
5 June Robert Villemain, Philadelphia	W	15
(Won vacant Pennsylvania World middleweight title)		
9 Aug. Charley Fusari, Jersey City	W	15
(Retained World welterweight title)		
25 Aug. Jose Basora, Scranton	KO	1
(Retained Pennsylvania World middleweight title)		
4 Sept. Billy Brown, New York	W	10
16 Oct. Joe Rindone, Boston	KO	6
26 Oct. Carl (Bobo) Olson, Philadelphia	KO	12
(Retained Pennsylvania World middleweight title)		
8 Nov. Bobby Dykes, Chicago	W	10
27 Nov. Jean Stock, Paris	KO	2
9 Dec. Luc Van Dam, Brussels	KO	4
16 Dec. Jean Walzack, Geneva	W	10
22 Dec. Robert Villemain, Paris	KO	9
25 Dec. Hans Stretz, Frankfurt	KO	5

1951

14 Feb. Jake LaMotta, Chicago	KO	13
(Won World middleweight title)		
5 Apr. Holley Mims, Miami	W	10
9 Apr. Don Ellis, Oklahoma City	KO	1
21 May Kid Marcel, Paris	KO	5
26 May Jean Wanes, Zürich	W	10
10 June Jan de Bruin, Antwerp	KO	8
16 June Jean Walzack, Liège	KO	6
24 June Gerhard Hecht, Berlin	DNC	2
1 July Cyrille Delannoit, Turin	KO	3
10 July Randy Turpin, London	L	15
(Lost World middleweight title)		
12 Sept Randy Turpin, New York	KO	10
(Regained World middleweight title)		

1952

13 Mar. Carl (Bobo) Olson, San Francisco (Retained World middleweight title)	W	15
16 Apr. Rocky Graziano, Chicago (Retained World middleweight title)	KO	3
25 June Joey Maxim, New York (For World light-heavyweight title)	KO	14
18 Dec. Announced retirement		

1953
(Inactive)

1954

20 Oct. Announced return to ring		
29 Nov. Gene Burton, Hamilton	Exh.	6

1955

5 Jan. Joe Rindone, Detroit	KO	6
19 Jan. Ralph (Tiger) Jones, Chicago	L	10
29 Mar. Johnny Lombardeo, Cincinnatti	W	10
14 Apr. Ted Olla, Milwaukee	KO	3
4 May Garth Panter, Detroit	W	10
22 July Rocky Castellani, San Francisco	W	10
9 Dec. Carl (Bobo) Olson, Chicago (Retained World middleweight title)	KO	2

1956

18 May Carl (Bobo) Olson, Los Angeles (Retained World middleweight title)	KO	4
10 Nov. Bob Provizzi, New Haven	W	10

1957

2 Jan. Gene Fullmer, New York (Lost World middleweight title)	L	15
1 May Gene Fullmer, Chicago (Regained World middleweight title)	KO	5
10 Sept. Otis Woodward, Philadelphia	Exh	2
10 Sept. Lee Williams, Philadelphia	Exh	2
23 Sept. Carmen Basilio, New York (Lost World middleweight title)	L	15

1958

25 Mar. Carmen Basilio, Chicago (Regained World middleweight title)	W	15

1959

14 Dec Bob Young, Boston	KO	2

1960

22 Jan. Paul Pender, Boston (Lost World middleweight title)	L	15
2 Apr. Tony Baldoni, Baltimore	KO	1
10 June Paul Pender, Boston (For World middleweight title)	L	15

3 Dec. Gene Fullmer, Los Angeles (For NBA middleweight title)	D		15

1961

4 Mar. Gene Fullmer, Las Vegas (For NBA middleweight title)	L		15
25 Sept. Wilf Greaves, Detroit	W		10
21 Oct. Denny Moyer, New York	W		10
20 Nov. Al Hauser, Providence		KO	6
8 Dec. Wilf Greaves, Pittsburgh		KO	8

1962

17 Feb. Denny Moyer, New York	L		10
27 Apr. Bobby Lee, Port of Spain		KO	2
9 July Phil Moyer, Los Angeles	L		10
25 Sept. Terry Downes, London	L		10
17 Oct Diego Infantes, Vienna		KO	2
10 Nov. Georges Estatoff, Lyons		KO	6

1963

30 Jan. Ralph Dupas, Miami Beach	W		10
25 Feb. Bernie Reynolds, Santo Domingo		KO	4
11 Mar. Billy Thornton, Lewiston		KO	3
5 May Maurice Rolbnet, Sherbrooke		KO	3
24 June Joey Giardello, Philadelphia	L		10
14 Oct. Armand Vanucci, Paris	W		10
9 Nov. Fabio Bettini, Lyons	D		10
16 Nov. Emile Sarens, Brussels		KO	8
29 Nov. Andre Davier, Grenoble	W		10
9 Dec. Armand Vanucci, Paris	W		10

1964

19 May Gaylord Barnes, Portland	W		10
8 July Clarence Riley, Pittsfield		KO	6
27 July Art Hernandez, Omaha	D		10
3 Sept. Mick Leahy, Paisley	L		10
28 Sept. Yolande Leveque, Paris	W		10
12 Oct. Johnny Angel, London		KO	6
24 Oct. Jackie Cailau, Nice	W		10
7 Nov. Baptiste Rolland, Calen	W		10
14 Nov. Jean Beltritti, Marseilles	W		10
27 Nov. Fabio Bettini, Rome	D		10

1965

6 Mar. Jimmy Beecham, Kingston		KO	2
4 Apr. East Basting, Savannah		KO	1
28 Apr. Rocky Randall, Norfolk		KO	3
5 May Rocky Randall, Jacksonville	W		8
24 May Memo Ayon, Tijuana	L		10
1 June Stan Harrington, Honolulu	L		10
24 June Young Joe Walcott, Richmond	W		10
12 July Ferd Hernandez, Las Vegas	L		10
15 Sept. Neil Morrison, Norfolk	NC		2
23 Sept. Young Joe Walcott, Philadelphia	W		10
1 Oct. Peter Schmidt, Johnstown	W		10

20 Oct. Rudolph Bent, Steubenville	KO	3
10 Nov. Joey Archer, Pittsburgh	L	10

Randy Turpin
Born: 7 June 1928, Leamington, Warwickshire, England

1946

17 Sept. Gordon Griffiths, London	KO	1
9 Nov. Des Jones, London	W	6
26 Dec. Bill Blything, Birmingham	KO	1

1947

14 Jan. Jimmy Davis, London	KO	4
24 Jan. Dai Jones, Birmingham	KO	3
18 Feb. Johnny Best, London	KO	1
18 Mar. Bert Hyland, London	KO	1
1 Apr. Frank Dolan, London	KO	2
15 Apr. Tommy Davies, London	KO	2
28 Apr. Bert Sanders, London	W	6
12 May Ron Cooper, Oxford	KO	4
27 May Jury VII, London	W	6
3 June Mark Hart, London	W	6
23 June Leon Fouquet, Coventry	KO	1
9 Sept. Jimmy Ingle, Coventry	KO	3
20 Oct. Mark Hart, London	D	6

1948

26 Jan. Freddie Price, Coventry	KO	1
17 Feb. Gerry McCrea, London	KO	1
16 Mar. Vince Hawkins, London	W	8
26 Apr. Albert Finch, London	L	8
28 June Alby Hollister, Birmingham	W	8
21 Sept. Jean Stock, London	KO by	5

1949

7 Feb. Jackie Jones, Coventry	KO	5
21 Feb. Doug Miller, London	W	8
25 Mar. Mickey Laurent, Manchester	KO	3
3 May William Poli, London	WF	4
20 June Cyrille Delannoit, Birmingham	KO	8
22 Aug. Jean Wanes, Manchester	KO	3
19 Sept. Roy Wouters, Coventry	KO	5
15 Nov. Pete Mead, London	KO	4

1950

31 Jan. Gilbert Stock, London	W	8
6 Mar. Richard Armah, Croydon	KO	6
24 Apr. Gustave Degouve, Nottingham	W	8
5 Sept. Eli Elandon, Watford	KO	2
17 Oct. Albert Finch, London	KO	5
(Won British middleweight title)		
13 Nov. Jose Alamo, Abergavenny	KO	2

12 Dec. Tommy Yarosz, London	WF		8

1951

22 Jan. Eduardo Lopez, Birmingham		KO	1
27 Feb. Luc Van Dam, London		KO	1
(Won vacant European middlweight title)			
19 Mar. Jean Stock, Leicester		KO	5
16 Apr. Billy Brown, Birmingham		KO	2
7 May Jan de Bruin, Coventry		KO	6
5 June Jackie Keough, London		KO	7
10 July Ray Robinson, London	W		15
(Won World middleweight title)			
12 Sept. Ray Robinson, New York		KO by	10
(Lost World middleweight title)			

12 Feb. Alex Buxton, London		KO	7
22 Apr. Jacques Harrabedian, London		KO	3
10 June Don Cockell, London		KO	11
(Won Vacant British Empire light-heavyweight title)			
21 Oct. George Angelo, London	W		15
(Won Vacant British Empire middleweight title)			

1953

19 Jan. Victo D'Haes, Birmingham		KO	6
16 Feb. Duggie Miller, Leicester	W		10
17 Mar. Walter Carter, London	W	Dis	2
9 June Charley Humez, London	W		15
(Retained European middleweight title)			
21 Oct. Carl (Bobo) Olson, New York	L		15
(For vacant World middleweight title)			

1953

30 Mar. Olle Bengtsson, London	W		10
2 May Tiberio Mitri, Rome		KO by	1
(Lost European middleweight title)			

1955

15 Feb. Ray Schmidt, Birmingham	WF		8
8 Mar. Jose Gonzalez, London		KO	7
26 Apr. Alex Buxton, London		KO	2
(Won British light heavyweight title)			
(Retained British Empire light-heavyweight title			
19 Sept. Polly Smith, Birmingham	W		10
18 Oct. Gordon Wallace, London		KO by	4

1956

17 Apr. Alessandro D. Ottawio, Birmingham		KO	6
18 June Jacques Bro, Birmingham		KO	5
21 Sept. Hans Stretz, Hamburg	L		10
26 Nov. Alex Buxton, Leicester		KO	5
(Retained British light-heavyweight title)			

1957
11 June Arthur Howard, Leicester   W   15
  (Retained British light-heavyweight title)
17 Sept. Ahmed Boulgrourne, London   KO   9
28 Oct. Sergio Burchi, Birmingham   KO   2
25 Nov. Uwe Janssen, Leicester   KO   8

1958
11 Feb Wim Snoek, Birmingham   W   10
21 Apr. Eddie Wright, Leicester   KO   7
22 July Redvers Sango, Oswestry   KO   4
 9 Sept. Yolande Pompey, Birmingham   KO by   2

1959–1962
(Inactive)

1963
18 Mar. Eddie Marcano, Wisbech   KO   6

1964
22 Aug. Charles Seguna, Malta   KO   2

Jimmy Wilde
Born: 12 May 1892, Quaker's Yard, Wales

1911
18 Feb. George Luke, Pontypridd   D   6
20 Mar. D. Thomas, Pontypridd   W   Pts   3

1911–12
    Lewis Williams   W   KO   3
    Dick Jenkins   W   Pts   6
    Fred Chappell   W   Pts   6
    S. Jenkins, Pontypridd   W   RSF   11
    Jim Easton, Edinburgh   W   Pts   10
    Young Baker   W   Pts   6
    Young Avent   W   KO   4
    Ted Powell   W   KO   3
    Joe Rogers   W   KO   5
    Kid Pearson   W   KO   2
    Joe Gaps   W   KO   7
    Lewis Williams   W   KO   5
    Mike Flynn   W   KO   8
    Young Powell   W   KO   3
    Ted Roberts   W   KO   3
    Ted Roberts   W   KO   4
    Dai Roberts   W   KO   3
    Young Langford   W   KO   2
    Eddie Thomas   W   KO   2
    Steve Thomas   W   KO   3
    Billy Panke   W   KO   3
    Archie Grant   W   KO   2
    Young Towell   W   KO   4

Young Towell	W	KO	3
Young Rice	W	KO	4
Walter Hall	W	RSF	3
Harry Stuckey	W	KO	7

1912

20 Jan. Matt Wells' Nipper, The Ring	W	KO	1
20 July Kid Morris, Cardiff	W	Rtd	5
17 Aug. Jim Stuckey, Tonypandy	W	RSF	8
9 Nov. Phil Davis	W	Rtd	2
16 Nov. Young Ransford, Tonypandy	W	Rtd	2
30 Nov. Alf Williams, Tonypandy	W	Pts	12
14 Dec. Stoker Staines, Tonypandy	W	KO	1
21 Dec. Billy Yates, Cardiff	W	Rtd.	4
31 Dec. Billy Padden, Glasgow	W	Rtd	18

1913

18 Jan. Tommy Hughes, Tonypandy	W	KO	7
1 Feb. Dicky Jenkins, Tonypandy	ND		7
15 Feb. Kid Fitzpatrick, Tonypandy	W	KO	2
Feb. Harry Stuckey, Tonypandy	ND		6
Feb. Ben Hardwick, Tylerstown	ND		8
8 Mar. Dai Matthews, Tonypandy	W	KO	8
Mar. Harry Taylor, Swansea	W	KO	3
12 Apr. Will Rees, Tonypandy	W	KO	2
19 Apr. Billy Yates, Tonypandy	W	KO	3
24 May Dai Davies, Tonypandy	W	Pts	12
Kid Levine, Tonypandy	W	KO	· 12
Harry Brooks, Manchester	W	KO	8
Harry Curley	W	KO	12
14 June Billy Paddon, Tonypandy	W	Pts	15
21 June Gwilym Thomas, Tonypandy	W	RSF	5
1 July Dick Lewis, Tonypandy	W	Rtd	3
12 July Tommy Lewis, Tonypandy	W	Pts	12
19 July Young Dando, Tonypandy	W	Pts	15
4 Aug. Darkey Saunders, Cardiff	W	Pts	10
28 Aug. Young Dyer, Liverpool	W	RSF.	3
6 Sept. Dick Jenkins, Ferndale	W	Rtd.	10
8 Sept. Kid Levine, Hanley	W	Rtd.	7
22 Sept. Young Dando, Cardiff	W	Pts	20
1 Nov. Darkey Saunders, Tonypandy	W	rsf	11
13 Nov. Young Baker, Liverpool	W	Rtd	10
21 Nov. Young Dyer, Manchester	W	Rtd.	10
22 Nov. Dido Gains, Swansea	W	Pts	15
6 Dec. Young Dando, Merthyr	W	Dis.	10
13 Dec. Billy Charles, Tonypandy	W	Rtd	6

1914

3 Jan. Kid Nutter, Tonypandy	W	Pts	15
8 Jan. Young Beynon, Liverpool	W	Pts	15
29 Jan. Billy Paddon, Liverpool	W	Rtd	5
2 Feb. Kid Nutter, Birkenhead	W	Pts	15
9 Feb. Tom Thomas, Manchester	W	KO	7
12 Feb. Paddy Carroll, Liverpool	W	KO	2
16 Feb. George Jaggers, Sheffield	W	RSF	5

26 Mar. Bill Kyne, Liverpool	W	RSF	4
30 Mar. Euyene Husson, NSC	W	KO	6
13 Apr. Jack Madden, Ashton-under-Lyme	W	KO	4
16 Apr. Bouzonnie, Liverpool	W	Rtd	6
27 Apr. Alf Mansfield, Leeds	W	Pts	20
11 May George Gloria, NSC	W	RSF	9
22 June Charlie Banyard, Aberdare	W	RSF	9
18 July Charley Jordan, Tonypandy	W	RSF	10
23 July Artie Edwards, Liverpool	W	Pts	15
19 Aug. Young Baker, Leicester	W	Pts	15
28 Sept. Alf Mansfield, W. London Stadium	W	Rtd	10
16 Nov. Joe Symonds NSC	W	Pts	15
(British flyweight title eliminator)			
3 Dec. Sid Smith, Liverpool	W	KO	9

1915

25 Jan. Tancy Lee, NSC	L	Rtd	17
(British and European flyweight title and Lonsdale Belt)			
25 Mar. Sid Shields, Liverpool	W	KO	2
24 July Driver Benthew, Sheffield	W	Rtd	5
14 Aug. George Clarke, Sheffield	W	Rtd	8
23 Sept. Walter Buchan, Liverpool	W	Rtd.	5
20 Oct. Tommy Hughes, Barrow	W	Rtd	8
27 Nov. Tommy Hughes, Barrow	W	Rtd	8
9 Dec. Johnny Best, Liverpool	W	RSF	14
16 Dec. Danny Elliot, Bradford	W	KO	2
20 Dec. Sid Smith, RSC	W	RSF	8

1916

8 Jan. Billy Rowlands, Swansea	W	RSF	7
24 Jan. Tommy Noble, New Cross	W	Rtd	11
27 Jan. Jimmy Morton, Liverpool	W	KO	2
14 Feb. Joe Symonds, NSC	W	Rtd	11
(British and European flyweight title and Lonsdale Belt)			
9 Mar. Sam Kellar, W. London Stadium	W	Rtd	8
27 Mar. Sid Smith, Hoxton	W	KO	3
24 Apr. Johnny Rosner, Liverpool	W	Rtd	11
(World flyweight title)			
29 Apr. Benny Thomas, Cardiff	W	Pts	
13 May Darkey Saunders, Woolwich	W	RSF	3
13 May Young Magnus, Woolwich	W	KO	2
29 May Tommy Harrison, Oxford Music Hall	W	Rtd	8
26 June Tancy Lee, NSC	W	RSF	11
(British and European flyweight title and Lonsdale belt)			
31 July Johnny Hughes, Kensal Rise	W	KO	
9 Nov. Tommy Noble, Liverpool	W	RSF	15
18 Dec. Young Zulu Kid, Holborn	W	KO	11
(World flyweight title)			

1917

12 Mar. George Clarke, NSC	W	Rtd	4
(British and European flyweight title and Lonsdale Belt outright)			
22 Mar. Frankie Russell, Holborn	W	RSF	3

1918

28 Mar. L/Cpl. Jacobs, Aldershot	W	RSF	4
29 Apr. Dick Heasman, NSC	W	Rtd	2
31 Aug. Joe Conn, Stamford Bridge	W	RSF	12
11 Dec. Pte. Joe Lynch, Albert Hall	W	Pts	3
11 Dec. Digger Evans, Albert Hall	W	Pts	
12 Dec. Pal Moore, Albert Hall	L	Pts	3
(Final of bantamweight class of ISBA King's Trophy Competition)			

1919

31 Mar. Joe Lynch, NSC	W	Pts	15
21 Apr. Jimmy Buck, Liverpool	W	KO	5
16 May Alf Mansfield, Holborn	W	RSF	13
17 July Pal Moore, Olympia	W	Pts	20
6 Dec. Jack Sharkey, Milwaukee	ND		10

1920

8 Jan. Babe Asher, St Louis	ND		8
29 Jan. Mike Ertle, Milwaukee	W	KO	3
19 Feb. Mickey Russell, Jersey City	W	KO	7
3 Mar. Patsy Wallace, Philadelphia	ND		6
12 Mar. Frankie Mason, Toledo	ND		12
12 Apr. Zulu Kid, Windsor, Ontario	ND		10
21 Apr. Battling Murray, Camden, New Jersey	W	KO	8
1 May Bobby Dyson, Lawrence	W	KO	1
13 May Battling Murray, Philadelphia	W	KO	2
24 May Patsy Wallace, Toronto	W	Pts	10

1921

13 Jan. Pete Herman, Albert Hall	L	RSF	17

1923

18 June Pancho Villa, New York	L	KO	7
(World flyweight title)			